PROPERTY IN
THE EIGHTEENTH CENTURY

By the same author:

Marxian Socialism (Cork: Purcell & Company; London: P.S. King & Son, 1917)

Economics and the Worker (Cork: University Press, 1937)

Economics and Its Frontiers (Cork: Mercier Press, 1957)

PROPERTY IN THE EIGHTEENTH CENTURY
WITH SPECIAL REFERENCE TO ENGLAND AND LOCKE

by

PASCHAL LARKIN

M.A., D.Econ.Sc. (N.U.I.), Ph.D. (Lond.)
Emeritus Professor of Economic Theory
National University of Ireland

WITH A NEW INTRODUCTION

by the author

HOWARD FERTIG

New York · 1969

First published in 1930 by Cork University Press

HOWARD FERTIG, INC. EDITION 1969
Published by arrangement with the author

Introduction to the 1969 edition
copyright © 1969 by Paschal Larkin

Library of Congress Catalog Card Number: 68-9655

PRINTED IN THE UNITED STATES OF AMERICA
BY NOBLE OFFSET PRINTERS, INC.

PREFACE BY PROFESSOR J. L. STOCKS

THE conviction of the cardinal importance of property for
social and political analysis seems to be a distinguishing
characteristic of the modern world. In 1789 the French
Revolutionary Convention solemnly declared private property
to be a sacred and inviolable right of man. In the nineteenth
century the revolutionary movements of which Paris was the
centre were understood by the world as attacks on this same
sacred right. In 1840 a voice from Paris announced that
property was theft. Socialism—a creed of Parisian origin—
meant for the nineteenth century primarily a denial of
the right of private property. When, for example,
John Stuart Mill described himself as developing in his
maturity into something of a socialist he had in mind his
doubts as to the legitimacy of existing property-rights.
" I cannot believe," he wrote in 1856 to an Italian corres-
pondent, " that private property, as understood to-day, is
the last word of society." Property, in short, has been the
watchword at different times both of those who defended
and of those who attacked the existing order ; but always
it has remained a centre of controversy.

Throughout this modern period there has been a predominant tendency to conceive property in terms of a theory
which early found its classic expression in a short chapter of
John Locke's *Essay concerning the True Original, Extent, and
End of Civil Government*. The chapter comes significantly
before the account of the institution of government. Property
exists, like marriage and the family, antecedently to government, and belongs to the state of nature on which government
is superimposed : it is natural in a sense in which government
is not. The position dictates an incompleteness of treatment,
which has certainly led to misapprehensions, but has probably
also increased, by the freedom thus left to inference and

interpretation, the influence of the principles laid down. According to Locke's theory, when government is instituted, nature is abrogated only in its defects : for the rest it remains intact, a source of fundamental social rights and obligations. Thus this account of natural property, except so far as it reveals defects in nature's provision, is correctly taken as defining in principle the property which, in Locke's view, it is the primary end of government to preserve. But the defects of nature's provision, which would legitimate government action, are not clearly brought out ; and there is no discussion of the forms which, since the institution of government, property has actually taken. Therefore the theory is available for all parties. One will jump at the absolute guarantee of property which seems to be inserted in the very definition of the State ; another, seeing how nature is said to give a man property in the product of his labour, condemns the society in which he lives for refusing this natural right ; while a third, taking ' estate ' as the external condition of ' life ' and ' liberty,' sees a blow struck at state-absolutism and rejoices in the cause of freedom.

Of this doctrine a careful account will be found in the following pages, marked by an evident desire to do justice to a great thinker. Our author is not, of course, writing as a historian of philosophy ; he cannot track the theory of natural rights to its source and follow it into all its applications. His main concerns are more concrete ; with the institution of property itself as it dominated a certain stage of human development, with the theory as springing from this soil and flourishing in it, suffering continual distortion and exaggeration in response to the fluctuations of social and economic circumstance. John Locke was a true philosopher : he had the wide vision and open mind, the ' leisure ' or disengagement, by which Plato characterised the philosophic attitude. But his candour and detachment only give him a certain relative advantage over his contemporaries. He remains the child of his time ; and from such a study as this we come to understand him better by seeing him in this light.

A concrete study such as this throws much light on that common, but palpably unjust, mode of assessment which judges a principle only in the light of its immediate practical application, which approves or condemns a doctrine by the use which is actually made of it. There are in fact few people at any time who can judge, with any approach to fairness, a doctrine which impinges at all closely on practice. The theory of the practical man is largely the formal justification of conclusions to which he has already come. He sees in a general principle only its cutting edge, its present practical application. He accepts or rejects it, picks it up or throws it down, according as it favours or discountenances the practical decision that he wants. Thus the City of London saw great merit in the essentially revolutionary propositions of Dr. Richard Price when they were advanced as a ground for condemning the British government's behaviour to the American colonists. Thirteen years later they were fully prepared to accept the French Revolution as the belated recognition by the French nation of principles asserted in England in 1688. It was not any refutation of the doctrine of natural rights, but the Terror and the War with Napoleon that brought them to a different view. Locke's theory of property was as capable of operating in criticism of existing property-rights as in defence of them ; and the fact that during the eighteenth century it was applied mainly in one direction must not be allowed to force on us a one-sided interpretation.

The question however of doing justice to the historical individual, John Locke, important as it is, is a very subordinate element in the problem which our author has set himself in this book. His is the historian's task—a task perhaps even more impossible of fulfilment than that of the philosopher—the effort to do justice to a whole age. With increasing distance, we are gradually becoming more appreciative and indulgent in our attitude to the eighteenth century. We still find its manners and morals hard to understand ; but they do not stir in us the contempt and disgust which they stirred in the more enlightened minds of the nineteenth century. Mill said of Bentham, who was born in 1748, that " his own lot was cast in a generation of the leanest and barrenest men whom England had yet produced, and he was an old man when a better race came in with the present century." As a historical statement that would be hard to substantiate. It probably represents mainly the common illusion by which the blackest spot in recent history is seen to lie about a hundred years back from the present. We are in a position now to do justice to the eighteenth century. The historian in every reader is anxious to do it justice, and welcomes a careful study of facts and tendencies, like the present, as an effort in this direction. But, as a citizen, the reader will also expect from it, in accordance with an ancient tradition, some enlightenment in regard to the problems of his own day, and he will not be disappointed. From this, I believe, as from all true historical studies, the reader will rise, not rejoicing pharisaically in his superiority, but chastened rather by the reflection, *de te fabula*.

J. L. STOCKS.

Professor of Philosophy, University of Manchester,
Sometime Fellow of St. John's College, Oxford.

April 3, 1930.

AUTHOR'S INTRODUCTION

THE title of the present work is not, perhaps, sufficiently comprehensive, for the matter discussed includes more than property and the period surveyed is not confined to the eighteenth century. The danger of making clear-cut divisions in the history either of ideas or of institutions is now generally recognised. Nevertheless there seemed to be good reason for confining ourselves, in this study, principally to the period which divides the Civil War in England from the French Revolution.

Special reference is made to England because she was the first country to adopt on a grand scale a new philosophy of property, and the first to carry out on a national scale a new experiment in economic organisation. Her pioneer work in industrialism has served as a guide and a warning to other countries. Its results both for good and evil were never so much the subject of discussion as they are to-day when England's industrial leadership is in the balance, and great numbers of her people are unemployed.

The evils which have accompanied the growth of private wealth in modern communities are intimately connected with the ideas which people have held as to the rights and duties, or lack of duties, of private property. In the following pages special attention is given to John Locke's theory of property because he is frequently represented as the English apostle of economic individualism. But his views were less individualistic than is commonly supposed, and many writers in the past have neglected the human and democratic elements in his theory.

The difficulties which beset the present study were obviously very great though the subject itself was undoubtedly attractive. The dearth of specific works on property in the eighteenth century entailed very wide reading. Points had to be touched on therefore which, at first sight, seem to have but a remote connection with our subject. But as views on property are inevitably affected by the attitude adopted towards such questions as religion, morality, education and State policy, it was thought that some reference to these subjects would throw light on the dominant theory of property held in England in our period. That meant the compression within a few paragraphs of subjects to which separate treatises might be devoted. The need for generalisation, however, imposed itself.

Though it may be natural to philosophise, philosophic vision or the capacity to see things steadily and as a whole is largely an acquired characteristic. Granted that all the relevant facts connected with a particular subject of research have been collected, the difficult question of interpretation and emphasis remains. Assuming that the facts are representative, who shall decide their relative value ? Here the personal equation inevitably intervenes, and thus the material at hand, or rather the judgement formed of it, is bound to be affected by subjective influences.

The reader may be inclined to question the wisdom of attempting to deal in a single volume with the theories of property held in three countries. It should, however, be remembered that America was a colony of England until practically the end of our period. There is good reason therefore for devoting some attention to the influence which English thought on property exercised on American writers and publicists in the eighteenth century. It is, perhaps, less easy to justify a chapter on France. The main reason for its inclusion is because of the broad contrast between English and French conditions in the eighteenth century. Again, the application of Locke's theory of property was attended by different results in the two countries. In England it proved a conservative instrument ; it appeared to sanction the individualistic arrangements following the Revolution of 1688. In France Locke's theory of property, in so far as it had any positive influence on events, tended to act as a revolutionary force—to free the French people from the vexatious interference with their property practised by the

Crown and nobility. But the abolition of the feudal régime owed more to the writers who regarded property as a social creation—a view which had many influential supporters in France—than to Locke.

The sources, primary and secondary, on which this book is based are, I trust, sufficiently indicated in the foot-notes. It is a pleasure as well as a duty to note also the kind assistance accorded to me by friends. Amongst English scholars my chief indebtedness is to Mr. R. H. Tawney. As supervisor of my research at the University of London, he has generously aided me with suggestions and criticisms. For these, and for the stimulus which his published works have given me, I desire to express my best thanks. I am also grateful to Professor H. J. Laski for the kind manner in which he gave me some information as to sources for Chapter vi. I have profited much by the criticisms of Professor J. L. Stocks, who acted as one of the Examiners of the manuscript when presented for the degree of Ph. D. (Econ.) in the University of London. For his kind interest in the work and for the prompt manner in which he responded to my invitation to write the preface, I thank him sincerely.

On this, as on a former occasion, Professor Alfred O'Rahilly has been ever ready to facilitate my work by procuring books for me. For this service, for making the Index, and for his supervision of the work while going through the press, I wish to express my appreciation. I desire to thank also the other Directors of the Cork University Press. I wish to thank my Superiors also for their kind interest and encouragement. The assistance which the Librarians of the London School of Economics, the University of London, including the Goldsmiths' Library, the British Museum, the Bibliothèque Nationale, Paris, and University College, Cork, have given me, is hereby also gratefully acknowledged.

Messrs. Purcell & Co., Printers, are to be congratulated on the careful manner in which they have executed a difficult task.

W. PASCHAL LARKIN.

University College, Cork,
  27th June, 1930.

INTRODUCTION TO THE 1969 EDITION

THE title of the present work is not, perhaps, sufficiently comprehensive, for the matter discussed includes more than property and the period surveyed is not confined to the eighteenth century. The danger of making clear-cut divisions in the history either of ideas or of institutions is now generally recognized. Nevertheless, there seemed to be good reason for confining ourselves, in this study, principally to the period which divides the Civil War in England from the French Revolution.

Special reference is made to England because she was the first country to adopt on a grand scale a new philosophy of property, and the first to carry out on a national scale a new experiment in economic organization. Her pioneer work in industrialism has served as a guide and a warning to other countries.

The evils which have accompanied the growth of private wealth in modern communities are intimately connected with the ideas which people have held as to the rights and duties, or lack of duties, of private property. In the following pages, special attention is given to John Locke's theory of property because he is frequently represented as the English apostle of economic individualism. But his views were less individualistic than is commonly supposed, and many writers in the past have failed to recognize the wide sense in which he used the term "property." For Locke it included a man's "life, liberty, and estate."

The difficulties which beset the present study were obviously great, though the subject itself was attractive. The dearth of specific works on property in the eighteenth century entailed very wide reading. Points had to be touched on therefore which, at first sight, seem to have but a remote connection with our subject. But as views on property are inevitably affected by the attitude adopted toward such questions as religion, morality, education and State policy, it was thought that some reference to these subjects would throw light on the dominant theory of property held in England in the period. That meant the compression within a few paragraphs of subjects to which separate treatises might be devoted. The need for generalization, however, imposed itself.

Though it may be natural for man to philosophize, philosophic vision or the capacity to see things steadily and in whole is largely an acquired characteristic. Granted that all the relevant facts on a particular research subject have been collected, the difficult question of interpretation and emphasis remains. Assuming that the facts are representative, who shall decide their relative value? Here the personal equation inevitably intervenes and thus the material at hand, or rather the judgment formed of it, is bound to be affected by subjective influences.

One may question the wisdom of attempting to deal in a single volume with the theories of property held in three countries. It should, however, be remembered that America was a colony of England until practically the end of our period. There is good reason therefore for devoting some attention to the influence which English thought exercised on American writers and publicists in the eighteenth century. It is, perhaps, less easy to justify a chapter on France. The main reason for its inclusion is because of the broad contrast between English and French conditions in the eighteenth century. Again, the application of Locke's theory of property was attended by different results in the two countries. In England it proved a conservative instrument, apparently sanctioning the individualist arrangements following the Revolution of 1688. In France Locke's theory of property, insofar as it had any positive influence on events, tended to act as a revolutionary force—to free the French people from the vexatious interference with their property practiced by the Crown and the nobility. But the abolition of feudalism as an economic and social regime during the Revolution owed more to the writers who regarded property as a social creation than to Locke.

The first edition of this book, published by the Cork University Press in 1930, was favorably received by scholars in the English-speaking world and in France and Belgium. Although it devoted little space to the views on property held by eighteenth-century lawyers and bypassed the mysteries of jurisprudence, two eminent professors of law found the book very interesting.

Professor J. E. de Montmorency of the University of London wrote a courteous and informative review article, "The Nature of

Property," in *The Contemporary Review* (January, 1931); Professor W. H. Hamilton of Yale University, in an appreciative and enlightening article, "Property According to Locke" in the *Yale University Journal*, XLI (1931–32), clarified for me the complex constitutional and legal problems of the American scene. Both reviewers realized that I was concerned mainly with the economic side of a very difficult theme.

There has been a revival of interest in the life and writings of John Locke in the present century. This is mainly due to the tercentenary of his birth in 1932, and to the acquisition by the Bodleian Library, Oxford, in 1948 of the hitherto unpublished massive material which Locke had bequeathed to his cousins, the King family. The authentic biography of Locke is that by Maurice Cranston,[1] who had access to the thousands of manuscripts, letters, notebooks, and private diaries of Locke. The complex and mysterious character of Locke portrayed in this biography offers interesting material for psychologists. Mr. Cranston, at the end of a patient and painstaking study, endeavors to summarize the nature of Locke's influence in these words: "Locke did not merely enlarge men's knowledge, he changed their ways of thinking." Others prefer to attribute Locke's importance in the history of thought to the problems which he raised—the questions he asked —rather than to the solutions he offered.

Locke's political philosophy, however, seems to have a more enduring interest. Utilizing the new material now available in the Bodleian Library, Mr. J. W. Gough has made an admirable attempt to extract the static from the dynamic in Locke's thought on various topics.[2] Locke's views on government, "the law of nature," "property" and "toleration" are clearly presented and charitably discussed.

The relations between Church and State were a great storm center of controversy in seventeenth-century England, and Locke spent a good deal of time trying to solve the problem. Though frequently represented as the pioneer or apostle of religious toleration, his views on the subject were less liberal than many of his contemporaries. Roman Catholics and atheists should not be

1.—*John Locke* (London: Longmans, Green, 1957).
2.—*John Locke's Political Philosophy* (Oxford: The Clarendon Press, 1950).

tolerated by the State. The number of atheists in Locke's England must have been few and their atheism was not aggressive. He must have been disappointed with the Toleration Act of 1689. Although the Act was confined to the Nonconformists, it did not, even for them, establish the principle of toleration. This Act allowed them freedom of worship behind closed doors, provided they took an oath of allegiance to the King and signed a declaration against "Popery." They were not granted full civil rights. "They were," in Ernest Barker's phrase, "only half citizens," subject to "a triple body of religious disabilities."[3] They could not hold municipal office or any civil or military office of the State, and their sons were debarred from entering the universities of Oxford and Cambridge. These "disabilities" or handicaps were not removed until 1828, and it was not until 1871 that Nonconformists were fully admitted on terms of equality to the universities of Oxford and Cambridge. Unlike other countries, the division of political parties in England was based on religion for centuries. Ernest Barker holds that "the development of English life and politics" can never be understood "unless we use the key of religion to unlock its secrets."[4]

Broadly speaking, the same considerations apply to a full understanding of American history. For good and evil the Puritan religion, and the political philosophy associated with it, had a profound influence both before and after the rise of the United States as an independent political power. It is probable that a false emphasis has been placed on the relation between Locke's political philosophy and the constitutional struggles which preceded the Declaration of Independence.

I think that the American colonies would have adopted the course which they did had Locke never lived. The Treaty of Paris (1763), ending the long war between France and England for supremacy in North America, gave the colonists a great sense of security, and an opportunity to reflect on their right to exist as a separate political entity. One might say that the American Revolution was predestined in 1763. Like all great historical innovations,

3.—*Britain and the British People* (London: Oxford University Press, 1943), pp. 86–87.
4.—*Ibid.*, pp. 25–26.

the American movement owed as much, if not more, to practical exigencies as to formal theorizing.

The problem to what extent Locke's writings have been responsible for the social theory which triumphed when the constitutional and military issues were no longer in doubt now seems to me incapable of a dogmatic solution. Admirers of John Locke, however, must rejoice that his theory of property comes to life again in one of Mr. Gough's skillful and judicial studies. He defends Locke against those critics who blamed him for not mentioning a well-known traditional theory of property of medieval origin, the theory of eminent domain (*dominium eminens*). This theory stressed the State's right to control the exercise of the rights of private property in the interest of the common good. It did not suit Locke's purpose to emphasize the State's power in an age which had suffered so much from the arbitrary interference of governments. Moreover, the Common Law of England, which was well known to Locke, took no cognizance of this medieval theory. On the contrary, it highlighted the "absolute" or unconditional character of rights of property.

Although Locke regarded political power as a trust to be held and used for the benefit of the people, he naïvely assumed that the good of the people as a whole would be best served by the minimum of State interference with their property as well as with their life and liberty. This assumption disposed him to dispense with any discussion of the concept of the common good. It seems fairly well established not only that he failed to make a distinction between the common good and the particular goods of individuals, but that he was unaware of its existence.[5] It is undoubtedly difficult to define the common good. It has, however, a positive content, although that content is relative to every organized community and to every historical period. In every age, each class in society tends to regard the common good as whatever promotes or at least does not impede its own special interests.

Blackstone in the eighteenth century thought that the laws of England were so perfect that they made provisions for the good of

5.—Gough, *op. cit.,* pp. 33–34.

all its citizens, including their economic good or welfare. His complacent optimism irritated Bentham. In the *Commentaries*, Blackstone wrote: "The law not only regards life and protects everyman in the enjoyment of it, but also furnishes him with everything necessary for its support. For there is no man so indigent or wretched, but he may demand a supply sufficient for all the necessities of life from the more opulent part of the community." The second sentence seems to summarize one of the main aims of modern social endeavor. In the undemocratic parliamentary government of eighteenth-century England little was done, beyond the Poor Law, to implement the indigent or wretched man's demands. Even the interests of many small landowners or peasants were sacrificed to those of pheasants, or rather to the social prestige attaching to the possession of large landed estates.

Early in this century a great English economist, Alfred Marshall, blamed the growth of "extreme rights of private property in land," and their acceptance by the State, for many of our modern urban problems. Large private gains accrued to landowners, he maintained, "not merely through causes which are public rather than private in their character, but also at the expense of one of the chief forms of public wealth," that is, the health of the people.

The food-supplies aspect of the land question, which was the great social problem of Europe for over a thousand years, has been solved in Europe by science, organization, and the revolution in transport. The improvement in transport made possible vast urbanization and this has brought into relief a land-space scarcity problem, creating a chronic housing headache in large towns and cities.

Important as the rights to property in land are, they form today only an island in a vast sea of other property rights. In highly industrialized countries, the great majority of property rights consist of legal claims to money incomes. Money in all its varying forms and degrees of acceptability is, in developed countries, the most important category of property rights. The social and ethical implications of that fact have not yet been fully grasped.

*   *   *   *   *   *

Amongst English scholars my chief indebtedness is to the late Professor R. H. Tawney, who supervised the research work connected with this book when I was a student at the London School of Economics and Political Science.

I wish to express my gratitude to Howard Fertig, Inc., Publisher, New York, for making this American edition possible.

PASCHAL LARKIN

St. Bonaventure's, Cork.
   December, 1968.

CONTENTS

ERRATA

Page 89, line 2 : "Addison" should read "Steele"

line 11 : "Addison's" should read "this"

line 15 : "But despite his literary claims to
a hearing" should read "Steele"

Page 112, line 9 from bottom of text : "centre of
political gravity" should read "political
centre of gravity"

Property In
The Eighteenth Century

CHAPTER I.

LOCKE'S PREDECESSORS.

To understand Locke's theory of property it is necessary to give some account of its antecedents. In this chapter we propose to set his theory in relation to the conception of property held in the later Middle Ages and, indeed, in the sixteenth century. To appreciate Locke's significance it seems desirable to trace also in brief outline the changes both in social theory and social organisation which prepared the way for his teaching. And since property is a concept which takes part of its colour from the general economic and social environment, it has seemed wise to include some reference to opinion on the wider subject of business transactions and social organisation.

The essential features of his theory were that private property [1] is a natural right anterior to the State, and to protect which, *inter alia*, the State came into existence. Private property is the outcome of human personality ; it is founded on the dominion which man has over his own exertions ; it represents the fruits of his labour. Since man has an inherent right to own as well as to possess property, he is in no way obliged to obtain the consent, tacit or explicit, of his fellowman or the State in order to appropriate the products of his industry. Indeed, a man's right to his

---

1.—It is important to observe that Locke used the word " property " in a wide sense. It included, as we shall see below, " lives, liberties and estates."—*Civil Government*, ed. H. Morley, 1884, bk. ii., ch. ix., § 123, p. 256.

property is so absolute that the State or " supreme power "
cannot take from him " any part of his property without his
own consent "[1] or that of his parliamentary representatives.
The absence of any reference to the moral obligations of
ownership, and the emphasis laid on individual right rather
than on social purpose in his theory, present a striking
contrast to the ideas which we are now to consider.[2]

The main characteristics of mediaeval social theory,
including the mediaeval conception of property, were derived
partly from the teaching of the Church, as expounded by the
Fathers;[3] partly from the writings of Aristotle ; and partly
from the feudal organisation of society. The background of
it all is religion. Man has a definite end to attain ; the
object of his existence, as made known by revelation, is to
know, love and serve God in this life and thus attain to
eternal happiness. The supreme criterion, therefore, of all
individual actions, as well as of all social institutions, was
whether they helped or hindered man to attain his final
supernatural end. Every department of life, the actions of
princes as well as those of peasants, must be judged by this
standard. A powerful aid to this judgement was afforded
by the doctrine of natural law, because though known to us
by the light of reason, it was in reality a part of the Divine
Law. And since man had fallen from the supernatural state
to which he was raised in the beginning, a legal system to
give effect to the consequences of the truths discovered by
reason was considered essential to the very existence of social
life. But no individual actions, much less any positive laws,
had any moral value unless they conformed to the requirements of natural reason or justice[4] as interpreted by the

1.—*Civil Government*, ed. Morley, bk. ii., ch. xi., § 138, p. 264.

2.—It should be noted that Locke's theory of property was influenced by
his historical environment. It was a defensive theory designed to protect
the individual against the encroachments of the Crown in England in the
seventeenth century, and not a complete philosophy of property.

3.—For a good account of the social and political ideals of the Fathers,
see Otto Schilling, *Die Christlichen Soziallehren*, Köln, 1926. The alleged
communism or socialism of the Church Fathers is ably refuted by
A. Vermeersch, S.J., *Quaestiones de Iustitia*, Brugis, 1904, no. 210, pp. 266f,
and by Rev. Dr. John A. Ryan, *Alleged Socialism of the Church Fathers*, 1913.

4.—St Thomas, *Summa Theologica*, 1. 2., q. 95, art. ii.

Canon Law of the Church. The individual was bound to lead a virtuous life, not only for his own interest, but for the sake of the community.[1] And the Church, being the custodian of those eternal interests which far transcend the secular interests of this life, claimed the right to interfere in every sphere of life.

Mediaeval social theory naturally could not ignore the facts of feudal organisation. But while, on the whole, accepting the economic and social environment in which he lived, the mediaeval theorist endeavoured to leaven the feudal mass with a mystic or spiritual significance. That was done by applying the Pauline conception of the Church to society.[2] Just as in the Church there are different orders having distinct functions and all united in one body of which the head is Christ, so also in the social body there must be a hierarchy of classes, each with its distinct functions and all animated and united by the idea of the common good.[3] The members within a class are equal and must discharge the duties attaching thereto. Between classes, however, inequality was considered necessary in order that each class might perform its functions or enjoy its rights. To the modern mind this dependence of rights on class inequality sounds strange. But we must remember that symbolism exercised a great sway over the mediaeval mind, and left its mark on social thought also. Everything in this world is linked up with something beyond it ; the most ordinary things have a deep significance ; their meaning is not exhausted by their functions ; their ultimate significance reaches into another world. This combination of the terrestrial and celestial ; this spiritual interpretation of all the facts of life did not, however, as is sometimes suggested, prevent mediaeval writers from

1.—St. Thomas, *Summa*, 1. 2., q. 92, a. 1. ad. 3.

2.—*Romans*, xii. 4. 5.

3.—John of Salisbury in the twelfth century expresses it thus : " Then and then only will the health of the commonwealth be sound and flourishing when the higher members devote themselves to the lower and when similarly the lower members cooperate with the higher, so that each and all are as it were members of one another and each believes his own interest best served by what he knows to be most usefully provided for others."—*Policraticus*, vi. 20 (Webb ii. 59) cf vi. 25 (Webb ii. 73) : "An injury to the head reacts on all the members and a wound unjustly inflicted on any member tends to the injury of the head."

discussing in a scientific manner [1] those institutions which lie at the basis of social life.

Whatever differences of opinion may exist as to Aquinas' superiority in the realm of metaphysics, few will question his primacy in the field of mediaeval social theory. His views as to the attitude which man should adopt towards material wealth, and, above all, the masterly manner in which he fits the social into the moral order, had such an enduring influence—his views on usury were quoted by English writers in the sixteenth century to whom parts of his theological system appeared an effete superstition [2]—that a brief notice of his economic and social views may help us to understand both their power in a predominantly religious civilisation, and their weakness in a growing commercial civilisation like that of sixteenth century England.

In his treatment of property St. Thomas distinguishes clearly between the right to property in general and the right to specific or individual forms of property. [3]   Man has a natural right to the use and ownership of some indeterminate amount of property ; that follows from his nature.   But while nature itself does not effect any division of property, private property is not opposed to natural law. [4]   In fact private property is founded on natural law in as much as it is prescribed by the *ius gentium* which is a deduction from the natural law. [5]   The right to private property, therefore, is not a mere positive right ; something dependent upon human enactments.   Experience shows that private owner-ship of the instruments of production and distribution stimulates enterprise, promotes order and secures social

1.—To what extent mediaeval thought can be considered ' scientific ' depends largely upon one's view of ' science.' See Dr. F. Aveling's article in *St. Thomas Aquinas*, ed. Rev. C. Lattey, S.J., 1925, p. 102.

2.—See, for example, Miles Mosse, *The Arraignment and conviction of Usurie, that is, the iniquitie and unlawfulness of usurie, displayed in sixe sermons*, 1595, p. 18, and *passim*. He quotes St. Thomas' *Summa* to show " why usurie shoulde not bee practised of a Christian (especiallie not of an Englishman)."—*Op. cit.*, p. 145. See *S.P.D. Elizabeth*, lxxv., no. 54., or *Tudor Economic Documents*, ed. Tawney and Power, 1924, vol. iii., p. 361.

3.—*Summa Theologica* 2. 2., q. 66, a. 1 and a. 2.

4.—*Summa Theologica* 2. 2., q. 66, art. 2, ad. 1. " Proprietas possessionum non est contra ius naturale."

5.—*Summa Theologica* 2, 2., q. 57, art. 3. The principles of the *ius gentium* are proper only to the human species.

peace. Thus the principle of private property, however much its concrete expression may vary, is not a mere juristic category.[1] If private property is a convenience or convention, it is a convenience founded on moral necessity. Finally, private ownership was not introduced on account of sin or the " Fall " ; [2] it would arise apart from the Fall, owing to the necessities of social life and the diversities of human capacities.

While however Aquinas regarded private ownership of the means of production and distribution as morally necessary, he would allow no such exclusive right to the individual with regard to the *use* or consumption of property. While he does not advocate common ownership as regards the use of things, he insists that private property is not an end in itself, and that it is in reality not so much an absolute right as the best means, in the present circumstances of human nature, of respecting the requirements of natural right. " The temporal goods which by God's providence are conferred on man are his indeed so far as relates to property, but in their use they should belong not only to him but also to others, who can be supported from what is superfluous to him." [3]

It is only within certain limits, therefore, that an individual may do what he likes with his property. Whenever property is used or abused so as to prevent the satisfaction of the essential needs of the community, it would seem, according to St. Thomas, that the community has the right to assert its claim to such ill-used wealth. Production in the Middle Ages not being the social process that it is to-day, St. Thomas did not consider the possibility of State or group ownership of such means of production as might be used in an anti-social manner. Even had he foreseen the development of the modern State, there is no reason to suppose that he would have considered it an ideal mechanism for righting the evils of the mal-distribution of wealth.[4] But he clearly

1.—*Summa Theologica* 1. 2., q. 95, art. 4.
2.—*Summa Theologica* 1., q. 96, a. 4.
3.—*Summa Theologica* 2. 2., q. 32, a. 5, ad 2.
4.—See the able article by Prof. A. O'Rahilly on " St. Thomas's Theory of Property " in *Studies*, Sept., 1920, pp. 343-9 ; and Rev. Dr. M. Cronin's articles on " The Moral, Social and Political Philosophy of St. Thomas " in *St. Thomas Aquinas*, ed. Lattey, 1925, pp. 176f.

admits the social character of wealth. Thus a person, in extreme necessity, who is refused assistance, is morally entitled to take from his better circumstanced neighbour what is necessary to sustain life. One who possesses superfluous wealth, that is, wealth over and above what is required for his state of life and that of his dependents—*superfluum non solum respectu sui ipsius, . . . sed etiam respectu aliorum quorum cura ei incumbit*—[1] is bound by the moral law to give alms to those in extreme need. Outside extreme necessity the obligation to give alms is not of justice but of charity, but that may also be binding.

Although for Aquinas the principle or institution of private property is eminently in accord with human reason and will, unlike Locke he laid no emphasis on the argument for private property based on the necessity of individual liberty. That argument which looms so large in the constitutional struggles of seventeenth century England, and in the anti-socialist literature of to-day, had not the same point in an age when the moral supremacy of the Church was generally accepted[2] and the modern State had scarcely begun to emerge. He is more careful than Locke and some other writers who seem to regard human personality as the cause, rather than as the condition or end, of the right of private property. The right of private property, like every other right, supposes a law which confers moral power and imposes obligations. The ultimate basis of the right of private property, therefore, is not the fickle will of the individual, but the unalterable moral law which is founded on the nature of things. Again, unlike most eighteenth century writers, St. Thomas is never weary of warning his readers against the allurements of avarice—the *immoderatus amor habendi*[3] Nor is he indifferent to the social and individual importance of labour. His whole teaching, or rather that of the Church of whose doctrine he was the most eminent exponent, on usury, prices

---

1.—*Summa Theologica* 2. 2., q. 32, art. 5.
2.—See Otto Gierke, *Political Theories of the Middle Ages*, tr. F. W. Maitland, 1900, p. 82. The Church taught that " every individual by virtue of his eternal destination is at the core somewhat holy and indestructible."
3.—*Summa Theologica* 2. 2., q. 118, art. 1.

and profits was designed to protect the economically weaker members of society. Even John of Paris,[2] who seems to anticipate Locke's individualistic conception of property, regarded it as the duty of the temporal authority to interfere with property whenever the common good demanded such interference.

The practical application of such doctrines was seen in the view taken of the obligations of landlord and tenant, of trade and industry, and of the duties of the rich towards the poor. The owners of large estates were political functionaries rather than economic adventurers. If they were supported by the labour of others, in the shape of customary rents, such payments were justified by the fact that they performed the function of protecting the people and preserving social order. The rent which the feudal lord received did not depend solely upon the impersonal forces of supply and demand ; the customary standard of living of his tenants was regarded as a controlling factor which it was immoral to ignore. Indeed, broadly speaking, one might say that the bonds which united landlord and tenant were conceived of as a matter of ethical obligation rather than as merely a cash nexus. To say this is not to ignore the many instances where practice fell short of theory ; or to deny the narrowing effect on human character which the economic atmosphere of the mediaeval peasant tended to produce. But if at times the peasant felt the sting of poverty in addition to the dis-advantages of dependence, his sufferings were normally regarded as the result rather of personal oppression than of inexorable economic law. It might have been imagined that

2.—*Tractatus de potestate regia et papali*, 1305, in Melchior Goldast, *Monarchia*, Franckfurt, 1614, t. ii., ch. vii, p. 116. . . . "Exterior possessions of the laity are not conferred on the community as are ecclesiastical possessions ; rather they are acquired by individuals through their own art, labour and industry. Individual persons, in so far as they are individual, have in themselves right, power and true ownership ; and each one may deal with his own—by disposing of it, distributing it, retaining it, or alienating it—as he pleases without injuring anyone else, since he is its owner." But the ruler may interfere when, as sometimes happens, men " loving their own goods too much, do not share them in accordance with the necessity or utility of their country." Paulus, the Roman jurist, anticipated John of Paris's labour theory of property. See F. Girard, *Manuel élémentaire de droit romain*, Paris, 1901, p. 316.

the comparatively static economic organisation of the Middle Ages would offer a more agreeable soil for the growth of a theory of immutable economic laws than the dynamic environment of later centuries. An age which is convinced of the contingency of the present world naturally exhibits traces of that conviction in its social and economic theory.

The conditional or contingent character of property rights was, indeed, an essential element in the feudal theory of landownership. The same idea was insisted upon with even greater emphasis, though from a different point of view, by religious thinkers. The opposition of the Church to the teaching of Roman Law in the early thirteenth century was probably prompted as much by a desire to counteract the absolutist conception of property rights which Roman Law was introducing, as it was to uphold the supremacy of the Canon Law.[1] Many feudal lords were but too willing to find a justification for their robbery and oppression of the poor in a law which put force above function, and conquest above charity, as titles to private property.

Property and contract are conceptions which are closely related ; and the mediaeval theory of prices and of interest was inspired by motives of a similar kind. Like its theory of landownership, it had its origin in the grand idea that we are all brothers of a common Father who intended the goods of this world to be so used that none should possess super-fluities while others lacked necessaries. Not to succour one's neighbour in economic distress was to forget the essential equality of all men in God's sight, and the levelling influence of the grave. Though the mediaeval doctrine of equality was " closely akin to a *memento mori* "—equality of wealth or of rank was considered neither natural nor desirable—it does not follow that it was, in practice, devoid of " social purport." [2] The elaborate machinery, both civil and ecclesiastical, dealing with unconscionable bargaining, un-neighbourly action, and injustice generally, what was that

1.—See Gabriel Ardant, *Papes et Paysans*, Paris, 1891, pp. 40-41. Cf. Ernest Tarbouriech, *Essai sur la Propriété*, Paris, 1904, pp. 255f.
2.—As Prof. J. Huizinga, *The Waning of the Middle Ages*, tr. F. Hopman, 1924, pp. 53-4, seems to imply.

but an attempt to secure at least a rough economic equalitarianism ?

The attempt to enforce the ' just price ' even in the comparatively simple economic life of the Middle Ages did not always meet with success,[1] but it was, nevertheless, not abandoned. Though the economic background of mediaeval social theory contained many elements which are surprisingly modern, it did, on the whole, lend itself to regulation. Broadly speaking, a natural rather than a money economy prevailed. The production of wealth was carried on mainly in response to, rather than in anticipation of, demand. Custom rather than competition regulated prices ; and custom, on the whole, though with many exceptions, tended to protect the weak.

The application of moral rules to economic transactions, at no time an easy matter, becomes much more difficult when new and more complex economic relationships arise. It is to the credit of the social theorists of the later Middle Ages that they attempted to deal with the new problems to which the growth of urban classes and a commercial economy gave rise. Village communities became less and less economically self-sufficient and feudal relations gradually dissolved. In the fifteenth century one finds St. Antonino [2] re-stating the traditional doctrine of the ' just price ' in the light of the complex economic environment in which he lived. Financial capitalism was carving its impersonal career in his native Florence ; and consequently he was led to take more account of individual or subjective forces in the determination of just prices than it was possible for St. Thomas to do. But St. Antonino in the fifteenth century is as emphatic as St. Thomas in the thirteenth in proclaiming that the pursuit of wealth as an end in itself is unlawful ; and that all economic activity must be governed by a moral purpose.

1.—See the interesting article by A. S. Walker in *History*, Octobei, 1921, p. 163.
2.—*Summa Theologica* ii. 8, 1 and ii. 16, 3. See also Fr. Bede Jarrett, O.P., *St. Antonino and Mediaeval Economics*, 1914 ; and *Social Theories of the Middle Ages*, 1926, p. 161.

Though St. Thomas shared Aristotle's predilection for agriculture, he recognised the necessity of commerce and justified it by the ends for which it was conducted. "A man may intend the moderate gain which he seeks to acquire by trading for the upkeep of his household, or for the assistance of the needy ; or, again, a man may take to trade for some public advantage, for instance lest his country lack the necessaries of life, and seek gain not as an end but as a payment of labour." [1] That view of profits as a payment for labour or services rendered to the community, held even in the tenth century,[2] seems to offer a formula sufficiently elastic to cover that modern theory of profits which regards them as the payment which society gives the business man for takings its risks.

It is difficult to say how far, if at all, the production of wealth in the Middle Ages was impeded by the moral restrictions placed on the pursuit of gain. There is no necessary antithesis between the religious and the practical mind. Has not Carlyle, as much as Aquinas, emphasised the fact that " No man has worked, or can work, except religiously ; " and that if men do not work " as in a Great Taskmaster's eye," they " will work wrong, work unhappily for themselves and you." [3] On the other hand, the practical efficacy of mediaeval social ideals is sometimes questioned. The tendency to oversystematise is commonly alleged to have been the greatest weakness of the mediaeval mentality. In extenuation, however, it is sometimes suggested that this characteristic was the defect of a good quality ; the product of a " profound idealism " which sought out general principles, standards and models, rather than exceptional and individual variations. Whatever truth this view may contain as a criticism of the mediaeval treatment of purely speculative problems, it is quite misleading if applied to mediaeval social ethics. The latter could not be " impersonal." [4] The

1.—*Summa Theologica* 2. 2., q. 77, art. 4.
2.—*The Colloquy of Archbishop Alfric*, by Alfric the Grammarian, in Library of National Antiquities, ed. Thomas Wright, 1857, vol. i., p. 8.
3.—" Past and Present " in *Works*, 1870, vol. xiii., p. 257.
4.—Prof. J. Huizinga, *Op. cit.*, p. 196, says that to the mediaeval mind " what is important is the impersonal."

dominant feature of mediaeval social thought was the concept of moral purpose and personal responsibility.

A more pertinent criticism of mediaeval social theory is that it was not sufficiently dynamic : that its principles were too abstract to permit of detailed application ; and particularly that its characteristic doctrine of usury was not thoroughly applied to the big financial operations of the age.

It is beyond the scope of this essay to enter into a detailed examination of these points. It may, however, be observed that while a good end never justifies the employment of immoral means, it is a matter for rejoicing rather than for ridicule if some of those who attained great wealth by morally doubtful methods did, by way of restitution, devote part of that wealth to promoting the beauty of God's house. Again, all principles are of course general and their application can never be made automatic. And it must not be forgotten that even in the Middle Ages the Church regarded itself as primarily a spiritual institution ; and therefore, *qua* Church, was not divinely commissioned to lay down a detailed programme of economic and social reform. Its principal concern was the eternal interests of man. Its eagerness to hold and to extend the temporal power conferred on it, as well as its apparent indifference to serfdom as an institution,[1] are both explained by that fact.

It is a comparatively easy task to discover examples of how practice falls short of principles in any age.[2] It is less easy to say how far the disturbing facts cited are representative or typical of the period under consideration ; much less to conclude that the principles of the period were never taken seriously. The things, both good and bad, which men have said about the Middle Ages would probably

1.—Though the Church was slow to recognise the utility of free labour, it endeavoured to check the abuses of feudal lords. The Council of Lateran, for example, condemned arbitrary taxes in 1179 ; and a certain number of theologians inveighed against serfdom. See Prof. P. Boissonnade, *Le Travail dans l'Europe chrétienne au Moyen-Age*, 1921, pp. 191-193.

2.—See the very interesting book by Dr. G. G. Coulton, *The Mediaeval Village*, 1925, and Sir W. Ashley's review of it in *Economic Journal*, June, 1926, pp. 142f.

have taxed the credulity of the mediaeval peasant himself !
It would seem that certain social critics in the past showed
greater acumen, in some respects, than their modern
imitators.

Langland, who exposed the evils of society in his day,
distinguished between the office and the man when in Piers
Plowman [1] he satirised the clergy's leaning towards avarice.
His poem not only reveals the dangers to which the growth
of wealth was exposing the Church in the fourteenth century,
but also throws much light on the independent spirit which
characterised even the English labourer of that period. The
Statute of Labourers (1349), adjusting wages to the new
economic conditions created by the Black Death, also
illustrates the growing mobility of the British labourer,
and his increasing emancipation from manorial authority.[2]
Langland's poem gives one a good insight into the " haukes
maneres " [3] of the age ; the social injustice practised, and
the pity for the poor which sometimes did not exceed that
which a " pedlere hath of cattes." [4] Himself, no advocate
of doctrinal changes, he seemed to feel that if religion did not
change men, men would be driven to change religion.

From the fifteenth century onwards there were a number
of forces at work making for an individualistic conception of
society and social relationships, which, in England, was almost
complete at the time Locke wrote. The development of
commerce following the great discoveries of the fifteenth
century ; the breakdown of the feudal system ; the increased
mobility of labour ; the rise of a middle class ; the
Renaissance which was far more than a revival of learning ;
the religious revolution in the sixteenth, and the development
of mathematical and physical science in the seventeenth
century ;—all contributed their share to the new outlook
towards life and social relations which characterised England
at the Restoration.

1.—W. Langland, *Piers the Plowman*, 1377, ed. Walter W. Skeat, 1906.
See also D. Chadwick, *Social Life in the days of Piers Plowman*, 1922.
2.—See Sir Frederick Morton Eden, *The State of the Poor*, 1797,
vol. i., p. 31.
3.—*Piers the Plowman*, ed. Skeat, 1906, p. 58.
4.—*Ibid.*, p. 52.

It is possible that some writers have attached more importance to the part played by the religious revolution in bringing about that change than the facts would seem to warrant. Though in its initial stages it was less a cause than a consequence of a contemporary movement towards economic and social individualism,[1] it did ultimately give an enormous momentum to other forces acting in that direction. It is, however, historically incorrect to say that the Reformation produced an immediate breach in traditional social theory. To many of the religious innovators the Reformation represented an attempt to restore not only what they considered the primitive Church but also a purified society.[2] Curiously enough, the Church which to-day is sometimes criticised for its antiquated views, was then charged with modernity. Edward VI's tutor accused the Norfolk rebels in 1549 of preferring " the Bishops of Rome afore Christ, men's invention afore God's law," and of neglecting the " examples " supplied by the Primitive Churches.[3] During the debates on the Elizabethan Act of Supremacy, nine years later, the Archbishop of York told his audience that " If you answer that the Church of Rome is not of God but a malignant Church, then it will follow that we have not yet received any benefit of Christ when we have received no other doctrine, no other faith, no other sacraments, than were sent us from the Church of Rome."[4]

As this is not a theological essay we must not dwell on the tremendous issues raised by the Reformation, or examine its motives, though indeed some of them were very " humaine & naughtie."[5] It is sufficient for our purpose to note that it was no part of the reformers' design to sweep away the

---

1.—Cf. Ashley, *The Economic Organisation of England*, 1914, p. 64.

2.—W. Tyndale, *The Obedience of a Christian Man*, 1528, vol. v., Christian Classics Series. See *Policies to reduce this Realme of Englande unto a Prosperus Wealthe and Estate*, 1549, printed in Tawney and Power, *Tudor Economic Documents*, vol. iii., pp. 311-45.

3.—Sir John Cheke, *The true subject to the Rebell or the Hurt of Sedition*. . . ed. Gerh. Langbaine, 1641, p. 59.

4.—*Parliamentary History*, vol. i., p. 647.

5.—R. Smith, *The Prudentiall Ballance of Religion*, 1609, Epistle to the Reader. See also p. 571 ; p. 567. Cf. Langbaine's preface to Sir John Cheke *Op. cit.*

traditional social theory of the Church,[1] although their opposition to, and hatred of, the authority which supported and gave it sanction acted as a powerful solvent of that theory. Luther, as a sixteenth century writer remarked, was as " vehement against al usurye whatsoever, as he was never more vehement against the Pope himself." [2] Though the subtlety of the canonists seemed but sophistry to him, he was animated by the same idea that the property-owner is a trustee as found expression in the Canon Law. Prices ought not to be left to the higgling of the market, but should be determined in accordance with the common estimation.[3] Both in the *Long Sermon on Usury* (1520) and in the pamphlet on *Trade and Usury* (1524), his social doctrine appears reactionary as compared with that of the later canonists. His attitude towards the new commercial and financial forces which were transforming society was one of profound distrust and even hatred. His outlook was that of a peasant ; his ideal was a rural civilisation with serfdom as its basis.

Quite different from Luther's was the attitude which Calvin adopted towards the economic environment of the sixteenth century. His treatment of the usury question [4] showed a profounder knowledge of the facts of business life than most of his contemporaries. His justification of moderate interest marked him out as an ethical Columbus ; and, apart from anything else which he wrote or did, would probably have secured for him a respectable following. His defence of moderate interest was welcomed especially by the commercial classes, who conveniently forgot the limitations with which it was surrounded. Calvin's alleged contribution to the

---

1.—See *Epistle Dedicatorie* in Miles Mosse, *Op. cit.* On p. 62 he writes : " In buying and selling men play the usurers in many wayes. As, for example, A man buyeth corne yet in the fielde (it may be in the blade) for five shillinges a coombe ; and it is likely that in the harvest it will be worth twelve or thirteen shillinges a coombe : *Tunc usuram facit.* Then that man committeth usurie."

2.—Thomas Wilson, *A Discourse upon Usury*, 1572, ed. R. H. Tawney, 1925, p. 360.

3.—*Werke*, ed. J. C. F. Knaake, 1883, Weimar, vol. xv., p. 295. See R. H. Tawney, *Religion and the Rise of Capitalism*, 1926, pp. 79f. For a full account of Luther's social theory see E. Troeltsch, *Die Soziallehren der Christlichen Kirchen*, 1912, pp. 549f.

4.—*Epistolae et Responsa*, Hanoviae, 1597, pp. 747f.

ethics of money lending consisted in showing that since money could, by its nature, be indifferently employed in purchasing a house, a piece of land, or in financing a business, it was unreasonable to make a moral distinction between income in the form of rent derived from letting a house or a piece of land and pure interest on loans for business purposes. Interest, however, ought not to exceed a certain maximum and the poor must not be asked to pay anything for loans.[1]

Calvin had no intention of introducing an unethical individualism into economic and social life. On the contrary, he believed that the man who tried to shut out God from his daily life was the most unhappy of beings.[2] And in his *Institutes* he sets forth the social character of wealth with an emphasis which is quite mediaeval. "All the blessings we enjoy," he writes, " are Divine deposits committed to our trust on this condition that they should be dispensed for the benefit of our neighbour. . . . So whatever ability a pious man possesses he ought to possess it for his brethren. . . . Let this then be our rule for benignity and beneficence that whatever God hath conferred on us, which enables us to assist our neighbour, we are the stewards of it, who must one day render an account of our stewardship."[3]

At a later stage we shall see how his doctrine of religious individualism took firm root on English soil from the time of Elizabeth, and became the ally of the commercial interests in their economic and political struggles with the Crown in the seventeenth century. But the England of the early sixteenth century which cast aside the traditional principle of Church supremacy in spiritual matters, witnessed, curiously enough, a vigorous restatement of its traditional social theory.

1.—Calvin, *Epistolae et Responsa* (Hanoviae, 1597), p. 750 lays down seven qualifying conditions for the lawfulness of interest-taking.

2.—*Catechismus Eccelsiae Genevensis* in *Opera Omnia*, Amsterdam, 1667, vol. viii., p. 12 : "Nihil posse homini infelicius contingere, quam Deo non vivere."

3.—*Institutes of the Christian Religion*, tr. J. Allen, 1838, vol. i., bk. iii., ch. 7, par. 5., p. 552.

Latimer,[1] Lever,[2] Becon,[3] Starkey,[4] Crowley,[5] Tyndale,[6] and many others stated the mediaeval social thory with even greater eloquence and force than that employed in the Middle Ages. Society is a corporate body ; it is the analogue of the human body ;[7] all members of the society must work for the common good. One must not have "to much *and* another to lytyl " ; social peace can only be attained when everyone is prepared to do his "offyce and duty."[8] Property is dependent on function. One must be content with one's position and have no desire "to be alofte."[9] Measures must be taken to prevent people from raising themselves in the social scale. "A certayn payne must be ordyrd and appoyntyd apon euery man that contentyth not hymselfe wyth hys owne mysterie, craft, and faculty."[10]

The occasion of these various and voluminous appeals to the social theory of the past lay in the rapidly changing economic environment of the sixteenth century. The balance of landed property was shifting from the nobility to the people since the Wars of the Roses broke the power of the nobles. The breakdown of feudalism involved the disappearance of the idea of landowning as a political function, at least in the south and midlands. The lords had not the same interest in preserving their tenants, whether copyholders or leaseholders. The agrarian changes of the first half of the sixteenth century, as has been frequently pointed out,[11] were directly related to the expansion of industry and commerce, and particularly to the growth of the woollen

1.—Hugh Latimer, *Sermons*, Everyman's Library.
2.—Thomas Lever, *Sermons*, ed. E. Arber, 1871, pp. 127-31.
3.—Thomas Becon, *The Jewel of Joy*, 1553.
4.—Thomas Starkey, *England in the Reign of Henry VIII.*, ed. J. M. Cowper, E.E.T.S., 1878.
5.—Robert Crowley, "An Informacion and Peticion," 1550, (*Select Works*, ed. J. M. Cowper, E.E.T.S., 1872), p. 157.
6.—Wm. Tyndale, *The Obedience of a Christian Man*, 1528 (vol. v., Christian Classics Series), pp. 125-6.
7.—Starkey, *Op. cit.*, pp. 45-8., p. 78.
8.—*Ibid.*, pp. 157-8.
9.—Robert Crowley, "The Voyce of the Laste Trumpet," 1550, (*Select Works*, ed. Cowper, E.E.T.S.), p. 64.
10.—Starkey, *Op. cit.*, p. 158.
11.—See R. H. Tawney, *The Agrarian Problem in the Sixteenth Century*, 1912, p. 195, *et passim*. Prof. Gay and Mr. Leadam, Articles in *Transactions Royal Historical Society*, vol. xiv., new series.

industry. From about the middle of the fifteenth century the development of the woollen trade had made pasture farming increasingly profitable. The old rural economy of England had received a severe shock long before it experienced, about the middle of the sixteenth century, the full effects of the flooding of the European market with American silver. But from the middle of the century the general depreciation of the currency acted as a powerful stimulus to the reorganisation of agriculture, and its effects, as we shall see below, were really revolutionary.

Fortunately it is unnecessary for our purpose to discuss the technicalities of what is vaguely termed the " enclosure " movement. But whether we regard the incisive criticisms to which it gave rise as evidence of the selfishness of the age, or see in them an attempt to set up a higher ideal than existed formerly, it must be admitted that the critics did not make sufficient allowance for the economic causes which made rural reorganisation a necessity. To say that, however, is not to condone all the evils committed in the name of desirable economic changes. If writers and preachers, like Latimer and Crowley, spoke much and felt deeply about the distress which they saw around them, one must remember that conservatism is always increased when new forces tend to widen the arena for anti-social action. The grave problems connected with the enclosure movement in England had exercised the minds of statesmen and reformers for almost a century before the Reformation. From 1489 to 1534 Parliament had on various occasions attempted to deal with them.[1]

Whatever may have been Henry VIII's real motives for introducing a " new religion," [2] traditional social theory did not change overnight when he broke with the Pope. He attempted, with varying measures of success, to apply on a

1.—4 Henry VII. C. 19 ; 6 Henry VIII. C. 5; 7 Henry VIII. C. 1; 25 Henry VIII. C. 13.

2.—An Italian writer towards the close of the Elizabethan reign said it was merely " a pretext " for exercising " a more absolute power " over his subjects. See Tommaso Campanella *A Discourse touching the Spanish Monarchy*, English tr. 1659, in Brit. Museum, Thomason Tracts, E. 1012, n. 817, p. 159.

From this point, T. T. will be used to denote Thomason Tracts.

national scale the regulative ideals and customs which governed the economic life of the local sovereignities of the Middle Ages. He endeavoured to carry out the traditional policy of making the State responsible for the welfare of all classes. Efforts were made to check enclosures which were not " beneficial to the commonwealth " or contravened " the statutes about the decay of houses." [1] The prices of food stuffs were fixed according to *25 Henry VIII. C. 2* whenever existing prices gave serious ground for complaint. Thus according to the above statute the Council was empowered to fix the prices of " cheese, butter, capons, hennes, chekyns, and other victualles," and the mayors in the cities, and the justices in the country, were to see that they were observed.

In Edward VI's reign elaborate legislation for the control of prices was passed. [2] Again the Canon Law as to usury, which was embodied in the legislation of 1487 and 1495, [3] was re-enacted in 1552. The doctrine of usury which was held by Latimer and Crowley was less discriminating than that held by the canonists of the later Middle Ages. Crowley, for example, deplored the concession which Parliament had made to practical necessities in 1545, when it allowed a rate of ten per cent. to be charged for the loan of capital. It was partly as a result of the protests made by him and others that Parliament was moved in 1552 to " call this act into question agayne," [4] prohibiting any payment in excess of the principal. Again the Statutes of Artificers, Forestallers and Regrators (1563), Tillage (1563, 1571, 1597), Frauds in Cloth-making (1559, 1593) were all, as economic historians have pointed out, modelled on mediaeval precedents. [5]

Even Edward VI himself, in truly mediaeval fashion, writes about " the reformation of many abuses." [6] The

1.—*Letters and Papers of Henry VIII.*, Appendix, vol. ii., p. 1546.
2.—5 and 6 *Edward VI.*, C. 14.
3.—3 *Henry VII.*, C. 5 ; 11 *Henry VIII.*, C. 8.
4.—R. Crowley, "An Informacion and Peticion," 1550, (*Select Works*, ed. Cowper, 1872), pp. 172-3.
5.—Sir Wm. Ashley, *Economic History*, part i., chaps. ii.-v., R. R. Reid, *The King's Council in the North*, 1921., R. H. Tawney, *Religion and the Rise of Capitalism*, 1926.
6.—"A Discourse about the Reformation of Many Abuses," c. 1550, printed in Gilbert Burnet, *History of the Reformation*, vol. v., pp. 96 f.

profiteering practised in his day is exposed ; the evils
arising from " enclosing commons," as well as those due to
the use of " exchange and usury," are denounced.[1] No one
should insist on his right to superfluities while his neighbour
lacks necessaries. " Wherefore as in the body no part hath
too much, nor too little ; so in a commonwealth ought every
part to have *ad victum et non ad saturitatem.*" [2]

Thus despite the revolutionary proceedings under Henry
VIII—the confiscation of Church property and the evils
which followed in the form of land speculation, increased
rents, evictions and the destruction of communal rights in
the process of converting arable land into pasture—an
attempt was made both by him and his successors to give
practical effects to the traditional social ideal, though
naturally it suffered a severe shock from the example of
economic greed which Henry himself had set. Whatever
opinion one may hold as to the comparative humanity or
inhumanity of pre-Reformation lay and ecclesiastical landlords,[3] it is generally admitted that the confiscation of
monastic and other Church property, and particularly the
open speculation to which it gave rise, tended inevitably to
produce a new type of landowner who embodied some of the
least reputable virtues of the economic man.[4] These " gredie
cormeraunts," who multiplied their " renttes to the
higheste," [5] had no illusions as to the power which property
confers. They were determined to teach the poor to know
" theyr betters." [6] The conception of property which such
conduct implied was obviously that of an absolute right.
Crowley in a memorable passage drew attention to its social
consequences.

1.—*Ibid.*, pp. 100-101.
2.—"A Discourse about the Reformation of Many Abuses," c. 1550, printed
in Gilbert Burnet, *History of the Reformation*, vol. v., p. 98.
3.—See Cardinal Francis Aidan Gasquet, *Henry the Eighth and the English
Monasteries*, 1898, ch. 22, pp. 462f. A. Savine, *Oxford Studies in Social
and Legal History*, ed. P. Vinogradoff, vol. i., pp. 263-7 ; pp. 245-60.
G. G. Coulton, *The Mediaeval Village*, 1925, p. 142.
4.—See *Star Chamber Proceedings* Henry VIII., vol. vi., n. 181, printed in
Tawney and Power *Tudor Economic Documents*, vol. i., pp. 19-29.
5.—R. Crowley, *An Informacion and Peticion*, 1550, ed. Cowper, 1872, p. 162.
6.—R. Crowley, *The Way to Wealth*, ed. Cowper, p. 143 ; Selden Society,
Select Cases in the Court of Requests, pp. 48, 49 ; pp. 198-200.

" If the possessioners," he wrote, " woulde consyder them selues to be but stuardes, and not Lordes over theyr possessions, thys oppression woulde sone be redressed. But so longe as thys perswasion styketh in theyr myndes,—' It is myne owne ; whoe shall warne me to do wyth myne owne as me selfe lysteth ? '—it shall not bee possible to haue any redresse at all. For if I may do wyth myne owne as me lysteth, then maye I suffer my brother, hys wyfe, and hys chyldrene to lye in the strete, excepte he wyll geue me more rent for myne house then euer he shall be able to paye." [1] That individualistic view of property rights, noticeable even in the middle of the sixteenth century, did not however become general until the seventeenth century.

Some evidence has been adduced to show that there was no deliberate and large scale abandonment of the traditional conception of property and social organisation at the Reformation period. How then did the transition take place ? And how account for the individualistic ideas of property and social theory which one finds in some of the pamphlet literature of the seventeenth century, and to which Locke merely gave philosophic precision ? An attempt to answer these questions will be made in the following chapter.

1.—*An Informacion and Peticion*, ed. Cowper, p. 157.

CHAPTER II.

THE RISE OF INDIVIDUALISM.

IT is a commonplace that there are no water-tight compartments in the history either of ideas or of institutions; and that thus every historical period is, in a sense, transitional. This truth, however, need not prevent one from regarding certain periods as transitional in the more fundamental sense of constituting watersheds between two distinct civilisations. Broadly speaking, from the beginning of the sixteenth century to the time of the Civil War there was such a transitional period in England. At the Restoration period one finds that the sense of the organic unity of human life of mediaeval civilisation has decayed; the secular and spiritual aspects of life are sharply severed; and the moral ties which bound social theory in the past, if not entirely broken, have at least been loosened.

While it was no part of the intention of the sixteenth century " Reformers " to abolish the supernatural criterion by which all individual actions should be governed, it is nevertheless certain that the disruption of the organic unity of Christendom in the sixteenth century, and the decline in religious authority which it inevitably involved, tended ultimately to act as a solvent not only of morality in general but of economic morality in particular. Even in Elizabeth's reign the number and variety of religious sects [1] which had grown up were not calculated to inspire confidence in any social theory which appealed to religious sanctions. By the middle of the seventeenth century, as a Protestant writer tells us, many people were " discouraged " at the spectacle of " minister preaching against minister, and one congregation separating from another," as a result of " liberty " being

1.—See *Parliamentary History*, vol. i., p. 644.

used "to invent and broach new errors."[1]   The same writer
complains : " Nor will we forsake any sinne, but what we
ourselves will call sinne : everyone will have his own way
to worship of God ; and everyone will have his own sinne to
dishonour God."[2]   But in addition to the effects which
divisions on religion tended to produce by way of substituting
an individual or subjective morality for an objective and
common ethic, there were two other sets of causes which
combined to overthrow the social theories and organisation
of the Middle Ages.

(1.) SPECULATIVE INFLUENCES.

The first was changes in the mode of thought.   Although
it is fruitless to ascribe the origin of a complex movement
like the Renaissance to any single cause,[3] some aspects of it
may be viewed as a reaction against the extreme attitude
towards property and life which certain phases of the
Franciscan movement assumed.   It is almost unnecessary
to point out that Franciscanism as such was the expression
of the highest form of humanism.   With all his love for
" Lady Poverty," St. Francis never adopted a Manichean
attitude towards wealth, much less towards rational or
irrational creatures.   St. Francis never intended his followers
to be standard-bearers of social pessimism or apologists of
economic oppression.   On the contrary, his Third Order,
founded for people living in the world, and prohibiting them
from taking up arms in purely secular disputes, was one
of the principal non-commercial factors in the breakdown
of feudalism.[4]   But whether we trace the Renaissance
movement to Franciscanism in the thirteenth century, to the
invention of printing in the fourteenth, to the infiltration

1.—George Smith, *England's Pressures, or the People's Complaint*, 1645,
p. 8, Brit. Museum, T. T., E. 295.   (9), *Cf.* R. Sherlock, *Catechism of the
Church of England*, 1663, Preface, p. 1.
2.—Smith, *Op. cit.*, p. 27.
3.—As Mr. A. J. Penty appears to do in *A Guildsman's Interpretation of
History*, 1920, p. 126.
4.—See *Thirde Order of Seynt Franceys*, edited from a fifteenth century
MS., by Walter W. Seton, *E.E.T.S.* (original series n. 148), 1914, p. 51 ; p. 58.

of Oriental and classical learning following the fall of Constantinople in the fifteenth century, to the sense of wonder and curiosity which gave rise to, and was increased by, the geographical discoveries in the same century, or see in it the combined result of all these factors, we must admit that, at least in its later stages, it represented far more than a revival of interest in classical philosophy and literature ; that it stood, in short, for a transvaluation of all accepted values.

Some of the Renaissance writers who did so much to make known to the world the refining influence of the classics did not, however, emerge from the pagan atmosphere of their studies with their moral and social outlook unimpaired. Their glorification of individual self-sufficiency tended to discredit religious restraints. The undue emphasis which they laid on the value of Latin and Greek lent support to the theory, which showed remarkable vitality even in the " enlightened " eighteenth century, that education should be the privilege of a leisured or monied class. It is well known that many of the Renaissance scholars and writers, particularly on the Continent, had something like hatred for the common people.[1] In England the latter were sometimes, as in Shakespeare's plays, described as " groundlings " or " base mechanicals." It was left to the humanitarianism of the eighteenth century to transmute such outspoken expressions into phrases of pity for the poor. Though some of the most enthusiastic scholars of the intellectual revival, such as Sir Thomas More [2] and Savonarola,[3] manifested a real love of the poor and a deep hatred of injustice in their writings, because they were true Christians, it is nevertheless true that the Renaissance movement, as a whole, tended not only to accentuate class divisions, but to remove one of the principal appeals by which economic and social inequalities in the past had been softened or held in check.

1.—Like Horace their motto was " Odi profanum vulgus et arceo." For Joachim Du Bellay, see *La Pléiade française*, ed. Ad. van Bever, 1912. See Lucien Pinvert, *Jacques Grévin*, (1538-1570), 1899. Georges Renard, *Guilds in the Middle Ages*, tr. D. Terry, 1918, p. 91.

2.—*Utopia*, 1516, Everyman's Library, p. 44, p. 26.

3.—Pasquale Villari, *The Life and Times of Savonarola*, tr. L. Villari. new impression, no date, pp. 125-7.

The tendency of Renaissance writers was to exalt "positive" at the expense of "natural" law, to which, with supernatural sanctions, the mediaeval theorists ultimately appealed. The effect was to discredit supernatural sanctions, and sometimes to make religion appear irrelevant to morality. They seemed to think that the "good life" of exceptional philosophers, like Socrates, was within the reach of the ordinary man provided he was sufficiently instructed. They thus forgot one of the important moral lessons, taught by Ovid [1] as well as by St. Paul, that it is one thing to know what is right and quite another thing to give practical effect to that knowledge. They did not see that morality or right living, unaided by religion, demands, as William James happily expresses it, an "athletic attitude" [2] of which few are capable. A further stimulus to the supersession of moral criteria in social and political life by the principle of expediency was added by certain objective factors, such as the decline in the political prestige of the Church, the developments in trade and commerce, and the rise of national states. Though it was not inevitable that a weakening of the political influence of the Church should involve a decline in its moral supremacy, fifteenth century politics conveniently assumed a causal connection ; became defiant towards religious restraint, and endeavoured to become a law unto itself. The most representative figure of this period was Machiavelli.

The important point about Machiavelli, as Dr. Figgis has shown, is "what he omits." [3] In his political works the mediaeval appeal to natural law is replaced by an appeal to pure expediency. Though Machiavelli did not create Machiavellianism any more than Adam Smith created what German writers call "Smithianismus," he did for political theory something similar to what Smith accomplished three centuries later in the economic sphere. He presented in an attractive form the unstated assumptions of the politics of his age just as Smith formulated with greater precision some

1.—*Video meliora proboque ; deteriora sequor.*
2.—*The Varieties of Religious Experience*, 1919, p. 46.
3.—J. N. Figgis, *From Gerson to Grotius*, 1916, p. 96.

of the working economic philosophy of England since the Restoration. While he had no intention of writing a formal treatise on government—his interests were on the whole patriotic rather than scientific—his erection of the non-moral principles and practices of his day into political maxims was a powerful factor in the secularisation of political theory.

Influenced by his environment, as well as by his study of past politics, he concluded that " men are naturally bad." [1] Religion for Machiavelli is only a means to government ; and morality, like religion, is good only when it is useful. A pessimistic appeal to expediency supplants the traditional appeal to the moral law. " For the manner in which men live is so different from the way in which they ought to live, that he who leaves the common course for that which he ought to follow will find that it leads him to ruin rather than to safety." [2] Even in that part of his writings [3] where his interests are doctrinal rather than patriotic, religion is made subservient to policy. The possibility of religion propounding a further end than policy dictates is not considered. Religion is merely an instrumental good. The State should uphold it because it keeps people " well conducted and united." [4]

Machiavelli's writings were known to English statesmen, for example to Thomas Cromwell, in the reign of Henry VIII. Shakespeare taking, strangely enough, the popular view, makes him appear the apotheosis of unscrupulosity. [5] Bacon, as we shall see below, seems to have been the first great modern English writer who fully realised the disastrous consequences of applying the Machiavellian rule of mere expediency to economic and social relations. About a half century after Bacon's death a less known writer refers to the

1.—*Works*, ed. C. E. Detmold, 1882, vol. ii., ch. xviii., p. 58.
2.—" The Prince " in *Works*, ed. Detmold, vol. ii., ch. xv., p. 51.
3.—" Titus Livius " in *Works*, ed. Detmold, vol. ii., ch. xii., p. 129.
4.—*Ibid ;* Cf. *The Works of Machiavelli*, ed. E. Farneworth, 1775, vol. iii., p. 54, note.
5.—*Merry Wives of Windsor*, Act iii., Scene 1 ; *Henry VI.*, part i, Act v., Scene 4 ; part iii., Act iii., Scene 2. Machiavelli admitted that " it is more praiseworthy for a prince always to maintain good faith, and practise integrity rather than craft and deceit," but, he adds, " the experience of our own times has shown that those princes have achieved great things who made small account of good faith."—*Works*, ed. Detmold, vol. ii., ch. xviii., p. 57.

author of *The Prince* as the "incomparable Machiavelli." [1] By the latter part of the sixteenth century, the movement towards the secularisation of political and social theory had made considerable headway in England.

One has but to contrast the social theory of Sir Thomas More, a typical product of the Christian Renaissance, or that of Tyndale, with the views expressed by Sir Thomas Smith in his *De Republica Anglorum,* to realise how wealth rather than moral worth was coming to be recognised as the hall-mark of complete citizenship.   More declared that the poor were more " profitable to the commonwealth " than the rich, and that the State, therefore, ought not to be " a certein conspiracy of riche men procuringe their own commodities under the name and title of the commonwelthe." [2]   Twelve years afterwards Tyndale stated that " the most despised person " in the realm " is the king's brother, . . .   and equal to him in the kingdom of God and of Christ." [3]   In neither of these writers does one find reference to a class of which " no account is made of . . . but onelie to be ruled," which Sir Thomas Smith thought good enough for " such lowe and base persons " as " day labourers, poore husbandmen, yea merchants or retailers which have no free lande, . . . and all artificers." [4]   Smith saw nothing surprising in the existing practice of excluding from active participation in the commonwealth those classes whose rights were not based on the ownership of property in land.

It must, however, be admitted that the absence of any reference to the religious basis of the State in Smith's work was, in a sense, a historical necessity.   The old view of society as an organism, held together by bonds of religion, was discredited in an age torn by religious strifes.   The boundaries between revelation or faith and reason were sharply defined.   The need for a clearer demarcation of the sciences was felt even by those who still valued traditional classifications.   Natural law,   now   that   the   individual

---

1.—Henry Nevile, *Plato Redivivus,* 1681, p. 181.

2.—T. More, *Utopia,* 1516, Everyman's Library, edn., p. 44 ; p. 26.

3.—W. Tyndale, *The Obedience of a Christian Man,* 1528 (vol. v., Christian Classics Series), pp. 125-26.

4.—*De Republica Anglorum,* 1583, ed. L. Alston, 1906, lib. 1. cap. 24, p. 46.

Englishman was free to form his own judgement of its import, might prove, it was thought, an explosive element if introduced into political and social theory. It was, in fact, a Janus, as Ireton realised in the following century when presented with the Levellers' programme, and as the social critics of the eighteenth century perceived when they began to read Locke for themselves.

Though the mediaeval synthesis, as worked out by St. Thomas, was far more rational and analytic than is sometimes suggested, its very symmetry proved a stumbling block to some of his contemporaries and an embarrassment to a more complex age. Scotus, for example, did not agree with the respective spheres which Aquinas assigned to reason and revelation. The former writer narrowed the realm of reason by excluding such subjects as creation and immortality from natural theology. His pupil William of Ockham went further, declaring that the truths of religion were beyond the powers of reason to establish. And in Gabriel Biel (1425-1495) one reaches what has been called the " Thomistic antithesis " [1]—the complete divorce of reason and revelation. The antithesis expressed by Biel leads up to a new synthesis with rationalistic writers like Herbert of Cherbury in the seventeenth century (1583-1648), who put Natural Theology or reason above Revealed Theology. What was above reason was erroneously considered as against reason. And thus theology began to be regarded as the handmaiden rather than as the mistress of all the sciences.[2] In Grotius and Locke one finds the counterpart of Biel's antithesis in a complete separation of Church and State. And with Hobbes we reach the conception of the unlimited sovereignty of the State, which has ever since exercised a strong influence on the political thought, if not on the political practice, of Englishmen.[3]

1.—See the interesting article by Rev. Dr. R. Downey in *St. Thomas Aquinas*, 1925, edited by C. Lattey, S.J., pp. 45 f.

2.—Cf. C. C. J. Webb, *Studies in the History of Natural Theology*, 1915, pp. 344f, and John Dryden " Religio Laici," 1682, in *Select Poems*, ed. W. D. Christie, 1901, p. 121, pp. 132f.

3.—In recent years the Austinian or Hobbesian view of the State has been subjected to brilliant criticism by writers like Prof. H. J. Laski, *Grammar of Politics*, 1925, and others. There is a return to the doctrine of natural right.

. . . " There would be," wrote Henry Nevile in 1681,
" but one inconvenience to have that Religion (Catholicism)
National again in England, which is, that the Clergy,
quatenus such, had and will have a share in the Sovereignty,
and inferior Courts in their own Power, called Ecclesiastical ;
that is and ever will be a Solecisme in Government". [1] . . .
Whatever autonomy or independence the Established Church
still enjoyed was also criticised by the influential and wealthy
followers of " honest John Calvin." [2] Nevile's Puritan zeal,
however, did not carry him so far as to approve of a
" Government and laws " which treated some of its subjects
as " little better than slaves." [3] His plea for the toleration
of Catholics, it is interesting to note, was based on business [4]
rather than on religious grounds. How laws could be so
good and yet so severe, or how Catholics could live
" quietly " under them, he prudently refrains from telling
his readers. All Christians, however, must be grateful to
him for not putting Catholics, as Locke seems to do,[5] on
the same plane as atheists in an age when unbelief was
becoming more and more fashionable.

The discoveries in the physical and mathematical sciences,
coupled with the cult of Cartesian philosophy in the
seventeenth century, contributed greatly to the overthrow
of the traditional or teleological view of the universe.
Naturalistic and mechanical conceptions not only affected the
speculative sciences, but influenced men's views on social and
political institutions. The idea of purpose seemed irrelevant
to an age whose knowledge had become " mechanical." [6]

1.—*Plato Redivivus*, 1681, pp. 178-179.
2.—*Ibid.*, p. 93. He speaks of " the little credit the Church of England
hath amongst the people, most men being almost as angry with that Popery
which is left amongst us . . . . as they are with those *Dogmas* that are
abolished."—*Op. cit.*, p. 188.
3.—*Ibid.*, pp. 184-185.
4.—*Ibid.*, p. 186. He would like to see " these People (who are very considerable, most of them, for Estates, Birth and Breeding) live quietly under
our good laws, and increase our Trade and Wealth with their expences here
at home, whereas now the severity of our Laws against them makes them
spend their Revenues abroad, and enrich other Nations."
5.—*Of Civil Government and Toleration*, Cassell's Library edn. 1905, pp. 181-2.
6.—-See Preface to Sir Dudley North, *Discourses upon Trade*, 1691, and
R. Cumberland, *A Philosophical Inquiry into the Laws of Nature*, tr. Towers,
1750, part 1, ch. 1, section 3, p. 6, and p. 76.

The astounding development of Mathematics influenced the practical as well as the theoretical sciences. In the economic sphere, for example, the quantitative method came to be regarded as the only approach to the truth about wealth. Men engaged in commerce, banking and insurance, the Childs, the Muns, and the Norths, set out to establish a science of Political Arithmetic which emptied economic questions of their human and social character. Social progress was reduced to mathematical formulae ; and social welfare was rarely envisaged in any other light than that of favourable trade-balances and banking returns. From their individualistic standpoint the question was not what is right or wrong in economic trans- actions, but what is expedient.

The consequences of allowing the Machiavellian principle of expediency to govern economic and social actions were pointed out by Francis Bacon towards the end of the sixteenth century. Despite his harsh criticism of the philo- sophical achievements of the Schoolmen,[1] his economic and social theory embodied many of their ideas, though not their language. He cannot be considered as the founder of a new social theory any more than he can be considered as the father of the inductive method. His modernity is often exaggerated. Certainly, from the standpoint of social theory, he was " old fashioned," or, at most, transitional. His namesake Roger Bacon, the Franciscan, told his thirteenth century readers that " Experience is worth more than Aristotle."[2] It is a regrettable fact that the Scholastic philosophers of subsequent centuries did not take that dictum more seriously. Had the principles of the Schoolmen been re-stated in the light of the new experiences furnished by religious, scientific, political and social developments, the disintegration of Scholasticism might have been averted. In the latter part of the sixteenth century a fresh effort was made to give new life and influence to the traditional philo- sophy and social ideals which Rabelais and the other

1.—" Of Studies " in *Essays,* (Chandos Classics edition, 1888), p. 91.
2.—See Paul Lacroix, *Science and Literature in the Middle Ages and at the Period of the Renaissance,* English tr. no date, pp. 88f.

Renaissance writers had done so much to discredit.

The need for a clearer demarcation of the sciences was recognised by Italian and Spanish Scholastic writers. Thus Giraldi,[1] while holding that in order to be a good citizen one must be a good man and multiplying quotations to illustrate the beauty of holiness, prescinded from theological considerations when he came to discuss the factors which make for social welfare. A more important methodological advance was made in 1586 and 1599 when the sons of the systematic St. Ignatius in their *Ratio Studiorum* selected the specifically philosophical questions in St. Thomas' *Summa* for special treatment. The result was the publication of Suarez's *Disputationes Metaphysicae* in 1597. This marked a stage in the advancement of learning ; or in the better understanding of what Bacon would call " the book of God's works." [2] Bacon seemed to think that men's works, particularly those connected with getting a livelihood, did not receive from philosophers that attention which they deserved. " But for the wisdom of business, wherein man's life is most conversant, there be no books of it, except some few scattered advertisements that have no proportion to the magnitude of this subject." [3] That this was far more than a plea for the utilitarian character of economic studies seems evident from other parts of the same essay. While doubting the sincerity of those who despised riches,[4] he had no admiration for those who attained to opulence by dispensing with " the laws of charity and integrity." [5]

Bacon's views illustrate the transitional character of economic and social thought towards the end of the sixteenth century. He had an almost mediaeval fear of riches. " The ways to enrich are many, and most of them are foul." [6]

1.—Giovanni Battista Giraldi, *Dialogues Philosophiques et très utiles Italiens-Francois, touchant la vie civile,* Paris, 1583. On p. 266 he writes : " Mais ayans à parler de la felicité ciuile, il n'est pas besoin d'entrer maintenant en ces considérations, qui appartiennent plus aux Theologiens, qu' aux naturelx, ou aux moraulx Philosophes."
2.—"Advancement of Learning," in *Essays,* p. 134.
3.—"Advancement of Learning," in *Essays,* p. 249.
4.—" Of Riches," in *Essays,* p. 66.
5.—"Advancement of Learning," in *Essays,* p. 264.
6.—" Of Riches," in *Essays,* p. 64.

" Usury " he considered "the certainest means of gain, though one of the worst, as that whereby a man doth eat his bread in *sudore vultus alieni*." [1] His qualified approval of interest or usury, as well as the emphasis which he laid on the social importance of an equitable distribution of wealth,[2] entitle him to an honourable place in the history of social as well as in that of physical science. And that the more because he lived in an age whose *primum quaerite* inclined more towards riches than towards religion.

The new attitude to the world appears more early with regard to political and religious institutions than it does in the field of social and economic relations. But the latter could not escape from its influence. The attitude of the commercial classes towards those divines who still preached the traditional doctrine on usury and other economic questions is summarised in the statement attributed to the merchant in Wilson's dialogue. " Merchants' doings must not thus be overthwarted by preachers and others, that can not skill of their dealings." [3] Even in the middle of the sixteenth century there were indications in England of a desire to understand and explain the laws of economic phenomena instead of laying down rules for economic conduct. In a book written about 1549 [4] we find quite modern views with regard to the principle of economic self-interest. One of the speakers in the dialogue says that a man is justified in using his land in whatever way he can make the most profit.[5] Men will not work hard unless they are permitted " to taike gaines and wealth as reward of theire labours." [6] The implication was that such rewards and returns should be determined by what the individual considered expedient, rather than by what the moral law allowed. And Crowley, as we saw, drew attention to the absolute character which landowners were beginning to claim

1.—*Ibid.*, p. 65.
2.—" Of Usury," in *Essays*, p. 75.
3.—Thomas Wilson, *A Discourse upon Usury*, 1572, ed. R. H. Tawney, 1925, p. 250.
4.—*A Discourse of the Commonweal of this Realm of England*, (probably by John Hales, published 1581), ed. E. Lamond, 1893.
5.—*Ibid.*, p. 50.
6.—*Ibid.*, p. 58.

for their property rights in 1550.[1]   Thus we see that, even early in the sixteenth century, moral restraints on economic self-interest were beginning to be regarded as old fashioned, and the idea of property as a conditional or derivative right was weakened.

In the second half of the sixteenth century more scope is claimed for,[2] and allowed to, individual self-interest.   Some economic theory, for example, with regard to money and exchanges, is quite modern.   The great public interest in foreign exchange questions, which the financial exigencies of the British Government occasioned about the middle of the century,[3] not only led to a fuller study of that part of economic phenomena which lends itself more easily to quantitative treatment, but also increased the forces tending towards an objective treatment of all economic questions unencumbered by considerations as to their ethical character.

The problems arising from an expanding trade financed largely by borrowed capital,[4] the increasing numbers and variety of credit transactions,[5] the large foreign debts which the Government had contracted by its continental wars, were complicated still more by a protracted period of currency depreciation in the sixteenth century.   State interference with economic enterprise, though practised on a great scale by Tudor governments, was beginning to be viewed more and more as an anachronism by the commercial classes.   Thus to the Elizabethan business world the government's proposal to nationalise exchange business, in order to check the export of bullion, appeared puerile.   Merchants knew by some centuries of experience that the bill of exchange was a good substitute for bullion in international transactions.   Their self-interest, it was urged, could therefore be relied on to check the shipment of bullion unless

1.—See above p. 20.
2.—See Tawney-Power, *Tudor Economic Documents*, vol. iii., pp. 339-341, vol. ii., p. 188.
3.—See *S.P.D. Elizabeth*, vol. cvi., no. 6.
4.—See Bacon, " Of Usury " in *Essays*, p. 76.
5.—Wilson, *A Discourse upon Usury*, 1572, ed. R. H. Tawney, 1925, pp. 304-9.

it were cheaper to do so.[1] Sir Thomas Gresham pointed that
out to Elizabeth in 1568 when he gave what was, in effect,
an outline of the modern theory of the " gold points." [2]
Four years later Wilson gave an explanation, though not a
justification, of the main types of credit transactions then
practised in England, and some of them were surprisingly
modern.

These changes visible even in the sixteenth century were
carried further in the seventeenth.

(2.) ECONOMIC AND POLITICAL ANTECEDENTS OF LOCKE'S THEORY.

The changes we have noted in the world of thought were
greatly strengthened by changes in the world of fact. The
sixteenth century was a period of rapid economic development. The first half was characterised by social and
economic dislocation. The second half saw the rise of new
forms of commercial and financial enterprise and of new
classes and interests based upon them.

Such changes as had taken place in the communal
framework of agriculture and land tenure from the thirteenth
to about the middle of the fifteenth century in England had
been mainly in the interests of the cultivators, and contributed to the rise of a prosperous peasantry. The Black
Death, and the development of commercial agriculture from
the middle of the fourteenth century onwards, gave a
powerful momentum to the forces and motives making for
the substitution of money payments for labour rents. Thus
at the beginning of Henry VII.'s reign we find the manorial
system undermined. The position of the small landholder
is greatly improved ; villein-tenure in the main has been
transformed into copyhold, and the majority of English

1.—*S.P.D.* Elizabeth, lxxv., no. 54, printed in Tawney and Power, *Tudor
Economic Documents*, vol. iii., p. 359.

2.—J. W. Burgon, *The Life and Times of Sir Thomas Gresham*, 1839, vol. i.,
Appendix, No. xxi., pp. 483-6.

peasants both are personally free and have a direct interest in the soil.

This economic freedom had scarcely been won by the peasants before it was seriously menaced in the sixteenth century by "trade's unfeeling train," which threatened to usurp the land and "dispossess the swain"; and later by an influx of money which widened the limits "between a splendid and a happy land." The great expansion of the cloth industry in the first half of the sixteenth century made sheep grazing on a large scale profitable, while later the depreciation of the currency, under Henry VIII. and Edward VI., compelled landlords or their agents to manage their estates in a more business-like fashion. The rise in prices led inevitably to an increase in customary fines and rents. Both landlord and tenant were faced with a situation hitherto unknown. The former was forced to re-organise his estate if he wanted to make it pay, and his tenants indulged the hope that such improvements would not involve their impoverishment, much less their disappearance. It was a vain hope for many of them.

The practice of leasing the demesne, which had been growing ever since the fourteenth century, was general in most parts of the country when the sixteenth century began; and with the demesne were often leased the manorial rights as a whole. The well-to-do farmers, into whose hands they had frequently passed, could introduce the new methods of farming demanded by the new conditions, and could offer the lord a higher and less precarious income than he could obtain from his tenants. Their interest naturally lay in clearing away customary restrictions on cultivation or in flouting the laws enacted against the conversion of arable land into pasture. It is unnecessary for us to enlarge on the social consequences of the agrarian changes of the sixteenth century. Their chief significance for us centres in the fact that they involved the destruction of many communal restrictions, and therefore acted as an additional stimulus to the other factors making for a highly individualistic conception of private property. Though such interference with customary rights was not directly related, as in Germany,[1] to the conscious adoption of Roman law, it certainly involved a sharp break with the traditional organisation of English agricultural life and rural society. It is true that early in the thirteenth century the Statute of Merton had recognised, while at the same time restricting, the right of the lord to enclose waste lands hitherto used as common pastures. But it was only with the economic changes of the fifteenth and sixteenth centuries that the situation became such as to give him a motive for doing so on a grand scale. Moreover, by that time, it was not only the common pasture which was threatened. In numerous cases, as is shown by the results of the Commission of 1517, manorial authorities enclosed arable holdings with the object of converting them to pasture, and evicted tenants holding by a customary title.[2] Some protection had, indeed, been extended to such tenants from the early fifteenth century onwards, first by the Court of Chancery, and then by the Common Law. But the courts only enforced the custom of the manor. In many cases, perhaps, in the majority of cases, the custom was unfavourable to the tenants, and, even when it was not, the social influence of the great landowner frequently made it a difficult matter for them to secure legal redress.

Landowners and merchants were never regarded as mutually exclusive classes in England. From the later part of the sixteenth century, however, the mantle of social prestige included within its folds more and more successful business men. The balance of landed property was shifting

---

1.—Johannes Janssen, *History of the German People*, English tr. 1896, vol. ii., pp. 179-81. Referring to the headway which Roman law was making in the German universities towards the end of the fifteenth century, Janssen states that the new jurists "looked on all German leases as limited, and applied the Roman slave law to the German manor rights. They invested avaricious and ambitious princes and landlords with legal authority not only to deprive the peasants of their communal rights, but to evict them from their life-lease possessions and to increase their taxes."—vol. ii., p. 181. But Janssen, as Maitland has pointed out, somewhat exaggerates the influence of Roman law on the continent. See F. W. Maitland, *English Law and the Renaissance*, 1901, p. 29 ; p. 91.

2.—See Rev. A. H. Johnson, *The Disappearance of the Small Landowner*, 1910, pp. 42f., Tawney, *The Agrarian Problem in the Sixteenth Century*, 1912, pp. 261-262.

in the fifteenth century.[1] The defeat of the feudal lords, followed in the sixteenth century by the confiscation of Church property, led to a " mighty alteration " in landed property. " In the course of one century," as an early eighteenth century writer remarks, a large part of the land of the country changed hands, passing " from the former powerful possessors . . . . into the hands of a numerous gentry and commonality." [2] The latter were frequently men who had acquired opulence by trade and commerce, and were glad to " exchange the hurry of Trade for the pleasures of Country Life.[3]

The extraordinary increase in exports in Henry VIII.'s reign were carried further in the Elizabethan age. The development of corporate economic enterprise which took place in the sixteenth century, though not created by the State, was fostered according to the ideals of Tudor Governments.[4] If the fifteenth century forms a landmark in the commercial history of Europe,[5] the sixteenth was one in the commercial and financial history of England. In Elizabeth's reign the isolated attempts at commercial expansion and exploration of previous centuries gave way to systematic and organised effort. Englishmen now competed successfully with Spaniards and Portuguese for commercial advantages in the New World, and for the eagerly guarded preserves of Eastern trade. Elizabeth cultivated the friendship of the Sultan. In 1583 she won for her merchants the right to participate fully in the trade advantages which the discovery of the Cape route to India had made possible for nearly a century.[6] The establishment of direct trading connections with the continent, particularly

1.—See Sir James Harrington, *Oceana*, 1656, ed. Morley, 1887, pp. 59-60.
2.—R. Harley, " Faults on both Sides," 1710, in *Somers' Tracts*, vol. xii., pp. 679f. Cf. Henry Nevile, *Plato Redivivus*, 1681, p. 37.
3.—Guy Miège, *The New State of England*, 1693 [2], part 2, ch. iv., p. 52.
4.—See *Select Charters of Trading Companies*, 1530-1707, (Selden Society Publications), edited by Cecil T. Carr. W. R. Scott, *The Constitution and Finance of English, Scottish and Irish Joint-Stock Companies to 1720*, 1910, vol. ii.
5.—The advance of the Turks in the eastern Mediterranean by blocking the communication with the East was a great blow to the economic supremacy of Italy.
6.—See *S. P. Venetian*, vol. xiii., no. 138.

with Germany and Russia, the incorporation of the Moscovy Company in 1555, the Levant in 1581 and the East India Company in 1600, and, above all, the development of a credit fabric with international ramifications, prepared the way for that cantonization " of the whole world almost . . . . amongst several societies " of British merchants about which Henry Parker, in 1647,[1] wrote with satisfaction from his home at Hamburg.

Widening markets in the sixteenth and seventeenth centuries were then, more than now, a cause rather than a consequence of trade specialisation and division of labour. The bridge which separated producer and consumer, whether the latter resided at home or abroad, was growing wider and wider. Merchants, instead of carrying their goods in person to other countries, appointed agents to do their buying and selling. That inevitably implied an increasing demand for the services of the money lender ; and even in Elizabeth's reign the number who were ready to provide credit for a consideration was not inconsiderable.[2] Throughout the following century financial organisation was becoming steadily more complex, and its influence more widely felt. Merchants found that " the art and mysterie " of exchange business was growing much more " profitable and beneficiall " than " the art of Merchandizing itselfe."[3] The foundation of the Bank of England in the closing decade of the century was an indication that the new body of interests based upon this financial development had achieved maturity, and were

1.—Of a Free Trade, London, 1648, p. 13.
2.—See S.P.D. Elizabeth, vol. cvi., no. 6 ; vol. clv., no. 65.
3.—Lewes Roberts, The Merchant's Mappe of Commerce ; wherein the universall manner and matter of Trade is compendiously handled, etc. London, 1638, ch. x., p. 47,—(Goldsmiths' Library).—"I have noticed then the first use of this exchanging, and the excellencie thereof, being preserved in times past in its true integritie and realitie ; but those honest and innocent ends are vanished with those innocent and honest days of our forefathers ; for since Trade by a more generall and universall Commerce and concurrencie of Nations, being growne to that height and perfection that now it is, this faire and candid manner and use of exchanging, and the most excellent commodities thereof, is in part given over ; for the subtilitie of these times hath made an art and mysterie thereof, which being reduced into heads and principals, hath proved in many places so profitable and beneficiall to the studious therein, that it is now a received opinion, that the excellency thereof exceeds the art of Merchandizing itselfe."

henceforward to occupy a recognised position of power in the State.

The economic progress which England had made during the preceding hundred years, despite the political disturbances which had intervened, was so great that it commanded the attention of foreigners like Guy Miège.[1]   Allowing for the natural tendency of a refugee to extol the people who extends to him hospitality, the picture he gives of the industrial qualities of Englishmen, their enterprise, their inventiveness, and their sense of equity in business, is not overdrawn.   The " Hollanders " were the only people comparable to them for " merchandizing and navigation." [2]   Evidence of their commercial greatness was afforded by their exports of " Woollen cloth of all sorts," as well as " Tin, Lead, Alum, Copper, Iron, Fuller's-earth, Salt, and Sea Coal, of most sorts of Grains but Wheat especially." [3]   The alleged happiness of the English people was, he thought, due in a great measure to the fact that they lived " under the best of governments, which saves them from the drudgery and hardships of other nations." [4]

Miège's praise of the present or " new State " of England was too great to be disturbed by doubts as to the future, or regrets as to the past.   Hence the absence of any discussion of the theory of property which triumphed at the Revolution. Some important phases in the evolution of that theory, before its philosophic formulation by Locke, must now be noted.

The above developments in commerce and finance led to the rise of a new and influential *bourgeoisie* on whom traditional ideas had no hold.   Its religion in the seventeenth century was predominantly Puritan which, since the days of Elizabeth, found many adherents amongst the commercial elements of the population.   Its emphasis on religious liberty and the doctrine of self-help, which brought it into collision with the Established Church in the sixteenth century, naturally affected its attitude towards the action of the Crown

1.— *The New State of England*, 1693 [2], part ii., chapters i-iv.
2.—Miège, *Op. cit.*, p. 11., p. 51.
3.— *Ibid.*, p. 51.
4.— *Op. cit.*, part 2, ch. i., p. 4.

in economic and political affairs. A considerable section of the landowners shared this Puritan spirit and outlook.[1] Being ill-disposed to brook regulation in economic as in religious affairs, opposition to the traditional conservative policy of the Privy Council was for them a matter of principle. Thus despite the intentions of its founder, and despite the conservative social theory of some of his followers, Puritanism, as a movement, tended to engender a social philosophy which, in practice, frequently sacrificed moral right to economic might.[2] "Temporall interest" must, at least, have been a temptation to many Englishmen to "follow the Puritan Ministers."[3] In 1644 a pamphleteer ascribed their great influence in England to the city of London, which was "the nest and seminary of the seditious faction and by reason of its universall trade throughout the kingdome, with its commodities conveying and deriving this civill contagion to all our cities and corporations, and thereby poysoning whole counties."[4] The same "proud" and "rebellious city of London,"[5] by reason of its "populousness and wealth" was, he said, "ambitious forsooth to be a free State."[6] That wealth, as we know, was given generously to finance the Parliamentary forces.

Whatever one may think of Puritanism as a religion,[7] it was eminently practical as a political and economic force in

1.—See Oliver Ormerod, *The Picture of a Puritane*, 1605, p. 8.

2.—We say *tended*, because numerous examples could be adduced both of Puritan merchants as well as of Puritan writers in the seventeenth century, and later, whose views on the moral responsibilities of property were quite mediaeval. The rich are "stewards of their wealth" says Sir Mathew Hale in *A Discourse touching provision for the Poor*, 1683, p. 25. John Cooke, *Unum Necessarium*, 1647, Brit. Mus., T.T., E. 425 (1), p. 36. Tho. Gouge, *The Surest and Safest Way of Thriving*, 1676, Brit. Mus. Tracts on Christian Practice, 1676-1824, p. 28, etc.

3.—R. Smith, *The Prudentiall Ballance of Religion*, 1609, p. 562.

4.—*An Orderly and plaine Narration of the Beginnings and Causes of this Warre*, 1644, p. 4., Brit. Mus., T. T., E. 54 (3).

5.—Samuel Butler, *A Letter from Mercurius Civicus to Mercurius Rusticus ; or London's Confession, but not Repentance*, 1643, printed in *Somers' Tracts*, vol. iv., p. 598. Butler says that one "could no more see a face of the Church of England" in London . . . "than . . . at Amsterdam."

6.—*An Orderly and plaine Narration of the Beginnings and Causes of this Warre*, 1644, T. T. E. 54 (3), pp. 4-5.

7.—See John Bunyan, *The Pilgrim's Progress*, ed. Rev. Robert Maguire, London, no date, pt. 1, p. 112.—"The soul of religion is the practical part." Bunyan's book is the "prose epic" of Puritan Protestantism.

seventeenth century England. Henry Parker [1] has noted
the curious things which it was supposed to represent in his
day. It was certainly opposed to many customs besides
that of " beating every bargaine " over a wine pot.[2]   Though
English Puritans were far from identifying the " commonweal
of merchants " with the commonweal of England,[3] a growing
number of the commercial and financial classes in the early
seventeenth century believed that both the interest of the
commonweal as a whole, as well as that of their own, would
be best served by allowing every individual to exercise his
industry as he wished.   It was those members of the House
of Commons, in the reign of James I. who shared that outlook,
that were responsible for the introduction of the Free Trade
Bill of 1604, which the Lords rejected.   In the instructions
touching the Bill for Free Trade the right of the individual
to trade freely, and to earn his livelihood in whatever industry
he desired, was claimed to be " natural " and beyond the
power of the State.   But " Merchandize being the chief and
richest of all other, and of greater extent and importance
than all the rest, it is *against the natural right and liberty*
of the subjects of England to restrict it into the hands of
some few as now it is ; for although there may be now some
five or six thousand persons, counting children and prentices,
free of the several companies of the merchants, in the whole ;
yet .   .   . the mass of the whole trade of all the realm is in
the hands of some two hundred persons at the most." [4]

That mild demand for economic freedom made no
impression on a King anxious to gather all power, economic
as well as political, into his own hands.   In his first speech [5]

1.—*A Discourse concerning Puritans*, 1641, p. 41, Brit. Mus., T. T., E. 204 (3).
2.—See " Epistole dedicatorie " to Tho. Gataker's Sermon, *The decease of
Lazarus*, preached in 1640, Brit. Mus., T. T., E. 204 (6).
3.—See Henry Parker, *Of a Free Trade*, 1648, p. 13. Parker was conservative in his economic views ; he believed in " a rightly governed and
ordered trade."
4.—*Journals of the House of Commons*, vol. i., p. 218.
5.—*Parliamentary History*, vol. i., p. 986—" The righteous and just King
doth, by the contrary, acknowledge himself to be ordained for the procuring
of the wealth and prosperity of his people, and that his greatest and principal
wordly felicity must consist in their prosperity. If you be rich I cannot be
poor ; if you be happy I cannot but be fortunate ; . . . and . . . as the head
is ordained for the body, and not the body for the head ; so must a righteous
king know himself to be ordained for his people, and not his people for him."

in Parliament he expressed a desire to carry out the traditional theory of the State ; a theory which made the Crown responsible not only for one, but for all classes. The Crown rather than Parliament was he thought the best judge of what was for the common good. Needless to say his views as to the best means of promoting the common good were not of a character to commend themselves to the propertied classes now grown conscious of their power. Above all, the extravagant claim that he was not subject to " any censure or correction upon the earth "[1] gave rise to serious apprehensions. It was a political bombshell.

The tactful Tudors knew how to use absolute power without emphasising their right to do so. The absolutism of an Elizabeth was also tempered by an economy in public expenditure which the personal prodigality of James I., amongst other causes, rendered impossible. The struggle between the Crown and Parliament over taxation in the seventeenth century has been discussed so often that it is unnecessary to dwell on it at length. Its interest for us centres in the fact that it was one of the most important issues which raised the question of private property, and sharpened ideas about it.

Dissatisfied with the grant which the Commons voted him in 1606, James determined to take advantage of the favourable decision which the Court of Exchequer gave in the same year respecting his right to levy impositions without the consent of Parliament. It was the theoretic basis of the Court's decision rather than the actual decision itself which alarmed Parliament, and particularly the commercial element in it. The Court claimed that all the ports of the kingdom were the King's property, and that, therefore, it was within his right to demand from merchants, and those who used the ports, as much money as he thought proper. Had such a principle gone unchallenged, every improvement in the economic life of the nation would, *pari passu*, strengthen the King's financial position, and finally make him independent of Parliament. After lengthy debates in Parliament over

1.—*Journals of the House of Commons*, vol. i., p. 314

the King's right to "impose,"[1] James agreed to a compromise. He would allow a bill to be brought in restricting his right to levy new impositions without the consent of Parliament, while retaining his right to levy existing impositions. The bill was lost in the Lords, probably because the Commons were now busy drawing up a contract by which the King would be put in possession of a definite revenue in return for the redress of their ecclesiastical and other grievances, such as impositions and feudal rights.

The Commons agreed to give James £200,000 which, at first, he accepted. Before proroguing Parliament, however, he refused to give a definite answer to the question of grievances. That answer, on which so much of the history of the seventeenth century hinged, was not favourable. Thus ended what is usually referred to as the "great contract."[2] James allowed the ecclesiastical grievances, which formed the main subject of disagreement before he prorogued Parliament, to go unredressed. He resolutely refused (October 1610) to alter the existing ecclesiastical system of the Church of England despite the fact that numerous people were opposed to it.[3] The words employed by a pamphleteer in 1646 reflect the religious and political temper of many people in the reign of James I. as well as in that of Charles I. "Every man" is "by nature . . . a King, Priest and Prophet in his own naturall circuite and compasse, whereof no second may partake, but by deputation, commission, and free consent from him, whose naturall right and freedom it is."[4] Behind the walls

1.—*Journals of the House of Commons*, vol. i., p. 430, p. 481.

2.—*Parliamentary History*, vol. i., p. 1146.

3.—See Oliver Ormerod, *The Picture of a Puritane*, 1605, p. 3. "These groaners," he writes, who dislike "not onely the Church of Rome but the Church of England also," have become so numerous "that one of their owne preachers said openly in a Pulpit he was persawded that there were 10,000 of them in England & that the number of them increased daily in euery place of al states & degrees."—*Op. cit.*, p. 8, p. 3.

4.—Richard Overton, *An Arrow against all Tyrants and Tyranny shot from the prison of Newgate into the Prerogative Bowels of the Arbitrary House of Lords, and all other Usurpers and Tyrants whatsoever*, 1646, p. 4., Brit. Mus., T.T., E. 356 (14).

Cf. Charles I.'s *Majesty in Misery*, written at Carisbrook Castle, 1648, and printed in 1681—" They will destroy the Crozier and Crown,
Churchmen are chain'd and Schismaticks are free'd,
Mechanicks preach, and holy Fathers bleed " . . .
Brit. Mus., *Poetical Broadsides*, nos. 1-92.

of Newgate prison the same writer made a profession of faith in individualism in words which exhibit a striking affinity to those used by Locke in the chapter on property in the *Civil Government*. " To every individuall in nature," writes Overton, " is given an individuall property by nature, not to be invaded or usurped by any : for every one as he is himselfe, so he hath a selfe propriety, else could he not be himselfe, . . . mine and thine cannot be, except this be : No man hath power over my rights and liberties and I over no man's ; I may be but an individuall, enjoy *myselfe* and my selfe propriety." [1]

London, the seat of Puritanism as well as of financial power in the seventeenth century, played a leading part in the constitutional struggles from which a strongly individualistic conception of property rights emerged. When Charles I. resolved to govern without Parliament he was compelled to have recourse to numerous financial expedients to replenish his treasury. The most famous, or infamous, of these was the revival of " ship-money." The levying of ship-money, as is well known, was a method used by the Crown to provide for the naval defence of the country. Originally it was confined to ports and maritime counties, but under Elizabeth it was levied on inland towns also.[2] The first writ issued by Charles in August 1634 to " the Mayor, commonlity and citizens " of London, did not arouse general indignation. But the second and third writs (1635, 1636) indicated that he was determined to convert this method of obtaining money into a general tax on the whole community, and that without consulting Parliament.[3] The number of " sad faces in England," which the new taxation " occasioned "[4] in 1635, must have increased considerably in 1637 when the majority of the judges, to whom Charles appealed for a final ruling on the question, declared in his favour.[5] The decision of

1.—*Op. cit.*, p. 3. Cf. Locke, *Civil Government*, ed. Morley, 1884, bk. ii., ch. v., §27, p. 204.
2.—See Tawney and Power, *Tudor Economic Documents*, vol. ii., p. 128.
3.—Gardiner, *The Constitutional Documents of the Puritan Revolution,* 1906, p. 105.
4.—Sir S. D'Ewes, *Autobiography*, ed. Halliwell, 1845, vol. ii., p. 132.
5.—Gardiner, *Op. cit.*, p. 108.

the judges was viewed as an invasion of property rights. If Charles might act as the " sole judge " of national necessities, levying money without the consent of Parliament, who could set limits to his interference with the people's property in the supposed interest of the nation ? [1]

The story of Hampden's refusal to pay ship-money is familiar to all, and " time, the mother of truth," as he himself said, was soon to vindicate his action.[2]   On August 7, 1641, an act was passed " declaring . . . the late proceedings touching ship-money . . . contrary to . . . the laws and statutes of this realm," and " the right of property." [3]

As already remarked the significance of the taxation struggle between Crown and Parliament has often been pointed out.   What is not always observed, however, is that there were other economic questions where the issue of the right of the State to interfere with property rights and contracts was involved, and on which the Crown came into collision with the propertied classes.   The right to trade freely was strongly urged under James I.,[4] and led to the passing of the Anti-Monopoly Act of 1624.[5]   The Act was largely ineffective as certain sections of it—particularly section ix.—offered a loophole to Charles to grant patents, thus enabling him to obtain money independent of Parliament.   The result was, as Bagshaw and Colepepper [6] pointed out, that the Act had intensified rather than removed the evils of monopoly.   And monopolists then, as now, were sometimes human enough to enrich themselves by charging high prices for inferior products.[7]   In that impressive indictment of Charles's rule, known as " The Grand Remonstrance " (1641), one finds " the monopolies of soap,

1.—Henry Parker, *The Case of Ship-money briefly discoursed*, 1640, pp. 2-3. Brit. Museum, T.T., E. 204 (4).   F. Corkayni(n), *England's Troubles Anatomized*, 1644, p. 26, Brit. Mus., T.T., E. 12 (15).

2.—Henry Parker, *Op. cit.*, p. 6.

3.—Gardiner, *Op. cit.*, p. 191.

4.—Even in Elizabeth's reign the Crown's policy of granting exclusive trading privileges led to such abuses that people were said to pray in public " God prosper those that further the overthrow of these monopolies."— *Parliamentary History*, vol. i., p. 936.

5.—21 James I., c. 3.

6.—*Parliamentary History*, vol. ii., p. 650 ; p. 656.

7.—See Misselden, *Free Trade*, 1622, pp. 57f.

salt, wine, leather, sea-coal, and in a manner of all things of most common and necessary use," mentioned amongst the " pressing miseries " and " disorders " which menace the " liberty, peace and prosperity " of the nation.[1]

The rights of individuals to their " goods and estates "[2] were also infringed in numerous other ways by Charles. The revival of various obsolete forms of revenue, such as forest claims ; the ancient law compelling, under penalty of fine, the owner of an estate worth £46 a year to be knighted ; the increased exactions of the court of Wards ; the enforcement of Depopulation Statutes—all these financial expedients served not only to incense the people, but to increase the reverence with which property rights are normally surrounded.

The revival of the forest laws was most unjust. The boundaries of English forests had been fixed for over three centuries, and things had greatly altered since Edward I. agreed to limit his power over forests. The forest of Dean, for example, was no longer the deer park it was then, but a land dotted with not less than seventeen villages. The application of forest law, with its irritating restrictions on all actions which might possibly interfere with the preservation of deer, was ludicrous since deer no longer " fed " there.[3] The exactions of the Court of Wards were so great that, according to Clarendon,[4] all the " rich families of England " were incensed at seeing " what the law intended for their protection and preservation " being now " applied to their destruction."

Again the administration of the Depopulation Statutes by Charles, though partly prompted by a genuine desire to secure a sufficiency of arable land for a growing population, was sicklied over with the selfish cast of finance. The evils connected with " enclosures," as we have seen, had engaged

1.—Gardiner, *Constitutional Documents of the Puritan Revolution*, 1906, p. 206 ; p. 212.

2.—See Wm. Prynne, *A Summary Collection of the principal fundamental rights, liberties, proprieties of all English Freemen*, 1656, pp. 1-2.

3.—See Bagshaw's speech in *Parliamentary History*, vol. ii., p. 649.— People " must be eased in their lands from Forests where never any deer fed." Gardiner, *History of England*, vol. vii., pp. 363f.

4.—*History of the Rebellion*, ii., 102, ed. Dun Macray, 1888, vol. i., p. 199.

the attention of Governments from the days when Henry VII. passed the first statute against depopulation.[1] If " rightly ordered," as a pamphleteer pointed out in 1653, enclosures should not " unpeople towns " or lead to the " decay of tillage." [2] In actual practice, however, the various enclosure movements involved considerable hardship. The Stuarts were not blind to that fact.[3] The three Commissions appointed between 1632 and 1636 formed part of an effort to check enclosures which involved depopulation, and to reconvert pasture to arable land where the essential needs of the people required it.

Those who refused to carry out the Privy Council's orders were fined heavily. The policy of fining was probably due to Sir Robert Osborne's " proposal for raising money by taking compositions for enclosures." [4] It was suggested that " all lands inclosed since the sixteenth of the late King should, within three months, be thrown back into arable on pain of a forfeiture of 20s., per acre, except such whereof the owners should compound." [5] During the years 1635-1638 several people compounded and the fines imposed reached a considerable figure.[6] But Charles's anxiety to secure revenue to carry on his personal government frequently led him to create " Depopulations, where never any farm was decayed, and . . . enclosures where never any hedge was set." [7]

The cloth industry affords another example of where the State's attempt to impose impracticable rules brought it into collision with the manufacturing and commercial classes. The regulation of the cloth industry both by Tudor and

1.—4 Henry VII., c. 19.
2.—*Considerations concerning Common Fields and Enclosures*, 1653, Brit. Mus., T. T., E. 719 (9), pp. 9-10. As, for example, the early forms of enclosure which merely meant a re-division of land and restrictions on open-field husbandry agreed to by the peasants themselves in the interest of efficiency. See Tawney, *Agrarian Problem in the Sixteenth Century*, 1912, p. 152.
3.—See *Acts of the Privy Council*, 1630, vol. vi., p. 199 ; p. 385.
4.—*S.P.D.* (1633-34), vol. cclx., p. 474.
5.—*Ibid.*
6.—According to Prof. Gonner, *Common Land and Enclosure*, 1912, pp. 166-7.—" Some six hundred persons were fined during this period," and the revenue obtained from compositions in thirteen counties amounted to £46,810.
7.—See Bagshaw's speech in the Long Parliament (1640) in *Parliamentary History*, vol. ii., p. 649. Gardiner, *Constitutional Documents*, pp .211-212.

Stuart Governments was prompted as much by financial considerations as by a desire to maintain a uniform standard of quality in home and foreign markets. In actual practice, as Mr. Heaton [1] has shown, quality was made subservient to revenue. For convenience of revenue collection the State had ordered that uniformity of dimensions be observed for all pieces of the same quality. Compliance with these regulations often involved a loss to the manufacturers ; and quite frequently the weight of the cloth was sacrificed to obtain the statutory requirements as to dimensions. To prevent such abuses Elizabeth prohibited all " stretching " and " tentering " [2] of the material, and charged the justices to see that the law was observed. " Searchers " were appointed and empowered to destroy all tenter-frames wherever found. The Act of 1597, which at first applied only to the North, was extended to the country as a whole in 1601. Those acquainted with the real facts of cloth manufacture recognised that the tenter-frame was an indispensable adjunct of the clothier's apparatus. The justices, therefore, in refusing to carry out this order were but giving effect to popular opinion. A compromise was reached in the reign of James I. ; tenter-frames were permitted, but certain regulations were laid down as to their construction and use. [3] Further attempts to control the textile industry by local organisations—such as the granting of monopolies to corporations like the cloth finishers under Charles I.—merely served to intensify the distrust which the Crown's policy created. [4]

In addition to the points noted above, there were two other cases where the Crown's policy aroused the opposition of the influential financial classes ; the attempt to obtain " forced loans and contributions " [5] and the re-erection of the ancient office of Royal Exchanger in 1627. [6] The revival

1.—For details see Herbert Heaton, *The Yorkshire Woollen and Worsted Industries*, 1920, chs. iv., vii.
2.—43 *Elizabeth*, c. 10.
3.—21 *James I.*, c. 18.
4.—See *S.P.D., Charles I.*, ccccviii., 15.
5.—Wm. Prynne, *Op. cit.*, p. 1. *S.P.D.*, Charles I. (1625-26), vol. xxxvi., p. 42 ; p. 435. Gardiner, *Constitutional Documents*, p. 67 ; p. 218.
6.—For details see Roger Ruding, *Annals of the Coinage of Great Britain and its Dependencies*, 1840, vol. ii., pp. 149-51.

of the office of Royal Exchanger was viewed as an attack on the money market, the growth of which had long rendered obsoletethe main function of the Royal Exchanger of the Middle Ages. Before the general adoption of the bill of exchange as an instrument of international commerce,the Royal Exchanger was the pivotal point around which international payments centred. Although the revival of the office in 1627 was primarily intended to safeguard the coinage rather than to control all exchange business, the idea was resented not only by the goldsmiths, who were supposed to have endangered the coinage by the export of heavy coins, but also by the financial classes generally.

By the foregoing and by other attempts at interference with the economic life of the people,

> . . . . " the springs of property were bent
> And wound so high they cracked the government." [1]

The ill-fated Charles, as well as his advisers, seemed to forget that power was now widely distributed because property was widely diffused.[2] If a section of the people believed that monarchical government should give way to Republicanism, it was less because kings were deemed " useless " than because they were considered " a clog to trade." [3] An early eighteenth century writer, interpreting the constitutional struggles of the previous century, admirably summarises the position. " The single authority of his (Charles's) prerogative proved but an artificial and precarious power, unable long to hold out against the real and natural power of property, which was now so largely vested in the people that when they had found the way to put their affairs into a method, and came to feel their own strength, they were able to bear down all before them." [4]

1.—See Dryden, "Absalom and Achitophel," 1681, lines 499-500, in *Select Poems*, ed. W. D. Christie, 1901, p. 101.

2.—Henry Nevile, *Plato Redivivus*, 1681, p. 37.—The wide distribution of property " has made the Country scarce governable by Monarchy."

3.—Dryden, *Loc. cit.*, p. 104.

4.—Richard Harley, "Faults on both Sides," 1710, printed in *Somers' Tracts*, vol. xii., p. 679. The wide distribution of property he considered the " second " and " less observed " cause of the " feuds and divisions " of the seventeenth century. The first cause was that the clergy since the Reformation were no longer on the popular side. The establishment of a State-Church led " men of aspiring tempers " to " flatter princes " by exaggerating their powers, whereas " in the times of Popery . . . the clergy were then as zealous as the temporality in defending the liberties of the people against the usurpations of the Crown."—*Ibid.*, pp. 682-3.

The unfortunate King, so willing to "pawn" his head to end the "business of Ireland,"[1] was destined to lose it to liberate the business of England. It must be remembered, however, that it was the *system* rather than the man or King that fanned to fire the revolutionary force of property. For when both Cromwell and Charles I. had passed through the gateway of death, we find the Short Parliament (1653-9) congratulating itself on the reasonableness, as well as on the reality, of its economic and political power. That independent business man as well as independent republican, Slingsby Bethell, to whom Dryden has given a place on his satirical roll of honour,[2] has left us an account of how he and other members "spent their time" in that Parliament.[3]

In the debate on the re-establishment of the House of Lords (Feb. 3, 1657), "the commonwealth's-men fell in, and showed, that where the cause is taken away, the effect must cease ; that as the House of Lords had anciently a *natural right to a superior jurisdiction, in that their property was five parts of six of the whole nation,* so it is now more natural for the Commons to have that superiority, their proportion of propriety being ninety-nine parts, or more, of a hundred ; and therefore moved, that if they would have another house, it might be so bounded as might suit with the people's interest."[4]

In this passage one sees that property is made to govern natural rights rather than natural rights to rule property. Verily we are at the parting of the ways in the history of English social theory and ideas about property. With such a doctrine in its sail, England was beginning to steer farther and farther from that world of the poet's vision, where "all may be supplied" even though "some may gain."[5] The disillusionment which speedily followed the Puritan revolution was crushing for many, but particularly for the poor and

1.—Charles I.'s words quoted by Gardiner, *History of England*, 1904, vol. x., p. 173.
2.—*Absalom and Achitophel.*
3.—"A true and impartial Narrative of the most material Debates and Passages in the late Parliament." . . . 1659, printed in *Somers' Tracts*, 1811, vol. vi., pp. 477f.
4.—*Ibid.*, p. 482. My italics.
5.—Dryden, "Annus Mirabilis," 1666. *Loc. cit.*, p. 61.

the small property owners. The Parliament, of which Bethell
writes, was the Parliament which in 1656 rejected after the
first reading " a bill for improvement of waste grounds
. . . and preventing Depopulations." [1] The " gentlemen
at Westminster " were not of that rare genus which hungers
and thirsts for social justice. They turned a deaf ear to the
Levellers' petition ; to the demand that the " right of the
poor, in their commons " be preserved ; that they be freed
from the " encroachments of all manner of projectors " ;
and that all " servile tenures of lands, as by copyholds, or
the like," be abolished.[2]

Even the " Protector " himself did little to protect the
" oppressed Commoners." [3] Then, as in modern times, some
soldiers thought they were fighting for a social ideal. But
then, as in all ages, when asked " what they fought for ;
. . . could not tell." [4] The Civil War led inevitably to
much interference with, and usurpation of, individual
property. The " Sword-Reformers," as Prynne [5] has shown,
had scant reverence for the property rights of those who
resisted them. Thus, as often happens during and after
periods of great internal disturbances, that reasonable respect
for property rights so essential to the existence of civilised
life tended to diminish. Probably it was that fact, more
than any inherent dislike of democracy, which led Ireton to
oppose Col. Rainborow's view that because " the poorest
hee that is in England hath a life to live as the greatest
hee," [6] everyone should have a voice in the appointment of
parliamentary delegates. Rainborow did not belong to that
type of commonwealth's men whose imperviousness to

1.—*Journals of the House of Commons*, vol. vii., p. 470.
2.—*The Fundamental Laws and Liberties of England, claimed, asserted and
agreed unto by several peaceable persons of the City of London, Westminster, etc.
. . . commonly called Levellers*, July 9, 1653, Brit. Mus., T. T., E. 705 (571),
p. 3 and n. 18.
3.—Gerard Winstanley, *The Law of Freedom in a Platform or True
Magistracy Restored*, presented to O. Cromwell, 1651, Brit. Mus., T.T.,
E. 655, p. 4.
4.—*Ibid.*, p. 7.
5.—Wm. Prynne, *Op. cit.*, pp. 50-59 ; See also John Jones, *Everyman's
Case or Lawyers Routed*, 1652, pp. 26-29.—" Common Lawyers " have usurped
rights which " Popes " never claimed such as divorcing men from their wives
" without " reason.
6.—*Clarke Papers*, Camden Society, N.S., ed. Firth, vol. i., p. 300.

reason would justify the employment of satire rather than syllogisms to confound him.[1] Accordingly Ireton sought to convince him of the reasonableness of restricting the franchise to those " in whome all land lies," and to " those in whom all trading lies." [2]

The arguments by which Ireton supported his position have a very interesting bearing on the question of property and natural right. " Now I wish wee may all consider of what right you will challenge, that all people should have a right to elections. Is itt by the right of Nature ? If you will hold forth that as your ground, then I thinke you must deny all property too, and this is my reason . . . By that same right of nature, whatever itt bee that you pretend, by which you can say, one man hath an equall right with another to the chusing of him that shall governe him, *by the same right of nature,* hee hath an equall right in any goods he sees, meate, drinke, cloathes, to take and use them for his sustenance . . . He hath the (same) freedome to anythinge that anyone doth account himself to have property in . . . If uppon these grounds you doe paramont (to) all Constitutions hold uppe this law of Nature, I would faine have any man shew mee their bounds, where you will end, and (why you should not) take away all propertie ?" [3]

Ireton's view that the requirements of natural law implied communism is as absurd as his fear that an extension of the franchise would lead to anarchy. Rainborow silenced him by pointing out that such interference with property as Ireton contemplated was impossible so long as men obeyed the Divine law, ' Thou shalt nott steale.' [4] In the above passage Ireton seems to confuse the right to property in general with the right to actual specific forms of property ;

1.—See the amusing poem *A Satyr against Commonwealths*, 1684, by H. P. In the preface he says he wants " to expose the giddy enthusiasts of those times," and that type of man " whom in the Country Language we may call substantial, who perhaps has got four score pounds a year, and joys in having a little Dove-coat annex'd to his Farm-house. . . . Such a man as this you can never convince by dint of Argument. . . . You would laugh in your Sleeve (if you have any) to hear his brisk and debonair reasonings about the Authority of the Commons of England."

2.—*Clarke Papers*, ed. Firth, vol. i., p. 302.

3.—*Clarke Papers*, ed. Firth, vol. i., pp. 307-8.

4.—*Ibid.*, vol. i., p. 309.

the former, as we have seen,[1] may be regarded as a natural right whereas the latter may or may not be so. Perhaps it was because he considered that natural right might prove a rather uncertain ground on which to justify some of the property arrangements of his day that he abandoned the doctrine. Others, however, have spoken more boldly and have claimed for individuals not only a natural right, but " an absolute power," to " dispose of all they have how they please."[2] That was the conception of the right of property which emerged at the Restoration period ; and for which many of the landed gentry and commercial classes had fought with great energy since the time of James I. When the question of the Crown's interference with property was uppermost in Englishmen's minds, a pamphleteer concluded his criticism of Gentili's *Three Regal Disputations*—a book dedicated to James I., and exaggerating his power " over the lives and estates of his people "—with the following exhortation :

Let us " who are English subjects . . . blesse God for His goodness who hath . . . *made us absolute proprietors of what we enjoy, so that our lives, liberties and estates,* doe not depend upon, nor are subject to, the sole breath or arbitrary will of our Soveraigne."[3] These words seem to represent far more than an appeal to the traditional sense of independence of Englishmen. They are an expression of faith in the wisdom of a political and social doctrine which, later on, will cause people to be sacrificed to property.

The same words, " lives, liberties and estates," Locke designated " by the general name " of property,[4] the protection of which was the chief object of the State's existence. Thus the word " property " or " propriety " had a rather wide connotation in the seventeenth century. It was

1.—See ch. i.
2.—Edward Chamberlayne, *Angliae Notitia,* 1669, pp. 447-8.
3.—*England's Monarch or a conviction and refutation by the common law of those false principles . . . of Albericus . . . etc.,* (London, 1644). Anonymous and no pagination. My italics.
4.—*Civil Government,* ed Morley, bk. ii., ch. ix., § 123, p. 256. See also *Civil Government and Toleration,* Cassell's Library, 1905, edn., p. 177.—Men enter into society "that by mutual assistance and joint force they *may secure unto each other their properties, in the things that contribute to the comfort and happiness of this life."* My italics.

frequently applied to constitutional liberties as well as to other matters.[1] In a sermon preached at Whitehall in 1665-(6), the Bishop of Lincoln referred to the "busie humour in the world, to lay all common," and "to fling down the inclosures" which protected the various "kinds of propriety." "Propriety of respect and honour," as well as "propriety in goods and possessions," [2] were, he thought, endangered by this Bolshevism born out of due season. But the Bishop's words, however pleasing to a small audience, could not ensure general respect for the authority which they represented. Ecclesiastical authority in England had long since been discredited in economic and social affairs as well as in religious and moral questions.[3] Locke was but reflecting the popular sentiment of several generations when, in 1689, he declared that ecclesiastical authority should have no jurisdiction in civil affairs, "nor anything at all to do with riches and revenues." [4]

The emphasis which Locke laid on the separate provinces of Church and State gave a new impetus to the individualistic tendencies of the age. His condemnation of arbitrary State interference with the fruits of one's labour, however, did not necessarily imply acquiescence in the view that the individual has no responsibility with regard to his property other than that arising from legal enactments. Unfortunately many of his successors tended to forget the point of view from which he approached the subject of private property, and Locke himself, as will be seen in the following chapter, did not sufficiently guard against possible misunderstanding.

1.—See Prynne, *Op. cit.*, 1656, R. Overton, *An Arrow directed against all Tyrants and Tyranny, . . . wherein the naturall and nationall rights, freedomes and properties of mankind are discovered*, 1646.—Brit. Mus. T. T., E. 356 (14).

2.—Brit. Mus., T. T., 694, d. 5, pp. 7-8.

3.—See "The Curate's Conference," 1641, in *Harleian Miscellany*, vol. i., p. 495, for an indictment of the higher ecclesiastics of the Established Church. They are accused of loving "preying better than praying." See Jeremy Collier, *Essays upon Several Moral Subjects*, 1698, part 1, p. 184. Collier regarded the inequality of incomes amongst the clergy as "the main ground of the contempt" in which they were held ; "one part of them grew cheap by their poverty, and the other by their covetousness."—*Op. cit.*, p. 51. See also *A Discourse upon the Commonweal of this Realm of England*, 1581, ed. Lamond, 1893, p. 133.

4.—*Civil Government and Toleration*, Cassell's Library, 1905, p. 186.

CHAPTER III.

LOCKE'S THEORY OF PROPERTY.

WHETHER we accept the high opinion which some have held with regard to the perspicacity of Locke's thought and the perspicuity of his style, or see in him a confused thinker who " does little more than guess," [1] the unique influence of his writings on the speculative and practical world of the eighteenth century can scarcely be questioned. He treated of many subjects even though he may not have adorned all those which he touched. What Dr. Johnson said of Milton—" scarcely any man ever wrote so much and praised so few " [2]—has, perhaps, a certain applicability to Locke. The latter departed somewhat from traditional methods of writing. Unlike many of his philosophical predecessors, Locke was more eager to note the authorities from whom he differed than to marshal those with whom he agreed. This characteristic of his has led some to view Locke as an intellectual Leviathan, who delivered mankind from the obscurities in which traditional philosophy was involved. Like all great writers, however, Locke was indebted to the intellectual inheritance into which he was born, though at times he appears to forget it. He " read much more than can be traced," [3] and thus, as Stewart

1.—H. A. Taine, *History of English Literature*, English tr. Van Laun, 1871, vol. ii., p. 70. W. Molyneux, writing from Dublin, December 24, 1695, congratulates Locke on the " admirable perspicuity " of his writing, " so clearly different from all the World."—*Letters between Mr. Locke and several of his Friends* in *Works*, 1714, vol. iii., p. 541. Though perfectly clear, his style was heavy and prolix, as Mr. Edmund Gosse has observed.— *A History of Eighteenth Century Literature*, 1891, p. 96.

2.—Samuel Johnson, *Lives of the English Poets*, ed. G. Birbeck Hill, 1905, vol. i., p. 94.

3.—E. Taggart, *Locke's Writings and Philosophy*, 1855, pp. 211-12. But Locke assimilated what he read . . . " 'Tis Thinking makes what we read ours."—*Of the Conduct of the Understanding*, § 19 in *Works*, 1714, vol. iii., p. 405.

shrewdly observes, he was " occasionally led to mistake the treasures of memory for those of invention." [1]

Locke's metaphysics has been placed on such a high pinnacle that some of his other writings seem to suffer in comparison. Thus it is sometimes suggested that the inductive method, which is supposed to be the crowning glory of his " Essay concerning Human Understanding," [2] was strangely neglected by Locke when he came to deal with political and social theory where its application was even more appropriate.[3] On the other hand, some have thought that Locke's reputation as a philosopher would still rank high if he never wrote anything but " the excellent chapter on property." [4] These opinions are open to criticism. The political and social theory of Locke was neither remarkably deductive nor strikingly original.

1.—*The Collected Works of Dugald Stewart*, ed. Sir W. Hamilton, 1854, vol. i., p. 213.

2.—This book passed through four editions from 1690 until Locke's death in 1704.

3.—Sir James Fitzjames Stephen, *Horae Sabbaticae*, 2nd series, 1892, Essay ix., pp. 150 f., writes, " The great singularity of the political theory of Locke is its striking incongruity with his metaphysics. The object of the *Essay on the Human Understanding* is to destroy the doctrine of innate ideas, and to reduce all knowledge to a generalisation of experience . . . The treatise on *Civil Government* . . . is the very reverse of all this . . . It is grounded on two conceptions of the state of nature and the law of nature, and it is difficult to see how Locke could arrive at either of these conceptions from experience." Stephen clearly had not mastered Locke's theory of knowledge. He is no champion of induction in any branch of thought, least of all in morals and politics. In the *Essay on the Human Understanding* (bk. iv., ch. iii., § 18, ed. Fraser, 1894, vol. ii., pp. 208-9), morals and politics are said to be the chief field outside mathematics in which real knowledge is possible, that is, in which the relations of ideas can be directly perceived and not merely presumed, as in regions given over to ' judgement.' " The idea of a Supreme Being, infinite in power, goodness, and wisdom, whose workmanship we are, and on whom we depend ; and the idea of ourselves, as understanding, rational creatures, . . . would, I suppose, if duly considered and pursued, afford such foundations of our duty and rules of action as might place morality amongst the sciences capable of demonstration."—*Ibid.*, p. 208. Again the political principle ' No government allows absolute liberty ' is, he thinks, akin to a mathematical principle. So also the proposition ' where there is no property there is no injustice,' if we understand by ' property ' a ' right to anything ' and by ' injustice ' an ' invasion or violation of that right,' is as true as " that a triangle has three angles equal to two right ones."—*Ibid.*, p. 208.

4.—H. Hallam, *Introduction to the Literature of Europe*, 1855, vol. iv. p. 203.

Property, as we have seen, was a revolutionary force in the seventeenth century. Various writers, like Harrington[1] and Nevile,[2] pointed out its political significance. Pamphleteers denounced the arbitrary interference of the Crown with the individual's right to do what he wished with his own.[3] After the Civil War had broken the power of the Crown, Englishmen rejoiced that they had now entered on that " most happy " state which results from the possession of " an absolute power " to " dispose of all they have how they please." [4] Those who disliked the social and political reforms, which Harrington had hoped to see Cromwell carry out,[5] were enthusiastic over his economic interpretation of the constitutional struggles. It seemed to confirm their view that those who had a stake in the country ought to rule the country. Indeed it is reasonable to suppose that the various currents of social democracy in the seventeenth century whether arising from a dissatisfaction with the system of land tenure which dated from William the Conqueror, or from an extreme emphasis on the rights of labour, or from both combined,[6] tended, by way of reaction, to strengthen the theory that social as well as political welfare was best served by allowing the individual the greatest possible freedom with regard to the use and disposal of his property. Nor is this surprising. For not only had property rights been arbitrarily interfered with by the Crown before the Civil War, but it is probable that a majority of Englishmen were, at any rate in some small measure, property owners. It is important, therefore, to remember that the

1.—*Oceana*, ed. H. Morley, 1887, p. 7, *et passim*.
2.—Henry Nevile, *Plato Redivivus*, 1681, p. 37.
3.—Richard Overton, *An Arrow against all Tyrants and Tyranny*, 1646, Brit. Mus., T.T., E. 356 (14), p. 3.
4.—Edward Chamberlayne, *Angliae Notitia*, 1669, pp. 447-8.
5.—*Oceana*, ed. Morley, p. 104.   In the ideal commonwealth no one should possess land exceeding the value of £2,000 ; and all offices should be for a limited period, and be filled by men chosen by ballot.
6.—Gerard Winstanley, *Op. cit.*, 1651, pp. 7-8 ; p. 12.—" No man can be rich, but he must be rich either by his own labors, or by the labors of other men helping him." He seems to think that riches are frequently due to the spoliation of the labourer ; and that the introduction of buying and selling was the economic original sin of the human race. See also *The Fundamental Laws and Liberties of England claimed by the Levellers*, 1653, T.T., E. 705 (571).

England into which Locke was born was one in which property was widely distributed. It is also necessary to bear in mind that his theory of property, in the modern sense of the word, was stated with a view to Politics.[1]

Although only ten years old when the Civil War broke out he must have been animated, even then, by some of that enthusiasm for individual liberty which caused his father to serve in the parliamentary forces. Locke himself suffered much for his political views. After his return from France, in 1679, he lived under a cloud of suspicion owing to his friendship with the Earl of Shaftesbury. In 1683 he was an exile in Holland, and the following year, by order of the King, he was deprived of his studentship and home at Christ Church, Oxford.[2] It was after returning from Holland, early in 1690, that the treatise on *Civil Government* appeared. In the first part of *Civil Government* Sir R. Filmer's political theory was severely criticised, or rather unconsciously caricatured.[3] His own theory of government, as well as his views on property, occurs in the second part of the same volume on *Civil Government*.

It contained a theoretical defence of the new conception of property and other rights which emerged after the storm of the Civil War. The leading ideas in the *Civil Government*[4]

1.—*Civil Government*, ed. H. Morley, 1884, bk. ii., ch. xix., § 222, p. 306.

2.—See "Prolegomena" to Dr. A. C. Fraser's edn. of Locke, *An Essay concerning Human Understanding*, 1894, pp. xxx-xxxv.

3.—For a fuller account of Filmer's views see the excellent article by Mr. J. W. Allen in *Social and Political Ideas of some English Thinkers of the Augustan Age*, edited by Dr. Hearnshaw, 1928, pp. 27-46.

4.—The title-page of the *Two Treatises of Civil Government* (Lond., 1694²) runs thus : "In the former [treatise], the false principles and foundation of Sir R. Filmer and his followers are detected and overthrown. The latter is an Essay concerning the true original, extent, and end of Civil Government." It seems unfair to Locke to regard the *Civil Government* as a mere apology for the particular circumstances that led to the Revolution of 1688. His Letters show that he never wrote anything merely to please. See below ch. iv. of the present work. The following passage from the preface to the second and revised edition (1694) may, however, have helped to stamp Locke's political philosophy with a partisan character. "Reader, thou hast here the Beginning and end of a Discourse concerning Government ; what fate has otherwise disposed of the Papers that should have filled up the middle, and were more than all the rest, 'tis not worth while to tell thee. These, which remain, I hope are sufficient to establish the Throne of our great Restorer, Our present King William ; to make good his Title, in the consent of the People, which being the only one of all lawful Governments, he has more fully and clearly than any prince in Christendom."

were in the air, so to speak, long before the Revolution of 1688. Untroubled by any of those fears which, at first, haunted the publisher of Nevile's *Plato Redivivus*,[1] who thought that the latter book might not "vend to profit" because it seemed to be largely "a Repetition of a great many Principles and positions" out of Harrington's *Oceana*, Locke presented his views on property to the public with an air of conviction and finality which disarmed criticism for almost a century. Serfdom had practically disappeared in England more than a century before Locke was born ; and the remaining feudal obligations were abolished in 1660.[2] Before the century closed a writer proudly remarked that the words which expressed "the servitude and slavery of other nations" were "wanting" in the English language.[3]

Locke, in a famous sentence, expressed the theory of the Revolution thus : "The supreme power cannot take from any man any part of his property without his own consent."[4] But "by property," he writes, "I must be understood here, as in other places, to mean that property which men have in their persons as well as goods."[5] When, therefore, Locke speaks of the preservation of "property" as the main object of the State, or as the primary reason why men formed political societies, he uses the term in a very wide sense. It includes the right to life and liberty as well as the right to

1.—"Publisher's Address to the Reader" in *Plato Redivivus*, 1681. Allowing for commercial considerations, the publisher's doubts are a fair illustration of the scientific temper of the age. His scruples vanished, however, when a friend told him that even Harrington was not quite original ; many others having "discoursed rationally" about the principle that "Empire is founded in property," including "an officer in Ireland," in a letter to Cromwell in 1653. Harrington himself admitted that the principle was known to the ancients. See *The Prerogative of popular Government*, 1657, p. 21. in Brit. Mus., T.T., E. 929 (7). Between 1641 and 1687 over two million acres of Irish land were confiscated, and Harrington's name appears amongst the list of "adventurers" who subscribed for land in Ireland. See John P. Prendergast, *Cromwellian Settlement of Ireland*, 1875, p. 431.— James Harrington, of Rand in Lincolnshire, £50.

2.—*A Collection of Important English Statutes*, 1885,[2] by F. B., p. 86. 12 Car. ii., cap. 24.

3.—Richard Baldwin, *A compendious history of the taxes of France and of the oppressive methods of raising them*, 1694, printed in *Harleian Miscellany*, vol. v., p. 273.

4.—*Civil Government*, ed. H. Morley, 1884, bk. ii., ch. xi., § 138, p. 264.

5.—*Ibid.*, bk. ii., ch. xv., § 173, p. 283.

property, as we understand it to-day. As Locke's principal aim in the second treatise on *Civil Government* was to discuss the origin, foundation and limits of civil authority, his treatment of property was merely incidental. The right to private property, like the right to liberty, is anterior to the State ; it is founded on the law of nature to protect which the State came into existence. Let us examine more closely Locke's idea of the " state of nature," and " the law of nature."

The " state of nature " represents that happy condition when all men were free and independent, with reason as their sole guide. Though a state of liberty, it was not a state of anarchy or license. It was pre-eminently a social state.[1] It had " a law of Nature to govern it, which obliges everyone, and reason, which is that law, teaches all mankind who will but consult it, that being all equal and independent, no one ought to harm another in his life, health, liberty or possessions ; for men being all the workmanship of one omnipotent and infinitely wise Maker ; all the servants of one sovereign Master, sent into the world by His order and about His business ; they are His property, whose workmanship they are, made to last during His, not one another's pleasure."[2] This extract is as characteristic of Locke's regard for human personality as it is of his style. Here he seems to imply that the law of nature is a creation of reason, but elsewhere he makes it clear that the function of reason is to discover or to declare that law. " Reason is natural revelation, whereby the Eternal Father of light and fountain of all knowledge communicates to mankind that portion of truth which He has laid within the reach of their natural

1.—The so-called distinction between political and pre-political society, or between the political and social state, which we find in Locke, is contained in a pamphlet by Henry Parker in 1644. Parker says " suppose any body of men not yet associated." He speaks of man as " animal sociale " and as " animal sociatum." See his *Jus Populi*, 1644, p. 35, Brit. Mus., T.T., E. 12. (25).

2.—*Civil Government*, ed. Morley, bk. ii., ch. ii., § 6, pp. 193-4. The comma after " whose workmanship they are " is left out in Morley's 1884 edition of *Civil Government*, but it is inserted in the Cassell's Library edition *Of Civil Government and Toleration*, 1905, p. 11, to which Morley contributes an introduction. We shall refer to the latter book as *Toleration* throughout this chapter.

faculties." [1] When, therefore, Locke makes the "law of reason" and the "law of nature" synonymous,[2] it is because he regards the law of nature as that part of the Divine law which is known to us by the light of reason as distinct from positive or revealed Divine law.

Locke made no discovery in dispensing with the metaphorical expression of "a moral law written on the heart." [3] Mediaeval writers had shown that man is not born with innate ideas of morality or of other things. They held, however, that a knowledge of at least the primary principles of the moral (or natural) law belongs naturally to the human mind, and is acquired when men are capable of reasoning. To say that Locke regarded the law of nature as "simply the pursuit of happiness in obedience to a natural impulse" [4] seems to imply a false antithesis between what is natural and what is moral, and is opposed to certain views held by Locke in some parts of his writings. The pursuit of happiness is natural to man ; but it is only by observing the moral law, and by availing of other helps, that man can travel in the direction wherein true happiness lies. Locke himself recognised that the moral law, as discovered by reason, was but a feeble guide in human life. "Experience," he writes, "shows that the knowledge of morality, by mere natural light (how agreeable soever it be to it) makes but slow progress, and little advance in the world," because of men's "passions, vices and mistaken interests." [5] So fallible is unaided reason in judging of the morality of things that Locke seems to regard it as impossible, even for a philosopher, to determine what is the *summum bonum*. He appears to go even further and to abandon the idea of an objective morality.

1.—*An Essay concerning Human Understanding*, bk. iv., ch. 19, § 4, ed. Fraser, vol. ii., p. 431.

2.—"Essay on the Reasonableness of Christianity" in *Works*, 1714, vol. ii., p. 477.

3.—As for example, Dr. J. Bonar, seems to think, *Philosophy and Political Economy*, 1922, p. 100.

4.—Bonar, *Op. cit.*, p. 100.

5.—"Reasonableness of Christianity" in *Works*, 1714, vol. ii., p. 532. In the same place he says, "He that shall collect all the moral rules of the philosophers, and compare them with those contained in the New Testament, will find them to come short of the morality delivered by our Saviour."—*Loc. cit.*, p. 533. See also p. 537.

Thus in the " Essay concerning Human Understanding," [1] he writes : " The philosophers of old did in vain inquire whether *summum bonum* consisted in riches, or bodily delights, or virtue, or contemplation ; and they might have as reasonably disputed whether the best relish were to be found in apples, plums, or nuts, and have divided themselves into sects upon it. For, as pleasant tastes depend not on things themselves, but on their agreeableness to this or that particular palate wherein there is great variety ; so the greatest happiness consists in the having of those things which produce the greatest pleasure, and in the absence of those which cause any disturbance, any pain. Now these, to different men, are very different." [2]   There is an element of inconsistency here, though it is often overlooked.[3]

1.—Bk. ii., ch. xxi., § 56, ed. Fraser, vol. i., p. 351.

2.—Contrast with the above the words of John of Salisbury : " Nothing but virtue is more glorious than liberty, if indeed virtue can be rightly severed from liberty ; for it is clear to all right-thinking men that true liberty issues from no other source. Hence, since it is agreed that the highest good in life is virtue and that it alone can shake off the heavy and hateful yoke of slavery, philosophers have held that, if the necessity arose, men should die for the sake of virtue, which is the only reason for living.   But virtue does not attain to perfection without liberty."—*Policraticus* vii.,   25 (Webb ii., 217).

3.—It is interesting to note a contemporary criticism of Locke's ethical theory. " It seems a peculiar way of speaking, not yet grown common in the World, when he (Locke) assigns the Names of *vice* and *vertue* to such actions, as are agreeable or disagreeable to common reputation, and for that reason, because they are so, whereas it always was, and still is the more usual way, not only of judging what things are in their own nature, but also, of denominating actions *vertuous* or *vicious* rather from theire agreeableness or disagreeableness to the dictates of reason, and the law of nature, rather than from the custom of the place. I grant indeed, that whatever is trully vertuous, is generally counted laudable, but it is not therefore vertuous, because laudable, but therefore laudable because vertuous."— Rev. J. Lowde, *Moral Essays*, (York and London), 1699, pp. 7-8. In reply to this criticism Locke stated that he was only reporting, " as matters of fact, what other men call virtue and vice." " Marginalia Lockeana " quoted by Fraser in his " Prolegomena " to *The Essay on the Human Understanding*, 1894, vol. i., p. cxi. Dr. Fraser himself, however, admits that Locke was sceptical about the *summum bonum* (vol. i., p. 352, note (2)), while at the same time he holds that Locke "always acknowledges what he calls the eternal and unalterable nature of right and wrong."—Fraser, vol. i., p. 353, note (1). Locke in one place, (*Essay on the Human Understanding*, bk. ii., ch. xxi., § 56, ed. Fraser, vol. i., p. 352), states that " men may choose different things, and yet all choose right ; supposing them only like a company of poor insects ; whereof some are bees delighted with flowers and their sweetness ; others beetles, delighted with other kinds of viands." But the word ' mistaken ' in the phrase from the *Reasonableness of Christianity*, cited above, shows that Locke thought there might be good grounds for telling people they were wrong in their choice. Virtue and knowledge, he wrote elsewhere, are the only things " that bring real satisfaction with them,"—See below p. 75, note 3.

Locke's inconsistency, or at least his distrust of ideals, helps to explain the limitations or defects in his treatment of property.

Amongst the institutions which existed even in the " state of nature," private property occupies a prominent position according to Locke.   Unlike Grotius,[1] he is less interested in the historic origin than in the philosophical basis of the right of private property.   Thus while Locke would allow that some consent may have been necessary to legitimise the retention of more property than the individual can use to advantage, he claimed that the principle of private property itself required no such justification.   It is the natural expression of human reason and personality. " Though the earth and all inferior creatures be common to all men, yet every man has a " property " in his own ' person.'   This nobody has any right to but himself.   The ' labour ' of his body and the ' work ' of his hands, we may say, are properly his.   Whatsoever, then, he removes out of the state that nature hath provided and left it in, he hath mixed his labour with it, and joined it to something that is his own, and thereby makes it his property.   It being by him removed from the common state Nature placed it in, it hath by this labour something annexed to it that excludes the common right of other men.   For this ' labour ' being the unquestionable property of the labourer, no man but he can have a right to what this is once joined to, *at least where there is enough, and as good left in common for others.*"[2]   It is only up to a certain point, therefore, that a man has a right of property in all he can effect with his labour.[3]

1.—Hugo Grotius, *The Rights of War and Peace.*   English tr. 1738, bk. ii., ch. ii., p. 146.   Private property "resulted from a certain compact and agreement, either expressly, as by division ; or else tacitly, as by seizure." Cf. Locke *Civil Government,* bk. ii., ch. v., § 25, p. 204.—"I shall endeavour to show how men might come to have a property in several parts of that which God gave to mankind in common, and that without any express compact of all the commoners."

2.—*Civil Government,* ed. Morley, bk. ii., ch. v., § 27, p. 204.   My italics.

3.—*Ibid.,* bk. ii., ch. v. § 46, p. 214.   In § 36 *Op. cit.,* p. 208, he writes, " The measure of property Nature well set, by the extent of men's labour and the conveniency of life."   The phrasing is better in the Cassell's Library edn. (p. 27).—" Nature has well set the measure of property by the extent of men's labour and the conveniences of life."

This was the first limitation of the right of private property in the state of nature. The second qualification which he laid down is really a corollary from this. One may not appropriate by his labour more than he can " use to any advantage of life before it spoils." [1] Similarly with regard to land ; only as much of it " as a man tills, plants, improves, cultivates, and can use the product of, so much is his property." [2] For, "the same law of Nature that does by this means (labour) give us property, does also bound that property too." [3] Thus the right to property is limited by its use even when the result of individual industry.

The first condition or limitation of private property cannot easily be observed in modern societies,[4] particularly with regard to land which is limited in quantity, unless some form of communism be established. Thus in trying to limit the right of property, Locke would have destroyed it were there not many forms of property, other than land, available. With regard to the second limitation men have devised a useful means of avoiding its practical inconvenience as a clog to effort. Thanks to " the invention of money, and the tacit agreement of men to put a value on it," [5] one may lawfully acquire an indefinite number of things by his labour. Money, being a store of value and a medium of exchange, prevents things from perishing. Thus perishability rather than use is the only real limit to appropriation.[6] That was agreed to in the state of nature. " Out of the bounds of society and

1.—*Ibid.*, bk. ii., ch. v.., § 31, p. 206.
2.—*Ibid.*, bk. ii., ch. v., § 32, p. 206-207.
3.—*Ibid.*, bk. ii., ch. v., § 31, p. 206.
4.—Locke said "that the same rule of propriety, viz., that every man should have as much as he could make use of, would hold still in the world without straitening anybody, *since there is land enough in the world to suffice double the inhabitants,* had not the invention of money, and the tacit agreement of men to put a value on it, introduced (by consent) larger possessions and a right to them."—bk. ii., ch. v., § 36, p. 209.
5.—*Ibid.*, p. 209.
6.—*Civil Government*, bk. ii., ch. v., § 46, p. 214. That fact seems to be overlooked in a recent essay on Locke in *The Social and Political Ideas of some English Thinkers of the Augustan Age,* ed. Hearnshaw, 1928, p. 92. Mr. C. H. Driver (*Loc. cit.*, p. 91) seems to accept the view that Karl Marx and the early English radicals were right in claiming Locke's authority for their labour theory of value. That view has, however, been ably combated by Mr. Max Beer, *History of British Socialism,* 1920, vol. i., p. 190.

compact," men consented to " a disproportionate and unequal possession of the earth." [1]

It was, *inter alia*, with a view to moderating the *amor sceleratus habendi*, which the institution of money tends to intensify, that men agreed to found the State. " The reason why men enter into society is the preservation of their property ; and the end while they choose and authorize a legislative is that there may be laws made, and rules set, as guards and fences to the properties of all the society, *to limit the power and moderate the dominion of every part and member of the society."* [2] It seems to follow from this and other passages [3] in the second book of the *Civil Government* that Locke regarded it as the duty of the State to limit the exercise of the right of property in the interests of society as a whole. He felt that men might sometimes perish if certain forms of property were preserved ; and that the existence of great possessions might prevent some from enjoying the fruits of their industry, a right which he was inclined to regard as axiomatic.

In the *Letters concerning Toleration* Locke refers again to the regulative functions of the State regarding property. . . . " The property of mankind," he writes, " being such that they had rather injuriously prey upon the fruits of other men's labours than take pains to provide for themselves, the necessity of preserving men in the possession of what honest industry has already acquired, and also of preserving their liberty and strength, whereby they may acquire what they farther want, obliges men to enter into society with one another, that by mutual assistance and joint force they may secure unto each other their properties, in the things that contribute to the comfort and happiness of this life." [4] . . .

1.—*Civil Government*, bk. ii., ch. v., § 50, p. 215.

2.—*Ibid.*, bk. ii., ch. xix. § 222 p. 305. My italics.

3.—*Ibid.*, bk. ii., ch. v., § 50, p. 215. *The Cassell Library* edition, 1905, p. 35, reads :—" For in governments the laws regulate the right of property, and the possession of land is determined by positive constitutions." This quotation from *Civil Government* (bk. ii., ch. v., § 50), does not correspond with the text of the second edition (1694, p. 202) which I have consulted in the British Museum, nor with Morley's (1884). But it corresponds with the sixth edition of Locke's *Works* (1759, vol. ii., p. 181), and with the eighth edition of *Works* (1777, vol. ii., p. 237).

4.— *Toleration*, Cassell's Library, p. 177.

The State is bound to provide " for the peace, riches, and public commodities of the *whole people.*" [1] Its duties, therefore, are not limited to protecting merely the propertied classes. " For the political society is instituted for no other end, but only to secure every man's possession of the things of this life." [2] In short, since for Locke the " property" [3] which the State is obliged to protect includes the " lives, liberties, and estates" of the people, it follows that the State would be neglecting its primary duty if it tolerated an economic and social arrangement that rendered a large body of its members propertyless. Indeed it might be argued that according to Locke's view of the State there should be no propertyless people. But he did not dwell on the full implications of the above statements.

His main object was to insist on the individual's right to his property as against the arbitrary interference of the State, and possibly that prevented him from recognising more explicitly than he does that private property is a social function as well as an individual right. He nowhere puts the responsibility which should accompany ownership on the same plane as the right to private property itself. He does not, like some previous writers, distinguish between the right to property in general and the right to specific pieces or forms of property. One might almost say that he tends to confuse the fact of private property with the right to private property. This weakness in his theory of property appears to be directly due to the subjective character of his ethical philosophy,[4] or to his lack of faith in social ideals.

1.—*Ibid.*, p. 178. My italics.
2.—*Ibid.*, p. 179.
3.—See above ch. i. of this essay for Locke's idea of ' property.'
4.—It appears from William Molyneux's letters to Locke that the latter hoped to write a *Moral Essay or Discourse of Morality*, but he never did so. See " Letters between Mr. Locke and several of his friends " in *Works*, 1714, vol. iii., p. 504. " I am wonderfully pleased," wrote Molyneux to Locke, Oct. 15, 1692, " that you give me Hopes of seeing a *Moral Essay* from your hand." Cf. p. 511 ; pp. 520, 521. Writing to Molyneux in 1696, Locke says "As to a *Treatise of Morals*, I must own to you, that . . . I so far incline to comply with your Desires, that I ever now and then lay by some Materials for it . . . But when I consider that a Book of Offices, as you call it, ought not to be slightly done, especially by me, . . . I am in doubt whether it would be Prudent, in one of my Age and Health . . . to set

What Taine[1] said of Locke's intellectual indecisiveness applies not only to his ethical views, but also to his treatment of labour as the foundation of property.   In one section of the chapter on property (§ 27), referring to the state of nature when the earth was "common to all men," Locke states that man has a natural right to whatever "he hath mixed his labour with."[2]   The next section (§ 28) contains an assertion which some find difficult to reconcile with that view.   But it is clear that in this section (§ 28) Locke is dealing with the origin of private property in the case of ' commons which remain so by compact.'   The following statement, therefore, does not refer to the state of nature :   "The grass my horse has bit, the turfs my servant has cut, and the ore I have digged in any place, where I have a right to them in common with others, become my property without the assignation or consent of anybody."[3]   Of course, rigorously interpreted, this statement not only denies that labour has a right to the whole product of industry when working with borrowed capital, but it seriously imperils the equitable claim of labour to its specific product in so far as that can ever be a known quantity.   If you put an employer's servant on the same functional level as the employer's horse with regard to the acquisition of property, you are treating man as a means rather than as an end in himself.   And thus the capitalist employer, as one interpreter of this clause has expressed it, would "be fully entitled to the entire product created by his servants, if he can manage to get it."[4]   That would be

about it.   Did the World want a Rule, I confess there could be no work so necessary . . . But the Gospel contains so perfect a Body of Ethicks, that Reason may be excused from that Enquiry, since she may find Man's Duty clearer and easier in Revelation than in herself."—*Works*, 1714, vol. iii., pp. 545-546.   He prefers to devote his remaining strength to other researches " wherein he finds himself more in the dark."

1.—*Op. cit.*, vol. ii., p. 70.   Locke "starts an opinion to advance and withdraw it by turns."   His views on morality are fragmentary, and leave the impression that what is good or evil is not related to eternal truth but depends on the individual's choice.   Cf.   Sir James Fitzjames Stephen, *Horae Sabbaticae*, 1892, Essay, viii., p. 123.

2.—*Civil Government*, bk. ii., ch. v., § 27, p. 204.

3.—*Ibid.*, bk. ii., ch. v., § 28, p. 205.

4.—D. G. Ritchie, *Economic Review*, vol. i., 1891, p. 30.   Mr. Ritchie errs, however, in thinking that § 28 refers to ' the state of nature.'   His essay will be found in a volume called *Darwin and Hegel* (Sonnenschein, 1893), pp. 178f.

opposed to Locke's idea of the dignity of human personality, and to his explicit opinion that human labour "puts the difference of value on everything." [1]

It is, perhaps, unnecessary to point out that what Locke and other seventeenth century writers meant by the expression "labour," when they speak of it as being the cause of value, was the labour of those who owned the land which they cultivated or the tools which they used in the workshop. If Locke did not distinguish between "capitalist labour" and property-less or wage-labour, it was because the economic conditions of his time rendered his meaning clear. The labourer was then, as a rule, a capitalist as well.[2]

The inadequacy of his explanation of property, outside that primitive but brief period of communism to which he refers, is quite apparent when one tries to apply it to present day economic conditions. In modern times the production of wealth, or the acquisition of property, is pre-eminently a social process. Labour to be effective or sometimes applied presupposes the right of property.[3] Even in the golden age of Locke's "state of nature," the workman must occasionally have been dependent upon the loan of his neighbour's tools or animals to make his labour effective. What was then the exception is now the rule. Again, so many people have 'mixed their labour' with nature that it is extremely difficult to say who should have the product. Locke saw the difficulty when he enumerated (*Civil Government*, bk. ii., ch. v., § 43) all the people and all the things that are involved in the production of a 'loaf of bread.' The product of labour to-day depends more, perhaps, on social and impersonal causes, financial organisation, marketing conditions, inventions, etc., than on individual

1.—*Civil Government*, bk. ii., ch. v. § 40, p. 211.
2.—Cf. Max Beer, *History of British Socialism*, 1920, vol. i., p. 190. Mr. Beer shows clearly how some modern socialists have misinterpreted the labour theory of value held by the great English economists of the seventeenth and eighteenth centuries.
3.—Grotius, in criticising the Roman Jurist Paulus who held a labour theory of property, showed that first occupancy was a more fundamental title to property than labour. One must own before one can apply labour. See *The Rights of War and Peace*, English tr. 1738, bk. ii., ch. iii., § 3.

exertion. To endeavour to find out how much property is due to the specific operation of labour is to attempt the impossible.[1]

Despite his plea for freedom of contract and liberty of exchange, Locke did not believe that the individual could, under all circumstances, work out his own economic salvation. While he argued against proposals for legislative interference with the rate of interest,[2] pointing out that the rate of interest does not depend upon statutory enactments any more than the "hire of houses, or ships,"[3] he admitted, with Bacon,[4] that some regulation of interest was desirable. "A stated rate of interest" was necessary to serve as a norm for the law courts when asked to assess debts and damages arising from contracts in which a definite rate of interest was not agreed upon.[5] In the second place a legal rate of interest was necessary in order to prevent "young men, and those in want," from being "too easily exposed to extortion and oppression."[6] "Money-jobbers" must not be permitted to take advantage of "the ignorance or necessity of borrowers." The root cause of the extortion practised in his day seemed to him to be due to what one might call a "money-trust." The existing power of moneylenders to prey on their debtors arises from the concentration of large sums of money in a few hands in London. That power would practically cease if "money were more equally distributed . . . according to the exigencies of trade,"[7] and thus the regulation of interest to protect the weak or necessitous would, it is implied, be no longer necessary.

Locke's main solicitude was for the landowner rather than for the manufacturer or merchant. But his denunciation of the evils of the "truck-system" as practised by

1.—Cf. D. G. Ritchie, *Natural Rights*, 1924, ch. xiii., p. 269.
2.—As, for example, that of Sir Josiah Child, *A New Discourse of Trade*, 1668.
3.—"Considerations of the Lowering of Interest and Raising the value of Money," 1691, in *Works*, 1714, vol. iii., p. 6.
4.—*Essays*, xli., "Of Usury," p. 76.
5.—Locke, *Works*, 1714, vol. iii., p. 31.
6.—*Ibid.*
7.—*Ibid.*

the clothiers,[1] for example, and his criticism of the growing army of middlemen who absorbed " too great a share of the gains of trade," [2] go to show that he did not love the labourer's interest less even if he loved that of the landlord's more. Locke's views may be considered, indeed, to have more affinity with those of the modern advocates of ' Distributivism ' than with those of the Marxian socialists. Whatever flaws we may find in his attitude towards the " idle " poor, it is gratifying to note his faith in industrial democracy. . . . " It is past question that all encouragement should be given to artificers ; and things so ordered, as much as might be, that those, who make, should also vend and retail out of their own commodities, and they be hindered, as much as possible, from passing here at home, through divers hands to the last buyer. Lazy and unworking shopkeepers in this being worse than gamesters, that they do not only keep so much of the money of a country constantly in their hands, but also make the publick pay them for the keeping of it." [3]

It would, however, be unfair to a man of Locke's business experience and associations—he was friendly with rich merchants and business men like Firmin, Freke, and was himself a partner with Sir W. Colleton in the " Bahamas trade " [4]—to see in the above passage a condemnation of business specialisation or a denial of the economic productivity of the middleman as such. His object was rather to call attention to the number of people in the retail business who were obtaining money altogether out of proportion to the value of their services. The practical desuetude into which the apprenticeship laws were falling was at least one

1.—*Works*, 1714, vol. iii., p. 13.—"And as for the Workmen, who are employed in our Manufactures, especially the Woollen one, these the Clothier, not having ready money to pay, furnishes with the Necessaries of Life, and so trucks Commodities for Work, which, such as they are, good or bad, the Workman must take at his Master's Rate, or sit still and starve : Whilst by this means, this new sort of Ingrossers or Forestallers . . . set the Price upon the poor Landholder, by that means starving the Labourer and impoverishing the Landholder, whose interest is chiefly to be taken care of."

2.—*Ibid.*, p. 17.

3.—*Ibid.*, p. 17.

4.—H. R. Fox-Bourne, *The Life of Locke*, 1876, vol. i., pp. 292-293 ; p. 311.

factor in the extraordinary growth of retail shops.[1] This
often enabled the less industrious and energetic of the
population to reap a golden harvest while many hardworking
artificers had only a "hand-to-mouth" existence.[2] His plea
for the industrious worker was a logical outcome of his labour
theory of property. His somewhat harsh attitude towards
the idle and ablebodied poor is partly explained by the
same fact, but probably it is still more due to Puritan
influences.

The doctrine, always acceptable to the well-to-do, that the
poverty of the poor is their own fault, a result of sin or
a sign of God's displeasure, found numerous adherents
amongst the commercial and financial classes of Locke's
generation. Poverty, said a Puritan writer, may result from
the neglect of one's "calling," or from "some secret sin,"
which "may justly bring a temporal curse."[3] However
much individual Puritans[4] might insist on the duty of alms
giving, and the "temporall blessings" with which it is
sometimes rewarded, Puritanism as a movement, by its
emphasis on the doctrine of self-help and labour, tended to
foster a harsh attitude towards the involuntary as well as
the voluntary idle poor. In the middle of the seventeenth
century a pamphleteer sighed for a return of some of the
practical charity of the "Papists," that it might serve as "a
load-stone to attract unto it all the iron hearts of this
obdurated age."[5] During the latter half of the century the
poor of England must have suffered much from political
disturbances, and the keen competition of foreign merchants,[6]

1.—See Ray Bert Westerfield, *Middlemen in English Business*, 1915, p. 341.
Another factor was the comparatively small taxes levied on merchants.
2.—Locke, *Works*, vol. iii., p. 12.—"The labourers, living generally but
from hand to mouth" . . . Cf. *Ibid.*, p. 28.
3.—Tho. Gouge, *The Surest and Safest Way of Thriving* . . . 1676, p. 10,
Brit. Mus. Tracts on Christian Practice, 1676-1824.
4.—For example, Gouge, *Op. cit.*, p. 14. See Sir Mathew Hale, *A Discourse
touching provision for the Poor*, 1683, Preface, and ch. i.
5.—Sir Balthazar Gerbier, *A New Year's Result in Favour of the Poore*,
1652, p. 6. Brit. Mus. Tracts on Trade Finance, etc., 1651-1707, 1029, e. 8.
6.—See *England's Safety in the Laws' Supremacy* . . . 1659, p. 19. Brit.
Mus., T.T., E. 988 (13).—"As to trade," writes this pamphleteer, "you cannot
but see at how low an ebbe it is at present, to the extreme discouragement, and
almost heart breaking of the merchant, Tradesman, and all other industrious
manufactures and occupations depending thereupon."

despite the industrial development which was taking place. Whatever improvement marked their position under the Protectorate [1] was menaced at the Restoration by the triumph of a new philosophy of poverty, which was profoundly indifferent to poor law administration. On the other hand, the Civil War led to a weakening of the central control over local administration formerly exercised by the Privy Council, so that it was less easy to carry out the poor law legislation of Elizabeth.

A statute passed in her reign (1576) was an improvement on its predecessors ; it recognised the principle of finding work for the poor. The treatment of the poverty-problem by the State in the first half of the seventeenth century was, on the whole, an advance on what it was in the previous century. But after the Restoration the view that poverty was due to individual rather than to social causes, and therefore not a matter for organised relief on the part of the State, was accepted as almost an axiom by the governing classes. To Sir Mathew Hale, England, in 1683, seemed " more deficient " in " prudent provision for the Poor than any other cultivated and Christian State." [2] The " laws of settlement," enacted by Charles II. in 1662, though designed as a protective measure against vagrancy, often prevented the industrious poor from seeking more remunerative work outside their own parish.

The problem of poverty was engaging Locke's attention almost twenty years before the Board of Trade, of which he was a member, presented its Report on the subject in 1697.[3] His views are a consequence and an illustration of his theory

1.—H. Levy, *Economic Liberalism*, 1913, p. 76, thinks that "the position of the working classes, including the able-bodied poor, greatly improved under the Protectorate " owing to the increased demand for labour, following the removal of restrictions on industry. It is also fair to add that the Commonwealth government passed an act in 1650 to help the poor and unemployed. For details as to the administration of the Elizabethan poor laws, particularly during the personal government of Charles I., see E. M. Leonard, *The Early History of English Poor Relief*, 1900, pp. 254-76.

2.—*A Discourse touching provision for the Poor*, 1683, Preface pp. 1-2.

3.—" Report of the Board of Trade to the Lords Justices," 1697, printed in *An Account of the Society for the promotion of Industry in Lindsey*, 1789, pp. 101 f. The main ideas in this Report are contained in an unpublished paper entitled *Atlantis*, which occurs in Locke's " Diary " for Feb. 20th, 1679, and available in Brit. Museum, *Add. MSS.*, 15642 f 41.

of property. Labour for Locke being the foundation of
property, he was inclined to argue that the poverty of the
able-bodied was due to their indolence. On the whole, he
was inclined to view the problem of pauperism as more one
of getting the poor to work than of getting work for the
poor. The great thing was to get the poor, especially the
young, to cultivate habits of industry.

"Could all the able hands in England *be brought to work,*
the greatest part of the burthen that lies upon the industrious
for maintaining the poor would immediately cease : for,
upon a very moderate computation, it may be concluded,
that about one half of those who receive relief from the
parishes are able to get their livelihood." [1] Characteristically
enough he admits that "the greatest part of the poor
maintained by parish rates are not absolutely unable, nor
wholly unwilling to earn their living." [2] The *Report* also
recommends the careful carrying out of the "statutes of
39 Eliz. cap. 4, and 43 Eliz. cap. 2 " ; and advocates new
legislation "for the more effectual restraining of idle
vagabonds." [3] Some of the suggestions for dealing with
those who were unwilling to work appear to us now rather
drastic. "All men sound of limb and mind, above fourteen
and under fifty years of age, begging in maritime counties
out of their own parish without a pass . . . shall be seized
on . . . and sent . . . not to the houses of correction
. . . but to the next sea-port town, there to be kept at
hard labour till some of his Majesty's ships coming in or
near there give an opportunity of putting them on board,
where they shall serve three years under strict discipline, at
soldier's pay (subsistence money being deducted for their
victuals on board) and be punished as deserters if they go
on shore without leave." [4]

Circumstances will always modify the ideals of the most
commonsense philosopher. In advocating such severe
measures for dealing with the sturdy and stubborn beggar,

1.—*Report*, p. 102. My italics.
2.—*Ibid.*, p. 109.
3.—*Ibid*, pp. 103-104.
4.—*Report*, p. 105. Cf. " Diary " f. 41.—"All beggars shall *ipso facto*
be taken to the publique house and there remain the rest of their lives."

Locke never meant to lend the weight of his authority to the view, sometimes expressed in the eighteenth century, that the poor generally are hardly full members of the State, an exceedingly " burdensome " class, who have no right to the freedom and protection of the property owner.[1]

It is less easy, however, to justify Locke's attitude towards the children of the poor. If personality is not to be stunted and self-expression thwarted, the education of a child scarcely arrived at self-consciousness ought not to be guided by purely commercial considerations. Locke, however, was thoroughly imbued with the disciplinary value of work as emphasised by Puritanism. Like Firmin, he seemed to think that the majority of poor children in England should have less play and more work.[2]

The idea of establishing " working schools," in which children were to be taught some trade, was probably due to Firmin who held up Holland as a model in that respect.[3] All poor children " above three years' old," found begging, Locke would send to a " working school," there to learn " spinning or knitting, or some other part of the woollen manufacture." [4] He would sacrifice the health and strength of some of the poor, and the cultural side of their education, to the prosperity of England's chief industry. In short, he here seems to put personalty above personality.

Locke's Report is sometimes regarded as a good refutation of the common objection that he was interested in the education of the higher classes only.[5] No doubt in the discourse on *The Conduct of the Understanding* he regretted " the small

1.—Indolence may have been pretty prevalent in the seventeenth century amongst some sections of the population, but it is difficult to prove that the majority of the able-bodied poor were more anxious to live as " drones " than as " bees." See, however, H. Levy, *Economic Liberalism*, 1913, p. 70 and the pamphlet *Considerations Concerning Common Fields and Enclosures*, 1653, p. 19, Brit. Mus., T.T., E. 719 (1).

2.—Thomas Firmin, *Proposals for the Employment of the Poor*, 1681, p. 3. Cf. Sir M. Hale, *Op. cit.*, p. 9, p. 26.

3.—*Op. cit.*, pp. 2-3.

4.—*Report*, pp. 113-15.

5.—Thus Dr. Mattoon Monroe Curtis, *An Outline of Locke's Ethical Philosophy* (Leipzig, 1890), p. 96, note (2), writes, " The common objection, that Locke was interested in the education of Gentlemen only, must be dismissed. In 1697 he addressed a remarkable document to the English Government on founding working schools for the children of the poor."

Pittance of Knowledge " possessed by the " Day-Labourer in a Country Village." He reprimanded the country gentleman for leaving " Latin and Learning in the University," and for associating with neighbours " who relish nothing but Hunting and a Bottle ; " [1] but, like the rest of his contemporaries, he was very far from sharing the modern view that the children of the poor have a right to the same quality of education as those of the rich.

Locke did not rise above the prejudices of his time and of his class. He numbered amongst his friends some of the leading business men of the age. He acted as financial adviser to the Whig government ; and was a subscriber to the capital fund of the Bank of England in 1694. He was so obsessed by the necessity of establishing the commercial supremacy of his country that he brushed aside as unimportant any consideration of the injury which the attainment of such supremacy might involve to the rights of individuals at home, or to those of nations abroad. It is legitimate patriotism to desire to see one's country avail of the natural advantages which it possesses for trade and commerce, but Locke seems to connive at covetousness and sharp practice where England's interests are at stake. He approved of the various measures taken by the British Government to crush the flourishing Irish woollen industry. In his letters to W. Molyneux in Dublin he pointed out the lines on which Irish economic development should take place so as not to interfere with English economic interests.[2]

1.—" Of the Conduct of the Understanding " § 3, in *Works*, 1714, vol. iii., p. 392. Yet he believed that " We are born with Faculties and Powers capable almost of anything . . . But 'tis only the Exercise of those Powers which gives us Ability and Skill in anything, and leads us towards Perfection."—*Works*, 1714, vol. iii., p. 393. Locke would like to see " every gentleman learn a Trade, a *Manual Trade* ; nay two or three, but one more particularly." Trade was not inconsistent with a gentleman's calling. See " Some Thoughts Concerning Education," § 201, in *Works*, 1714, vol. iii., p. 93.

2.—*Works*, 1714, vol. iii., p. 551 ; p. 575. For an account of the woollen industry in Ireland in the seventeenth century, see George O'Brien, *The Economic History of Ireland in the Seventeenth Century*, 1919, p. 226. " The encouragement of the linen industry," Dr. O'Brien observes, " was not an adequate compensation for the destruction of the woollen industry. The latter was a manufacture peculiarly suitable for Ireland ; . . . and the foundation of its success had been laid by the labour and enterprise of

Unlike his contemporary, Jeremy Collier,[1] Locke did not seem to worry too much about the possibility of the ' mystery of trade ' merging itself, at times, into the ' mystery of iniquity.'

If Locke did not accept the principle of expediency in economic and social affairs, there is at least no explicit condemnation of it from the standpoint of a definite moral or religious theory of society.[2]   The omission is all the more remarkable as Collier's work, referred to above, throws an interesting side-light on the ethical thought of the age.   " One would almost think," complained one of the speakers in the Dialogue, " that Right and Wrong lay rather in the Fancies of Men than in the Reason of Things ; and was bounded more by Seas and Rivers than by any unalterable Limits of Nature." [3]

Although it is beyond the scope of this essay to deal with slavery, some consideration of Locke's attitude towards it and serfdom may help one to form a judgement of his social theory as a whole.   In the *Civil Government*, as is to be expected, he argues against that form of slavery which involves " absolute arbitrary power " [4] over the life of

many years."—*Op. cit.*, p. 230. Locke believed that England had a right to direct Irish capital into the linen industry by acts of Parliament, although Molyneux, his friend, wondered how the author of *Civil Government* could justify such interference without Ireland's " consent " and representation. See *Works*, 1714, vol. iii., p. 582. See also p. 581 ; p. 584.

1.—*Essays upon Several Moral Subjects*, 1698,[3] part i., pp. 70-71.

2.—See, however, " Considerations of the Lowering of Interest and Raising the Value of Money," 1691, in *Works*, 1714, vol. iii., p. 4.—" I have heard very sober and observing Persons complain of the Danger Men's Lives and Properties are in by the frequency and fashionableness of Perjury amongst us.   Faith and Truth, especially in all Occasions of attesting it upon the solemn Appeal to Heaven by an Oath, is the great Bond of Society."   .   .   .

3.—It is interesting to note Locke's commendation of virtue.   In a letter to a pupil who had finished his University education, Locke wrote : " I have been always of opinion that a virtuous life is best disposed to be the most pleasant, for certainly, amidst the troubles and vanities of this world, there are but two things that bring real satisfaction with them, that is, virtue and knowledge."—Fox-Bourne, *The Life of Locke*, 1876, vol. i., p. 134. In another letter to a friend he says, " This world is a scene of vanity, .   .   . and affords no solid satisfaction but the consciousness of doing well, and the Hopes of another Life.   This is what I can say by experience, and what you will find, when you come to make up your Account."   Printed in *The Thoughts of Several Famous men concerning Religion and a Future State*, (London, 1724), p. 104., Brit. Mus., Tracts on Christian Practice, 1676-1824.

4.—Bk. ii., ed. Morley, ch. iv., § 23-24, pp. 202-203, Cf. bk. i., § i., p. 77.

another. A man may not be thus enslaved unless he has forfeited his right to life by committing some act deserving of death. " Drudgery," however, is not slavery. Locke neither approved nor disapproved of people binding themselves over to the service of others for a period of years, as was customary amongst the Jews.

In *The Fundamental Constitutions of Carolina*,[1] which was at least edited, if not actually drafted by Locke, a similar negative attitude towards servile conditions of labour is observed. Article CX of these constitutions states : " Every free man of Carolina shall have absolute power and authority over his negro slaves, of what opinion or religion soever."[2] Framed at a time (1669) when feudalism was practically dead in England, it is surprising to find such a provision appearing in them. Even granting that Locke was not mainly responsible for the document, he ought at least to have disassociated himself from the above provision as he did in the case of the article providing for the establishment of a State-Church.[3]

Locke's views seem occasionally, indeed, something of a psychological paradox. At one time he is posing as the arch-enemy of slavery,[4] while at another time he seems to be conniving at measures which would involve a servile state. Some statements as, for example, that which denies that " the first born " had " a sole or peculiar right by any law of God and nature "[5] to inherit the whole of his father's property, seem to be directed against the common practice

1.—Printed in Locke, *Works*, 1823, vol. x., pp. 175 f. Des Maizeaux, who included this constitution amongst a collection of Locke's Works published in 1720, was probably responsible for the erroneous opinion that Locke was the author of it. See H. F. Russell-Smith, *Harrington and his Oceana*, 1914, p. 159. In the latest edition of Locke's *Works*, 1823, *The Constitutions of Carolina* are included on account of Locke's association with them.

2.—*Works*, 1823, vol. x., p. 196.

3.—*Works*, 1823, vol. x., p. 194 note. In a letter to a friend Locke disapproved of Art. xcvi. : " It shall belong to the Parliament to take for the building of churches, and the public maintenance of divines, to be employed in the exercise of religion, according to the Church of England, . . . the national religion of all the King's dominions."

4.—*Civil Government*, ed. Morley, bk. i. ch. i., § i., p. 77.

5.—*Ibid.*, bk. i., ch. ix. § 93, p. 142. Cf. bk. ii., ch. xvi. § 190, p. 291.— " Every man is born with a double right. First, a right of freedom to his person, . . . Secondly, a right before any other man to inherit, *with his brethren*, his father's goods." My italics.

in England of primogeniture in the case of intestacy. In other passages he seems to favour whatever distribution of property amongst children is allowed by "the law and custom of each country."[1] Locke apparently was too preoccupied with upholding the right of children to their parents' property, as against the State or the rest of mankind,[2] to notice the various laws and customs which then governed the distribution of landed and other property in England in case of intestacy.[3] The right of children to inherit their father's goods was not due to "common tacit consent."[4] That would make their right purely "positive." It was grounded on their right to self-preservation and self-propagation, and must, therefore, be regarded as "natural." The universality of the practice of inheritance also points to its naturalness. But the children have not a natural right, according to Locke, to all their father's property. The father has a right "to dispose of his own possessions as he pleases" provided his children "are out of danger of perishing for want."[5] Locke seems to forget that the right to dispose by will, particularly in the case of landed property, had been much modified in the course of history. From the Norman Conquest up to the time of Henry VIII., all land was regarded as belonging to the King. He was absolute proprietor. Permission to dispose of land by will was not granted to the individual until 1540, and even then only with certain limitations.[6]

While Locke seems to recognise the importance of distinguishing between what one may call essential or natural and positive or institutional property rights, he appears, on the whole, to be so convinced of the pragmatic value of existing property arrangements that he is disposed to regard them as natural and necessary. Thus it is a matter of some difficulty to determine how far, if at all, he desired that the

1.—*Ibid.*, bk. ii., ch. vi. § 72, p. 227.
2.—*Ibid.*, bk. i., ch. ix. § 88, p. 139.
3.—See Evelyn Cecil, *Primogeniture*, 1895, ch. ii., pp. 26 f, *et passim*.
4.—*Civil Government*, ed. Morley, bk. i., ch. ix. § 88, p. 139.
5.—*Ibid.*, bk. ii., ch. vi., § 65, p. 223.
6.—See *A Collection of Important English Statutes*, (Cambridge, 1885²), by F. B., pp. 40-43.

criteria of labour and human needs, which limited the right of property at one period of the " state of nature," should be applied to the facts of property in his own time. A dogmatic solution of this question seems, perhaps, impossible. It seems to depend on the answer to another question, on which interpreters are divided, what did he mean by the " state of nature ? " To us it seems that Locke believed in the historicity of such a state,[1] and, as we have seen, he justified very unequal possessions even then on the plea that men had consented to them. If, therefore, he does not question the property arrangements of his time, it is because the political contract has already sanctioned unequal possessions. It is important, however, to note that the terms of the contract in Locke are not restrictive : the contract is a promise to abide by a majority decision. He never includes in a description of the contract any limitation to the defence of property. The State which was founded, *inter alia*, to protect such unequal divisions of property, cannot now interfere with their growth unless by a majority decision. To do so would be to transcend its power. Moreover, excessive property does not consist in the extent of one's possessions, but in " the perishing of anything uselessly " in them.[2] Probably Locke did not realise the far reaching consequences of this concession to self-interest, " the great idol " of the age,[3] anymore than he perceived the revolutionary import of his statement that human needs and labour set natural limits to the acquisition of property.

The net result, however, of his vacillating attitude was that a theory of property rights based on the legal *status quo* of his day tended to be substituted for one which traced the

1.—*Civil Government*, ed. Morley, bk. ii., ch. viii., § 102-103, pp. 243-4.— " Thus," he writes, " I have given several examples out of history of people, free and in the state of Nature, that, being met together, incorporated and began a commonwealth." See, however, Sir Frederick Pollock, *An Introduction to the History of the Science of Politics*, 1923, p. 75, who seems to think that the " state of nature " for Locke was a mere hypothesis. But see Locke, *Civil Government*, bk. ii., ch. viii., § 100-101, pp. 242-43, and David G. Ritchie, *Natural Rights*, 1924, p. 11.

2.—*Civil Government*, bk. ii., ch. v., § 46, p. 214.

3.—Sir Henry Vane, *The Retired Man's Meditations or the Mysterie and Power of Godliness*, 1655, Preface, p. 2. He thought the " selfish spirit " of the age was the " forerunner of Christ's second coming."

justification of property to its origin in human needs and human labour. In other words, the State's sanction could be regarded as a sufficient justification of large fortunes no matter by what means acquired. While disagreeing with Hobbes' explanation of the origin of property as " an effect of commonwealth,"[1] Locke seems to arrive at the same practical conclusion with regard to existing property rights. Thus the theory opens the road to the evils arising from the cupidity of enclosing landlords and unscrupulous employers. It seems unimportant whether one considers Locke's " state of nature " as an actual state existing antecedent to political society, or as existing in the heart of existing society,[2] since the main purpose which it serves in his hands is to rationalise the facts and tendencies of property in his time. It was a plea for the current view that natural rights, including the rights of property, were those rights which remained after the interference of the Executive had been removed.

The defects in his theory of property, however, must, in a large measure, be ascribed to the fact that he treated it as an incident to the wider problem of the origin, nature, and limits of civil government. The social question in his time was, if one may so speak, largely a political one. Locke was naturally led to emphasise the individual's right, as against the State, to whatever property he had acquired. The duties of property and the responsibilities of ownership were thus thrust into the background. Accordingly, his theory appears ethically inferior to that of some of his predecessors. St. Thomas, for example, had been much more explicit than Locke in showing that private property was not an ultimate category ; and that whether the effect of personal labour, or the result of occupancy, it must be limited

1.—*Leviathan*, 1651, Everyman's Library, edn., part ii., ch. xxiv., p. 131.

2.—See Frédéric Atger, *Essai sur l'histoire des doctrines du contrat social*, Paris, 1906, p. 208. The following sentence in Locke may perhaps be regarded as a justification of contemporary enclosures. " For the provisions serving to the support of human life, produced by one acre of enclosed and cultivated land, are . . . ten times more than those which are yielded by an acre of land of an equal richness lying waste in common. And therefore he that encloses land, etc." *Civil Government*, Cassell's Library edn., bk. ii., ch. v., § 37, p. 28. These words are omitted in Morley's edition, 1884, p. 209, though they are included in the 1714 edn. of Locke's *Works*, vol. ii., p. 169.

or conditioned by the needs of others. And as a defensive
theory, as an assertion of the individual's right to his property
against the arbitrary interference of the State, it contained
nothing new. Bodin, whose *De Republica* was well known
in England, said it was the duty of the State to " preserve
to every man his own, according to the law of nature." [1]
Several writers also like Paulus, the Roman jurist, and John
of Paris, had held that the justification of private property
was to be found in labour. The right of the individual to
the fruits of his labour was logically and historically anterior
to any positive or civil agreement. The State's sanction,
according to them, was merely declaratory and not con-
stitutive of the individual's right to acquire private
property.

Had Locke written a treatise rather than a chapter on
property our criticism of him might, perhaps, be more
indulgent. Our chief quarrel with him, however, is not for
neglecting to give an exhaustive account of the different
forms of property and the modes by which they had been
acquired in various countries at various periods, but for
omitting a moral analysis of the new forms of property in
commerce, finance and land, the growth of which was
characteristic of his period. That omission may have been
due to the limited scope of his inquiry or to the uncertainty
of his moral standards—for he never wrote the ethical treatise
which apparently he had planned—and to his aristocratic
associations. Though he preached the gospel of labour,
with a zeal worthy of a Carlyle, not only to parasitic
merchants but to all young men,[2] his respect for large

1.—Jean Bodin, *The Six Books of a Commonweale*, English trans.,
R. Knowles, 1606, bk. v., ch. ii., p. 571. Cf. H. Grotius, *The Rights of War
and Peace*, London, 1738, bk. i., ch. i., § 3, pp. 10-11.—" The law of nature
informs us that it is a wicked thing to take away from any man, against his
will, what is his own." S. Puffendorf, *The Law of Nature and Nations*, trans.
Kennet, 1749, bk. iv., ch. iv., § 2, pp. 362-363.

2.—" Some Thoughts concerning Education," § 201 ; 208 ; 210, in *Works*,
1714, vol. iii., pp. 93-95. If young men utilised their leisure time properly,
they could " learn almost any Trade " without interfering with their " main
Business " or " proper Callings."—§ 208, p. 95. Thus the " science " of
accountancy—" Merchant's Accounts "—though " not likely to help a
Gentleman to get an Estate, yet possibly there is not anything of more use
and efficacy to make him preserve the Estate he has."—§ 210, p. 95.

properties prevented him from applying to them the test of labour, or some of the criteria of that "exalted utilitarianism" with which his admirers [1] have credited him.

1.—Fox-Bourne, *Life of Locke*, vol. i., p. 164.

CHAPTER IV.

EIGHTEENTH CENTURY THEORIES.

THE high esteem in which Locke was held during his life might well have proved embarrassing to a less disinterested writer. His sole aim in writing was to exhibit the truth,[1] as he conceived it, rather than to put forward theories which might please the prejudices or promote the interests of parties. If, as in the case of the *Civil Government,* his political theory happened to be in agreement with the views of the dominant Whig party of the day, that was due to accident rather than to design. He told his friend, W. Molyneux, that he never published anything which was not due to reasoned conviction.[2] But he claimed no infallibility for his judgements ; and he thought some friends attached too much importance to his writings. Indeed, Locke himself did not at all feel sure that the popularity which his works enjoyed " amongst English Readers " was a guarantee that they would " satisfie the learned World." [3] If his style of writing could be detected by all, as a contemporary stated,[4] his meaning was not always equally obvious. The impression, for example, which the reading of his chapter on property leaves is not quite what one would expect from studying the works of an advocate of ' clear and distinct ideas.' [5] His ideas on property, however, might perhaps have led to more fruitful discussion in the eighteenth century if his reputation as a philosopher, particularly as the philosopher of the Revolution,

1.—" Letter of Mr. Locke to Mr. Molyneux," March 30th, 1696, in *Works,* 1714, vol. iii., p. 546.
2.—*Ibid.*
3.—*Ibid.*
4.—" Letter of Mr. Molyneux to Mr. Locke," Dec. 24th, 1695, *Loc. cit.,* p. 541.
5.—The phrase is Descartes's, but it occurs in Locke.

had not cast such a halo of reverence round everything which he had written. Not only did men of letters, like Addison and Pope,[1] look on Locke as a national glory and a master of English prose, but even philosophers were loath to disturb the smooth waters of their intellectual inheritance by any deep diving for truth.

(1.) THE SUCCESSORS OF LOCKE.

The great majority of writers who treated of property, down to the time of Godwin, merely repeated what Locke had said as to the right of the individual to acquire private property. They seemed to forget the political circumstances which gave point to that aspect of his theory ; that Locke's main design was to protect the individual's property against the arbitrary interference of the State. They laid no emphasis on Locke's idea that property is or should be the reward of labour. No attempt was made to analyse the existing economic organisation in the light of that conception. Instead of enquiring what forms of property were most conducive to public welfare, unprofitable disquisitions were instituted with regard to the historical origin or psychological basis [2] of private property as such. What Godwin said of the treatment of government by political writers may be applied to property : " its different forms have been estimated, not by the consequences with which they were pregnant, but the source from which they sprung." [3]   Thus many, following Grotius, confused one of the ways or modes by which property was historically acquired with the rationale of private property itself. The criticism of Locke indulged in by writers like Rutherforth and Paley was of such a character. They did not seem to realise that even if first

1.—Addison, *Spectator*, 1797 edn., vol. ii., n. 94, p. 73 ; p. 121 ; p. 215 ; vol. iv., n. 313, p. 367.   For traces of Locke's influence on Pope, see Pope, *Works*, 1770, vol. iii., " Essay on Man," Epistle iii., verses 244-8.

2.—Mandeville, for example, traces private property " to the love of dominion and that usurping Temper all Mankind are born with."—*The Fable of the Bees or Private Vices, Publick Benefits*, ed. F. B. Kaye, 1924, vol. i., p. 281.

3.—Wm. Godwin, *Political Justice*, 1796, vol. i., bk. ii., ch. i., p. 124.

occupancy with the tacit or explicit consent of the community were an adequate explanation of the existence of some property, it could not be applied to that property to which no consent was ever given, because its possessors had no need to obtain it. In short, they did not perceive that the chief value of an historical study of property forms and their legal recognition arises from the fact that it helps to throw light on, rather than serves as a substitute for, a philosophical theory of property.

Locke himself was partly responsible for this. He had abandoned the attempt to justify property as having its origin in labour, and his example was followed by less ingenious writers who might otherwise, perhaps, have been tempted to question the recognition of property forms whose connection with labour was even less obvious later than in the days when Locke wrote. The attitude of eighteenth century writers is all the more remarkable when we remember that it was an age when, on the whole, men were more interested in the validity than in the genesis of things. Perhaps in this, as in other matters of deeper significance, eighteenth century rationalism exhibits a " want of confidence " rather than " an excess of confidence " in reason.[1]

What strikes one most with regard to the eighteenth century is the illogical attitude adopted towards the labourers or " manufactors." In theory, the labourers were regarded as the creators of agricultural and industrial values—or, as Locke said, labour puts " the difference of value on everything "—but, in practice, their share of the wealth produced with the aid of the landlord's or employer's capital was limited to a bare subsistence wage. It was thought that if the labourers were well remunerated, national prosperity, which up to the time of A. Smith at least tended to be regarded as an end in itself,[2] would be endangered. Thus Mandeville

1.—See C. C. J. Webb, *The History of Natural Theology*, 1915, p. 358.
2.—We say tended, because writers, like Bishop Berkeley, held that the use to which riches was put rather than the amount accumulated was the true measure of national prosperity. See his *An Essay towards preventing the Ruine of Great Britain*, 1721, p. 11, in *Works*, ed. Fraser, 1871, vol. iii., p. 200.

considered it essential to the happiness and welfare of a country that " great numbers " of its people should be kept " ignorant as well as poor." [1] Low wages were necessary to maintain the incentive to labour, and thus lead to greater wealth production. Locke and Houghton,[2] amongst others, were, in part, responsible for that view ; for since the poverty of the poor according to them is largely due to indolence, the latter must not be encouraged by high wages. There were of course both in the seventeenth and in the eighteenth centuries many writers whose views transcended such prejudices. Men, like John Bellers, at the end of the seventeenth century insisted that the labourer's claim to a " comfortable living " was a matter of justice rather than of charity, or social expediency.[3] In 1721 a politician,[4] who in those days could not be suspected of soliciting labourers' votes, preached the economy of high wages with a conviction which contrasts favourably with A. Smith's rather vacillating attitude towards the subject half a century later. When people " are sure to be well rewarded," wrote Braddon, " they shall do much more work, and much better perform the same, than when under any Dejection, either from their small Wages or Just Fears." [5]

Even if Braddon's solicitude for labour was the outcome of a belief in the necessity of increased production to ensure a favourable balance of trade, it is gratifying to note that he deemed the attainment of that end quite compatible with a well paid labouring class. Unfortunately neither the views of Bellers nor those of Braddon had any effect on the main current of eighteenth century social thought. Nor had the traditional teaching of the Church, as to the stewardship of

1.—Bernard Mandeville, *The Fable of the Bees*, ed. F. B. Kaye, 1924, vol. i., pp. 287-8, 193-4.

2.—John Houghton in his weekly paper *A Collection for Improvement of Husbandry and Trade*, April 16, 1698.—" The majority of the poor are very lazy and expensive, especially, the manufactors."

3.—*Proposals for raising a Colledge of Industry*, 1696, (reprint 1916), p. 24.

4.—Lawrence Braddon, *A Proposal for Relieving, Reforming and Employing all the Poor of Great Britain*, 1721. (Goldsmiths' Library).

5.—*Op. cit.*, p. 78. Braddon seems to have recognised the necessity of Labour Exchanges. " But all Industrious Britons should at all Times know where they may be employed and well rewarded for their Art and Industry."—*Op. cit.*, p. 10.

wealth and the duties of ownership, any great weight in a century in which it was "fashionable to decry Religion."[1] A full discussion of the causes and consequences of the decay of religion as a practical force in eighteenth century England is beyond the scope of this essay, but certain points, which seem to have an intimate bearing on our subject, may be noted. The very vigour with which theological controversies were conducted contributed in no small degree to quench Religion's "sacred fires." That fact was humorously commented upon by foreign observers, like d'Argenson, who remarked that there were but two things which could arouse the enthusiasm of Englishmen : "commerce " and "religion of which they have none."[2] Again the reaction against Puritan austerity which set in at the Restoration, apart altogether from the doubts of theologians or the scepticism of philosophers, tended to spoil rather than to improve the taste and manners of the people. " Piety and virtue " were the only things, it was said, of which men were ashamed.[3] The drama in the early eighteenth century was also mainly used as an instrument to expose or ridicule the things which men regarded as serious or sacred.[4] Apart from occasional attacks on the selfishness and materialism of the age, the spokesmen of the Established Church could do little to check the growth of religious indifferentism or to prevent Christianity from becoming a merely spectral affair in human relations. Themselves, a part of the established order, they had neither the freedom nor the authority to enforce definite moral standards even if they possessed them. It is little wonder, therefore, that they practically acquiesced in that

1.—Bishop Berkeley, *Op. cit.*, p. 2. Cf. Robert Wallace, *Various Prospects,* 1758, p. 388.

2.—*Considérations sur le Gouvernement Ancien et Présent de la France,* Amsterdam, 1765, p. 37. Cf. Goldsmith, *The Goodnatured Man*, 1768. One of the speakers in the Comedy, Croaker, referring to the Jesuits, says : " Indeed what signifies whom they pervert in a country that has scarce any religion to lose."—*Poems, Plays and Essays*, edited by J. Aikin, 1835, p. 105.

3.—Bishop Berkeley, *Op. cit.*, p. 26.

4.—See Berkeley, *Op. cit.*, p. 17. And also *A Representation of the present State of Religion, with regard to the late excessive growth of Infidelity, Heresy Profaneness :* Drawn up by the Upper House of Convocation of the Province of Canterbury, etc., 1711, printed in *Harleian Miscellany*, 1809, vol. ii., pp. 19 f. Amongst the evils complained of is the denial of free-will which overturns "the foundations of all religion"—p. 20.

eighteenth century view of religion which made God also a
" constitutional " monarch to Whom the individual owed no
duties other than those laid down by an earthly sovereign.[1]

Despite his admiration for the man who was devoted to his
" Earthly " or " Temporal Calling," the typical seventeenth
century Puritan insisted that material interests should be
always subordinated to the spiritual or main interest of man.
The net effect of Puritan writings, however, was that man's
material success tended to be identified with man's salvation.
Steele, for example, while declaring that one " must remember
that, in the throng of his Business, he is a Christian," [2] under-
rated the difficulties of acting always in a Christian manner.
Defoe, at a later date, tended to make Christian practice
even less exacting by emphasising the need of keeping
religion in its place.[3] " Duties of Religion : these may be
call'd necessities too in their kind, and that of the sublimest
nature ; and they ought not by any means to be thrust out
of their places, and yet they ought to be kept in their places
too." [4] Defoe, however, as his condemnation of the financial
orgies of the early eighteenth century testify,[5] was not devoid
of a moral outlook. One can imagine, however, the satisfaction with which a business man read Defoe's exhortation
to curtail prayers if they interfered with one's economic
interests. For a thoughtless world will not take into consideration the piety of a man should he become bankrupt as
a result of spending too much time in the Church.[6]

Again, the tendency to emphasise the difficulty of practising
the Christian religion, which dates back to Christianity itself,
received a fresh impetus in the eighteenth century from the
writings of Mandeville, whose views were largely influenced

1.—Cf. Francis Thompson, *Works*, 1913, vol. iii., p. 34. Apparently
some of the duties imposed on the Clergy as, for example, that provision of
the Book of Common Prayer obliging them to " say daily the morning and
evening prayer in their Parish Church " were seriously neglected at times.
See complaint to Parliament in 1750, in *Virtue Reviv'd or Briton's Fall
Protracted*, p. 5, Brit. Museum, Tracts, 1750.

2.—R. Steele, *The Tradesman's Calling*, 1684, ch. i., p. 2.

3.—Daniel Defoe, *The Complete English Tradesman*, 1732, vol. i., p. 50.

4.—*Ibid.*

5.—*The Anatomy of Exchange Alley or a System of Stock-Jobbing by a Jobber*,
1719, pp. 10-15.

6.—*The Complete English Tradesman*, 1732, vol. i., p. 53.

by Pierre Bayle. The latter in his *Miscellaneous Reflections*,[1] which was translated into English two years after his death and six years before Mandeville's *Fable of the Bees*[2] appeared in prose form (1714), tried to prove that "the sense of a God" does not correct "the vicious inclinations of men"; and that, in practice, man "almost always follows the reigning Passion of his soul."[3] Mandeville applied Bayle's[4] ideas to justify the economic selfishness of the age, and tried to show that "private vices" were really "public benefits." This is not the place to consider Mandeville's false notion of virtue. The significance of his book for us centres in the fact that it tended to discredit religious and moral standards in economic and social life.[5]

Thus religion tended to be regarded as a department of life; something which should not be allowed to interfere with the serious affair of making the most of this world. The economic loss which the observance of religious feasts or holidays involved was stressed.[6] Aristotle's dictum that the end of labour is to gain leisure had little meaning in an age from which teleological conceptions were rapidly disappearing. In all ages the possession of a certain amount of wealth has been regarded as an indispensable condition of influence, but in the eighteenth, perhaps, more than in any other century, men's worth tended to be judged by the

1.—Pierre Bayle, *Miscellaneous Reflections*, English trans. 1708, 2 vols.

2.—Bernard Mandeville's *The Fable of the Bees* was first published as a satire in verse in 1705.

3.—*Op. cit.*, vol. i., p. 272.

4.—Bayle, *Op. cit.*, vol. ii., p. 347.

5.—Adam Smith, *The Theory of Moral Sentiments*, 1759, pp. 482-486, regarded Mandeville's "licentious system" as a reaction against "some popular ascetic doctrines which had been current before his time, and which placed virtue in the entire extirpation and annihilation of all our passions."—*Op. cit.*, pp. 485-6.

6.—Sir Walter Harris, *Remarks on the Affairs and Trade of England and Ireland*, 1691, p. 44.   Laurence Braddon, *Abstract of a Bill*, 1717, p. viii. For further quotations see E. S. Furniss *The position of the Labourer in a system of Nationalism*, 1920.   The following extract from a pamphlet entitled *An Enquiry into some of the causes of the ill situation of the affairs of Ireland with some Reflexions on the Trade. Manufactures &c. of England*, (Dublin and Lond., 1732, p. 55), illustrates the tendency of English writers to attribute the economic backwardness of Ireland to religious rather than to political causes.   "If some Gentlemen skilled in *Political Arithmetic* would calculate what *Irish* Holidays cost the Nation, it is probable a surprising sum would appear, and a large list of the worst *Absentees* would be brought to light."

amount of property which they held. Poverty became associated with guilt, and riches with innocence, as Addison poignantly pointed out in the *Spectator*. "It is here in England," he writes, "come into our very language, as a propriety of distinction, to say when we would speak of persons to their advantage, 'They are people of condition.' . . . The consideration of fortune has taken up all our minds and, as I have often complained, poverty and riches stand in our imaginations in the places of guilt and innocence." [1]

Had Addison's protest been taken seriously in the early part of the century, Goldsmith might have had less ground in 1766 for complaining of the extent to which virtue and all other qualifications were subordinated to economic self-interest.[2] But despite his literary claims to a hearing, Addison must have been regarded by more than Mandeville as a "parson in a tye-wig;"[3] and the views of parsons, particularly on economic and social questions, had, for many reasons, little influence in those days.[4] Accordingly, though the traditional view of property continued to be asserted during the century, it was not defended with sufficient ability or put forward with sufficient authority to counteract that view of it as an absolute right, entailing no duties other than those imposed by the State. While admitting that property rights were subordinate to human needs—at least in the "state of nature"—Locke, as we saw, was led to emphasise their absolute aspect owing to the constitutional struggles of the seventeenth century. But most eighteenth century writers, and some of his contemporaries, made that element in his theory preponderant to the neglect of the equally important point of the limitation or moderation of property rights by the State in the interest of the common good.

1.—*Spectator*, 1797, edn., vol. iv., n. 294, p. 244.
2.—*Vicar of Wakefield*, ed. Percy L. Parker, 1905, ch. xvi., p. 89 and ch. xix.
3.—*Gentleman's Magazine*, vol. 49, p. 597.
4.—Goldsmith in his essay on the "English Clergy and Popular Preachers" said that nowhere were the Clergy "so little thought of, by the populace, as in England."—*Poems, Plays and Essays*, ed. J. Aikin, 1835, p. 326. This was due, he thought, to their style of preaching which lacked enthusiasm and conviction.

At the end of the seventeenth century we find Locke's friend, James Tyrrell,[1] interpreting him thus. The existing division of property, as sanctioned by law, must not be "altered however, perhaps, hard and unequal it may prove to some particular persons."[2] This view is rather surprising when one remembers that Tyrrell was conscious of the necessity of a fuller and more exact division of the necessaries of life to meet the requirements of a growing population. In "well-inhabited countries," land was incapable of affording a "comfortable subsistence" to all without "foreign Trades or mechanick Employments."[3] Undoubtedly things ought not and cannot be altered to suit "everyman's particular fancies,"[4] but Tyrrell goes further and seems to imply that the present distribution of property is so necessary and convenient that no future circumstances could justify State interference with it. His attitude seems unreasonably conservative because he admits that the lawful appropriation of things, the use of which can be separated from their ownership, is due to social sanction.[5]

Another contemporary, William Wollaston, (1659-1724) tried to give almost mathematical precision to the absolutist aspect of Locke's theory of property.[6] Everyman has within himself "a principle of individuation, which distinguishes and separates him from all other men in such a manner, as may render him and them capable of distinct properties in things (or distinct subjects of property) . . . The labour of B cannot be the labour of C ; because it is the application of the organs and powers of B, not of C, to the effecting of something."[7] He defines the right of private property, but makes no effort to discuss how far this right to permanent and exclusive ownership[8] should be respected in the case,

1.—*A Brief Disquisition of the Laws of Nature*, 1701.²
2.—*Op. cit.*, p. 39.
3.—*Op. cit.*, p. 38.
4.—*Op. cit.*, p. 39.
5.—*Op. cit.*, p. 34.
6.—*The Religion of Nature⁷ Delineated*, 1738 edn., § 6. This book was first published in 1724, and passed through six editions in the following fourteen years.
7.—*Op. cit.*, § 6, p. 127.
8.—*Op. cit.*, § 6, p. 136.

for example, of non-essential goods. He assumes that property is always the " fruit " of a man's " cares and sweat," [1] and that it is not even in man's power to part with it, except in the sense of contributing some of it to the State " in order to preserve the rest." [2] " Men's titles to what they have " are founded " in nature " as well as " in law." Having taken so much for granted, one is not surprised that he did not perceive the possibility of legal titles predominating, at times, to the extent of making some property a species of forbidden fruit. Though few people to-day would regard Wollaston's intellectual stature as equal to that of Newton or Locke, it is interesting to note that a royal personage in the eighteenth century placed his bust with those of Locke and Newton in the royal garden at Richmond.[3] It is, perhaps, even more significant in our own days to see a book devoted to the *Ethics of Wollaston* containing no reference to his views on property.[4]

The optimism of Wollaston and Tyrrell was imitated by a whole host of eighteenth century writers who touched on the question of property. With the exception of a few writers, like Francis Hutcheson and, to a lesser degree, Wm. Paley, there is no attempt made to resolve what one may call the synthetic concept of property into its constituent parts until we reach the social critics of the last quarter of the century. Thus the right of property in land, for example, is seldom distinguished from the right of property which one has to the fruits of his labour. All property is considered equally sacred ; all property rights are exhibited as something absolute or natural ; though, in reality, many of them are but rights which English law has come to sanction. In most eighteenth century writers one finds a similar attitude of satisfaction with, or actual indifference to, the actual distribution of property ; or an implied or express belief in

1.—*Op. cit.*, § 6, p. 134.
2.—*Op. cit.*, § 7, p. 150. "A man cannot give away the natural right and property he has in anything, in order to preserve or retain that property ; but he may consent to contribute part of his estate in order to preserve the rest."—*Ibid.*, p. 150.
3.—See *Dictionary of National Biography*, 1900, vol. lxii., p. 311.
4.—Clifford Griffeth Thompson, *The Ethics of Wollaston*, (Boston, 1922).

political security as the decisive factor in a nation's wealth and welfare.

Adam Smith, for example, declared that " that security which the laws of Great Britain give to everyman . . . to enjoy the fruits of his own labour is sufficient to make any country flourish."[1] Though he recognised that the prosperity of a country must be judged by the distribution of wealth amongst its inhabitants, more than by the total amount of wealth available within that country,[2] he has very little to say about property in the sense which really matters, its personal distribution. He is more interested in classes than in individuals. Discussing the inequality of social classes, Smith refers to the " superiority of personal qualifications " such as strength, beauty, wisdom and virtue, as one of the causes which leads to subordination of classes in society ; but he does not say that any of these criteria should prevail over the very " plain and palpable " criteria of fortune and birth.[3] It must, however, be admitted that for Smith property's title to respect and superiority centred in the belief that it represented the accumulated labour of many generations.[4] This optimistic note is characteristic of Smith. At times, however, he seems to doubt the close connection between labour and property as, for example, in his discussion on value. He seems to think that profits and rents were deductions from the value created by labour,[5] and one eminent economist[6] is of opinion that Smith finally adhered to that view. In truly Lockeian language he pointed out the important place which labour occupies in the social order. " The property which everyman has in his own labour, as

1.—*Wealth of Nations*, bk. iv., ch. v., ed. Cannan 1920,[2] vol. ii., pp. 42-43.
2.—*Ibid.*, vol. i., p. 1.   See also the article by Prof. Cannan, "Adam Smith as an Economist," in *Economica*, June, 1926, pp. 123 f.   Prof. Cannan seems to exaggerate the originality of Smith.—*Loc. cit.*, p. 126.   He introduced no " Copernican change."   Berkeley, as we saw, combated the idea of making national prosperity synonymous with national riches.   " Men are apt to measure national Prosperity by Riches : it would be righter to measure it by the use that is made of them."—*An Essay towards preventing the Ruine of Great Britain*, 1721, p. 11.
3.—*Wealth of Nations*, bk. v., ch. i., pt. ii., ed., Cannan, vol. ii., pp. 203-4.
4.—*Ibid.*, p. 203.
5.—*Wealth of Nations*, bk. i., ch. viii., ed. Cannan, vol. i., p. 67.
6.—Prof. Cannan, *Theories of Production and Distribution*, 2nd edn., p. 202.

it is the original foundation of all other property, so it is the most sacred and inviolable." [1] Civil Government is an effect of property; [2] the protection of property, including the property which a poor man derives from "the strength and dexterity of his hands," [3] is the main object of its existence.

Smith, however, was conscious of the fact that protection of property did not always involve the protection of labour. He regretfully remarks that "for one rich man there must be at least five hundred poor." [4] It is difficult to justify his social fatalism when one remembers his sympathy for the industrious worker, and his emphatic declaration that labour was the original foundation of all property. He noted with satisfaction the improved condition of the labouring classes in the first half of the eighteenth century. Any improvement in what is by far "the greater part of every political society" can never be an "inconveniency to the whole . . . It is but equity, besides, that they who feed, cloath, and lodge the whole body of the people, should have such a share of the produce of their own labour as to be themselves tolerably well fed, cloathed, and lodged." [5] Smith's intellectual indecisiveness is, at times, as embarrassing as that of Locke's. Thus, in one part of the *Wealth of Nations*, the labourers or "those who live by wages" are made practically synonymous with society; and in other parts labour is represented as merely one, and only second in importance, of "the three great orders" of civilised society. [6] The interest of landlords—"those who live by rent "— is said to be "inseparably connected with the general interest of society" [7] just as much as that of those who live by wages.

With regard to merchants, Smith has even harder things to say than Locke—things which cannot easily be reconciled

1.—*Wealth of Nations*, bk. i., ch. x., pt. ii., ed. Cannan, vol. i., **p. 123.** Cf. vol. i., p. 80.
2.—*Ibid.*, bk. v., ch. i., pt. ii., ed. Cannan, vol. ii., p. 203.
3.—*Ibid.*, bk. i., ch. x., pt. ii., ed. Cannan, vol. i., p. 123.
4.—*Ibid.*, bk. v., ch. i., pt. ii., ed. Cannan, vol. ii., p. 203.
5.—*Ibid.*, bk. i., ch. viii, ed. Cannan. vol. i., p. 80.
6.—*Ibid.*, bk. i., ch. xi., pt. iii., ed. Cannan, vol. i., p. 248.
7.—*Ibid.*, p. 248.

with his belief in the beneficent effects of unregulated self-interest. The merchants are an order of men whose interests are never the same as that of the public. They " have generally an interest to deceive and even to oppress the public, and . . . have, upon many occasions, both deceived and oppressed it." [1] It would seem that his faith in the practical efficacy of economic self-interest meant little more than the substance of things to be hoped for in the future. Adam Smith had no clear ideas as to interest and profits ; they are often confused and represented as deductions from the product of labour.[2]

Despite the fact that he was no optimist with regard to the distribution of wealth, and notwithstanding his sympathy towards the industrious labourer, he nowhere attempts a systematic discussion of the causes governing the inequalities between individuals, as distinct from classes. He merely refers casually to the evils of inheritance and primogeniture.[3] He does not consider the question of property in the light of any moral or social ideal. Had he attempted a philosophical analysis of property or passed judgement on some ot its forms, he might have offended a self-satisfied generation, but then subsequent generations could, perhaps, less easily find

1.—*Ibid.*, bk. i., ch. xi., pt. iii., ed. Cannan, vol. i., p. 250.
2.—*Ibid.*, bk. iv., ch. vii., pt. ii., ed. Cannan, vol. ii., p. 67.—" Rent and profits eat up wages and the two superior orders of people oppress the inferior one."
3.—*Ibid.*, bk. iii., ch. ii., ed. Cannan, vol. i., pp. 360-361.—" But when land was considered as the means, not of subsistence merely, but of power and protection, it was thought better that it should descend undivided to one. In those disorderly times every great landlord was a sort of petty prince. His tenants were his subjects. He was their judge, and in some respects their legislator in peace, and their leader in war. . . . The security of a landed estate, therefore, the protection which its owner could afford to those who dwelt on it, depended upon its greatness.
" In the present state of Europe the proprietor of a single acre of land is as perfectly secure of his possession as the proprietor of a hundred thousand. The right of primogeniture, however, still continues to be respected, and as of all institutions it is the fittest to support the pride of family distinctions, it is still likely to endure for many centuries. In every other respect, nothing can be more contrary to the real interest of a numerous family than a right which in order to enrich one, beggars all the rest of the children." See also Josiah Tucker, *The Elements of Commerce and Theory of Taxes*, 1755, p. 14, (impression " not designed for public use " in Brit. Mus.). Tucker criticised primogeniture for its effects on population and the cultivation of the land. " These monopolies of land must occasion . . . a great diminution of people."

in him what suited their social philosophy ; particularly the opinion that political economy was the enemy of the working man. One consideration may be put forward to condone this sin of omission in the case of Smith, though obviously it is less applicable to nineteenth century economists. In Smith's time landlords and capitalists were, as a rule, more than landlords and capitalists ; they were producers or labourers as well. Thus their titles to income rested not only on property rights guaranteed by law, but also on their active participation in the production of wealth or in the performance of some public service. Probably very few of the landed gentry in the eighteenth century would fit precisely into Machiavelli's definition of a gentleman. As a class they certainly did more than " live idly upon the proceeds of their extensive possessions." [1] Though Smith did more than any previous or contemporary writer to make commerce respectable, he was not at all confident that, because a trader could be a gentleman, every trader would act in a gentlemanly fashion. Above all, he had not much faith in the justice which would be meted out to " workmen " in a State where the dominant counsels were those of property.[2]

Although the composition of the *Wealth of Nations* [3] was spread over more than a quarter of a century, it was impossible for Smith to foresee the multiplication of those "rarified and sublimated " [4] forms of property which the development of the factory-system and the growth of joint-stock enterprise made possible after his death ; forms of property which often stood in the way of the labourers' being " tolerably well fed, cloathed and lodged." [5] Adam Smith's main object, however, was to create an atmosphere favourable to the abolition of economic privileges. His enthusiasm for individual liberty and freedom of contract was inspired by

1.—Machiavelli, *Titus Livius*, bk. i., ch. lv., in *Works*, ed. Detmold, vol. ii., p. 210.
2.—*Wealth of Nations*, bk. i., ch. x., part ii., ed. Cannan, vol. i., p. 143.
3.—See Prof. Cannan's introduction to 1920² edition, p. xlvii.
4.—See the interesting book by John Sangster, *The Rights and Duties of Property*, 1851, p. 44.
5.—*Wealth of Nations*, bk. i., ch. viii., ed. Cannan, vol. i., p. 80.

the hope that labour would benefit ultimately by the removal of all restrictions on economic enterprise. Not only was he influenced by Locke's political philosophy, but he gave a distinctly optimistic interpretation to Locke's economic rationalism. For, according to Smith, man, by following his intelligent self-interest, is led by an " invisible hand " to promote the interest of society as a whole. With such a philosophy the sphere of State control was for him even narrower that it was for Locke. Had he lived in the nineteenth century his humanity and sympathy with the industrious worker would probably have led him to modify his views, and condemn the paradoxical position of property being found in the greatest proportions with those who often laboured least.[1] His failure to grasp the significance of the economic developments which he witnessed or to read correctly the signs of the time is, however, more excusable than his neglect to profit more by the wisdom of his friend and teacher, Francis Hutcheson.

The latter's views on property[2] illustrate, by way of contrast, the defects of the typical eighteenth century theory of property. While sharing some of Locke's passion for individual liberty, and holding that the right of property is founded on that strong desire within man of acting as he pleases, he recognised that that natural liberty for which man craves, and particularly that form of it which finds expression in the desire to enjoy the fruits of his own labour, was not a thing to be pursued irrespective of the requirements of the " public interest."[3] He distinguished very carefully between the psychological and moral aspects of private property. The psychological argument for private property ought not to be invoked to justify a state of things where property had ceased to be the protection of labour, or had in fact become the instrument of its repression. "As

1.—Cf. Sangster, Op. cit., pp. 244-5.
2.—Francis Hutcheson, 1694-1746. A System of Moral Philosophy, 1755, vol. i., pp. 319f.
3.—Op. cit., vol. i., pp. 319-320.—" From these strong fealings in our hearts we discover the right of property that each one has in the fruits of his own labour ; that is, we must approve the securing them to him, where no public interest requires the contrary " . . .

property is constituted to encourage and reward industry, it can never be so extended as to prevent or frustrate the diligence of mankind. No person or society therefore can by mere occupation acquire a right in a vast tract of land quite beyond their power to cultivate, as shall exclude others who may want work or sustenance for their numerous hands." [1]

Those who are able, and refuse to labour, should not be supported by the labours of others.[2] Communism, however, was no solution of the " inconveniences " arising from the present individualistic system of ownership. But these evils must not be regarded as inseparable accidents of a private property régime. " Most of them may be prevented . . . by a *censorial* power, and proper laws about education, testaments, and succession." [3] What a contrast with Locke and other writers who stressed the absolute or unlimited nature of property rights. It is only within the limits noted above that Hutcheson regarded the right of private property as implying a right to the " fullest use " and " disposal " of what one possesses.[4] The right of disposing of one's property as one pleases must be controlled by the needs of society as a whole. Thus the right of devising by will he considered natural only in the sense of being socially expedient ; if it were not permitted, industry might be " much discouraged." [5] While believing that property, particularly landed property, was the natural basis of power, he was careful to add that " it gives not any just right to power." [6] Like the entertainer in Goldsmith's *Vicar of Wakefield*,[7] Hutcheson could not see why the mere " defect of opulence " should disqualify learned men for high positions in the State. He regretted that political power had become the privilege of a class. Power being the natural accompaniment of property, there ought to be a " suitable division of property," and " such Agrarian laws as will prevent any immoderate increase of wealth in

1.—*Op. cit.*, vol. i., p. 326.
2.—*Op. cit.*, vol. i., p. 321.
3.—*Op. cit.*, vol. i., p. 323.
4.— *Op. cit.*, vol. i., p. 322.
5.—*Op. cit.*, vol. i., p. 352.
6.—*Op. cit.*, vol. ii., p. 245.
7.—L. Stein, edn. 1912, ch. xix., p. 133.

the hands of a few, which could support a force superior to the whole body."[1] Hutcheson was too sincere a student of human nature to hold that any interest—even Burke's glorified landed interest[2]—could safely be entrusted with a monopoly of political power.   The foregoing analysis not only illustrates the organic character of Hutcheson's conception of society as compared with Locke's individualism, but it also affords some grounds for doubting the identity of ideas which is sometimes said to exist between A. Smith and Hutcheson.[3]   With regard to property, at least, one would wish that Smith's assumptions embodied more of Hutcheson's thesis.

But if Hutcheson's views on property represent what is most human in the social philosophy of a century which, on the whole, distrusted ideals, those of his friend David Hume afford, perhaps, the best illustration of a social philosophy shorn of all enthusiasm save that for wealth production. The gloomy faith, the austere morals, and the perverted view of the passions for which Scottish Puritanism stood in the seventeenth century, helped to produce[4] that philosophical reaction in the eighteenth century of which Hume was the embodiment.   The emphasis laid on the beneficence of human liberty by Scottish philosophers—Hutcheson, Smith and Hume—was born of the irrational regulations and the " killjoy spirit " of the Church of Scotland.[5]   In a sense Hume's zeal for economic enterprise, and particularly the prominence which he gave to labour, may be regarded as a re-assertion of that element in Puritanism which had attracted those who cared little for the dreary dogmatism, or the false antithesis

1.—*Op. cit.*, vol. ii., p. 248 ; pp. 259-60.
2.—Edmund Burke, Letter iii., " Regicide Peace " in *Select Works*, ed. Payne, 1904, vol. i., pp. 243-4.
3.—W. R. Scott, *Francis Hutcheson*, 1900, p. 232.   Dr. Scott writes : " In both thinkers we find the same natural liberty, Optimism and Naturalism, with Smith as an assumption with Hutcheson as a thesis."
4.—There were other influences at work also as, for example, the writings of Pierre Bayle, *Miscellaneous Reflections*, English trans., 1706, vol. i., p. 272, who tried to prove that man is ruled by his passions rather than by reason or by religion, and that the love of riches, being ineradicable, cannot be checked.—vol. ii., p. 347.
5.—See H. T. Buckle, *History of Civilisation in England*, ed. J. M. Robertson, 1904, ch. xx., p. 792, pp. 782-5.

between spiritual and temporal interests which other elements in the system suggested.[1]

If Hume's admiration for merchants and manufacturers was great, it was because, for him, trade and industry represented "a stock of labour."[2]   If he favoured taxation of the poor, provided it did not fall on the necessaries of life, it was in order that they might perform more work.[3] The important thing was to awaken new wants ; to arouse the acquisitive instinct.   But while admitting that, "every person, if possible, ought to enjoy the fruits of his labour, in a full possession of all the necessaries, and many of the conveniences of life,"[4] he does not say how that rough economic equality, which adds more to the happiness of the poor than it takes from that of the rich, might be attained in actual life.   His positivism and optimism probably prevented him from considering more fully its practical implications.   Hume thought that the growth of manufacture and commerce would act as a great humanitarian force.   He seemed convinced that what sociologists call the "other-regarding" instincts would develop *pari passu* with every advance in wealth production.   "Industry, knowledge, and humanity, are linked together by an indissoluble chain, and are found from experience as well as reason to be peculiar to the more polished, and what are commonly denominated, the more luxurious ages."[5]

Commerce, no doubt, implies mutual dependence.   It promotes peace up to a point ; but Hume must have known that it can also provoke war and man's inhumanity to man. Unless the acquisitive instinct is controlled by some criterion less vague and more objective than Hume's "sympathetic naturalism"[6] affords, we shall look in vain for that

1.—See T. H. Green, "Four lectures on the English Revolution" in *Works*, ed. R. L. Nettleship, 1888, vol. iii., p. 286.

2.—David Hume, *Essays*, The New Universal Library, 1905, part ii., no. 1, p. 190.

3.—*Ibid.*, part ii., no. 8, "Taxes," p. 247.

4.—*Ibid.*, part ii., no. 1, p. 192.

5.—*Essays*, part ii., no. 2, p. 197.

1.—For a good summary of Hume's ethical views see Reginald A. P. Rogers, *A Short History of Ethics*, 1911, ch. iv., pp. 177 f.   See also Dr. W. Windelband, *A History of Philosophy*, tr. James H. Tufts, 1910, p. 516.

humanitarianism which he so lightly assumed to accompany the growth of commerce. Though he considered it unreasonable to expect that a piece of woollen cloth could be " wrought to perfection " in a nation " where ethics are neglected," [1] his own ethical system, despite the emphasis which it laid on the social consequences of man's actions, tended to make moral criteria a negligible force in actual life. For Hume, right and wrong were a matter of emotion rather than of reason ; a question of pleasant or painful feelings. The basis of morality was not metaphysics, but empirical psychology. A certain line of action is considered good because it is socially advantageous, rather than socially advantageous because it is good. Viewed in the most favourable light, his ethical system was a plea for a fuller recognition of the facts of life on the part of the moralist. Considered from another and more correct standpoint, it was an attempt to discredit objective standards and ultimate values. His attitude towards morality, and indeed his general philosophical position, naturally influenced his treatment of private property. No attempt is made to distinguish between the positive and nomative aspects of private property. The laws which guarantee or preserve our possessions are " the laws of justice." [2]

The definition which he gives of private property is not less significant. It is a " convention entered into by all the members of the society to bestow stability on the possession of those external goods, and leave everyone in the peaceable enjoyment of what he may acquire by his fortune and industry." [3] Since stability of possessions is for him one of " the three fundamental laws of Nature " [4] as requisite to the existence of society as private property itself is, it seems that property acquired by " fortune," however dubious in its nature or harmful in its consequences, is by virtue of this compact as sacred as that due to labour or industry.

1.—*Essays*, part ii., no. 2, p. 196.
2.—David Hume, *A Treatise of Human Nature*, 1738, ed. L. A. Selby-Bigge, 1896, part ii., bk. iii., § 2, p. 491. Everyman's Library edn., E. Rhys, vol. ii., p. 196.
3.—*Ibid.*, Selby-Bigge, p. 490. Everyman's Library edn., vol. ii., p. 195.
4.—Rogers, *Op. cit.*, p. 184.

Though he admits that the " avidity . . . of acquiring goods and possessions for ourselves and our nearest friends, is insatiable, . . . and directly destructive of society," unless controlled by considerations of justice, he seems to value the preservation of society less for the restraints which it imposes on " the interested affection," or acquisitive instinct, than for the security which it offers of making " much greater advances " in the acquisition of wealth than is possible under a system of " universal licence." [1] Since for him the " laws of society " are synonymous with " the laws of of justice " [2]—and justice itself is a human contrivance—it would seem to follow that if the State sanctioned a system of property rights which prevented a considerable section of its members from satisfying their minimal needs, one could not, according to that view, find fault with it. With all his positivism and utilitarianism the view of property which he favoured was one which obscured its social aspect. The right which a man has to a piece of property, whether acquired by occupation, or by the consent of the proprietor, can only be lost " by his own consent." [3]

This seems to be implied in the passage where he disposes of degrees of dominion.[4] His object apparently is to emphasise the subordination of the use to the right, rather than of the right to the use, of property. " However civil laws may talk of a perfect dominion, and of an imperfect, 'tis easy to observe that this arises from a fiction, which has no foundation in reason, and can never enter our notions of natural justice and equity. A man that hires a horse, tho' but for a day, has as full a right to make use of it for that time, as he whom we call its proprietor has to make use of it any other day ; and 'tis evident, that however the use may be bounded in time or degree, the right itself is not susceptible of any such gradation, but is absolute and entire, as far as it extends. Accordingly we may observe, that this

1.—*A Treatise of Human Nature*, Everyman's Library ed., vol. ii., bk. iii., § 2, p. 197.
2.—*A Treatise of Human Nature*, ed. Selby-Bigge, p. 491. Everyman's Library ed., vol. ii., p. 196.
3.—*Ibid.*, Selby-Bigge, p. 530.
4.—*Ibid.*, Selby-Bigge, p. 529.

right both arises and perishes in an instant ; and that a
man entirely acquires the property of any object by
occupation or the consent of the proprietor ; and loses it by
his own consent." [1]   Hume, however, was more consistent
than his contemporary, Thomas Rutherforth, who set himself
the task of disputing Locke's "first principles," [2] and yet
defined " full property in a thing " as " a perpetual right to
use it to any purpose, and to dispose of it at pleasure." [3]

In his lectures at Cambridge, Rutherforth subjected Locke's
labour theory of property to a keen criticism.   The ambiguity
of Locke's phrase that everyone has a right to the labour of
his body is exposed.   A man's labour " may mean either the
personal act of working, or the effect which is produced by
that act.   In the first sense, it must be allowed that a man's
labour is properly his own ; . . . but it does not follow
. . . that the effect of his labouring . . . must likewise
be properly his own." [4]   To prove that, one would have to
show that the materials worked on belonged exclusively to
the individual ; and that cannot be unless others have agreed
to separate ownership.   To prove that even in a 'state of
nature' a man had a right to the effects of his labour, " it
would be necessary to show that the labour of one man can
overrule or set aside the right of others." [5]   Following
Grotius he held that in the beginning all things belonged to
all in common, and that, therefore, some consent on the part
of the community was necessary to make the introduction
of private property consistent with justice.   In the early
ages of the world explicit consent for the division of property
was procurable ; but in later ages occupation, followed by
peaceable possession, was sufficient to legitimise private
ownership. [6]   Like Grotius he was more interested in
accounting for the historic origin of private property than in
the rationale of private property itself.   In certain passages,
however, he seems to regard human needs as a more

1.—*Ibid.*, Selby-Bigge, p. 530.
2.—*Institutes of Natural Law*, 1754, American edition, 1832, pp. 26 f.
3.—*Op. cit.*, 1832 edition, p. 34.
4.—*Op. cit.*, p. 26.
5.—*Ibid.*, p. 26.
6.—*Ibid.*, p. 25.

fundamental title to property than occupancy plus consent, tacit or explicit. "In some circumstances," he writes, "our common right to the use of things remains, even after those things have been appropriated and have their distinct and respective owners."[1] When a certain amount of property becomes "absolutely necessary for the preservation of individuals," they may assert their common right. But such circumstances, he thought, could not arise in a country like England "where the civil laws have provided for the poor."[2] There can be no necessity, therefore, which the law will consider sufficient to justify an individual taking and using the food or clothing of his neighbour since it has made adequate "provision for such wants."[3]

There was nothing original about Rutherforth's doctrine of communal property rights. The traditional teaching of moralists and theologians always recognised one universal limit to the right of private property, the extreme or quasi-extreme necessity of one's neighbour.[4] The concept of necessity is rather elastic.[5] In the interests of social stability that form of it which would morally justify any individual interfering with the property of his neighbour must necessarily be narrowly defined. According to Catholic moralists an individual is said to be in extreme necessity when he is in danger of dying or succumbing unless he receives prompt assistance. In such circumstances he may help himself from another's property to preserve his life when the owner's permission cannot be obtained, or is unreasonably withheld.

It is to Rutherforth's credit to have drawn attention again to the existence of such communal property rights, although his motive in doing so was rather to make a pedantic point against Locke than to suggest some solution of the paradox of property. If the space devoted to showing the

1.—*Ibid.*, p. 41.
2.—*Ibid.*, p. 43.
3.—*Ibid.*, p. 43.
4.—See A. Castelein, S.J., *Le Socialisme et le droit de la Propriété* 1896, pp. 508 f.
5.—See the interesting classification of " necessitie " given by G. Powel in *Theological positions concerning the lawfulnesse of borrowing upon Usurie,* 1605, Goldsmiths' Library, pp. 1-2.

supposed necessity of some consent to legitimise the introduction of private property had been devoted to the more
important question of how far the community's consent can
be presumed to be given to a state of things where property,
on the whole, or in part, fails to fulfil its primary function,
his criticism of Locke might have been more fruitful. This
brief outline of the development of what one may call an
absolutist conception of private property, which failed to
distinguish between property that is necessary and property
that is unnecessary for the reasonable development of
human personality, may be concluded by reference to two
other extravagant expressions of it in the eighteenth century ;
one by a legal luminary, and the other by a Church divine.

For Blackstone, private property whether arising from
continuous occupation as in the case of land, or from labour
as in the case of movable goods, was one of those absolute
rights to protect which the State exists. An individual can
use, enjoy, and dispose of his acquisitions " without any
control or diminution save only by the laws of the land." [1]
It is difficult to see how any right can be really absolute and
yet capable of being modified by law ; or, indeed, to reconcile
the existence of any absolute right with Blackstone's theory
of State omnipotence. Though the legislative power of
Parliament was for him limited only by the impossible,
extending to all objects spiritual and temporal, he did not
discuss what the State could do to modify private property
in the interests of the community. Parliament, however,
could not abrogate the natural law ; and all property,
according to his optimistic philosophy, partook of the sacredness of the natural law. This individualistic conception of
property was strengthened by two movements, the French
Revolution and the Industrial Revolution. The latter was
ultimately to throw discredit on the eighteenth century idea
of property ; but, to begin with, it fostered it. Surviving
restrictions on industry and trade must be removed in order
that a competitive régime, in which each would receive the
equivalence of his service, may be established. One of the

1.—Wm. Blackstone, *Commentaries*, 9th edition, vol. i., pp. 138, 124.

leading ideas of the French revolutionaries was to secure for the producer the right to use his property as he thought fit. But contemporary English thought, on the whole, was not inclined to view the Revolution merely as a movement for the abolition of economic privileges.

Some feared, with little reason as we shall see later, that the political and social fabric of England, as well as that of France, would be endangered by the proceedings of the States-General in 1789. Others, whose hopes were pitched in a higher key and whose reason moved in a rarer atmosphere, were inclined to see in these events the beginning of the fulfilment of their dreams of equality.[1] Behind Burke's passionate protest against the continental revolutionaries, there is a deep reservoir of political wisdom on which mankind can draw with profit for all time. The intellectual legacy of some other contemporary critics of the Revolution has not a similar interest for students of social philosophy. Due allowance being made for the emotional atmosphere created by the French Revolution, it is regrettable that Churchmen like Dr. Vincent, Dean of Westminster, did not observe more moderation. Property and privilege should not have been confused. It is out of such confusions that revolutionaries are made ; and the passion of a Paine becomes intelligible.

His *Sermons* at Westminster Abbey in 1798 contained some points which seem to be opposed to the traditional Christian doctrine of property. " Riches, perhaps, you may think, are abused ; but have not the rich a right over their own wealth, to use it or abuse it ? A man may be vicious, or a prodigal, or a fool ; but if he injures himself only, he is accountable to himself only, to his family, or to God."[2] It is difficult to see how the abuse of his property by a rich man should not produce undesirable reactions on many outside the immediate circle of his family. In fact an individual cannot injure himself by his wealth without injuring or benefitting others. To say that the rich are not " free from

1.—See " Letter of Thomas Paine to the People of France " in *State Trials*, ed. Howell, 1818, vol. xxiv. 495.
2.—W. Vincent, *Sermons*, ed. R. Nares, 1817, vol. i., pp. 281 f. These sermons were delivered on Nov. 25th and Dec. 16th, 1798.

misery," and " that anxiety is increased in proportion to
rank and eminence," [1] is a harmless platitude.   It would be
more important to observe that much " misery," both to
themselves, and to others, might be avoided if the rich were
occasionally content with a little less.   But the gospel of
resignation and contentment with a little was preached only
to the poor.   Another Churchman, William Paley, was for
less reason accused of removing from the poor " their only
consolation in distress, the hope of bettering their conditions." [2]   But in view of his criticism of the actual
distribution of property in *The Principles of Moral and
Political Philosophy,* his *Reasons for Contentment* [3] cannot be
taken as evidence of his indifference to the lot of the poor
anymore than Goldsmith's reference to the levelling effects
of the grave, and the consolations which the poor derive
from religion, can be interpreted as a want of sympathy
with their present condition. [4]   Dr. Vincent failed to make
any distinction between those who are poor through pre-
ventible causes, and those who are poor because they are
incapacitated.

" It is impossible for society to exist without a class of
poor."   History and experience confirm the word of God :
" ye have the poor always with you." [5]   God, of course,
being omniscient, foresaw that there would always be some
poor, owing to human improvidence, sickness or incapacity.
One cannot, however, reasonably invoke scriptural phrases
to justify the volume of poverty existing in any age ;   much
of which could be remedied or removed by human endeavour.
Vincent thought he had demonstrated the futility of altering
the actual distribution of wealth by pointing out that if
the land of England were " equally divided " amongst its
inhabitants, " it would amount to less than four acres a

1.—*Ibid.,* vol. i., p. 318.

2.—*A Reply to Wm. Paley from a Poor Labourer,* 1793, Brit. Mus., *Political
Tracts,* 1793-1833, p. 4.

3.—*Reasons for Contentment addressed to the labouring part of the British
Public,* 1793, Brit. Mus., *Political Tracts,* pp. 4-9.

4.—*Vicar of Wakefield,* ch. xxix., L. Stein ed., pp. 219-220.

5.—W. Vincent, *Sermons,* ed. Nares, 1817, vol. i., p. 359.   This sermon
was preached on May 13th, 1792, and was " printed by order of the Society
for preserving liberty and property against republicans and levellers."

man." [1]   He did not discuss the possibility or the desirability
of State interference with the rental receipts of the landowners in the interests of the poor.   He did not proclaim
that a living wage should be the first charge on industry in
an age when many workers had no definite property in
anything but their labour.   He had implicit faith not only
in the computations, but also in the social philosophy, of the
" political Arithmeticians." [2]   It was that philosophy which
a writer in 1795 had in mind when he observed that it had
been " a kind of religious faith to believe that the good
effects from commerce would rectify every mistake." [3]

From the foregoing analysis it will be seen that most of
the successors of Locke did little to modify the fundamental
characteristics of his teaching with regard to the nature of
property.   The essence of his doctrine had been an emphasis
on the absolute right of the property-owner as against the
State, which thrust into the background the conclusion that
might otherwise have been drawn from his statement that
the original foundation of property was labour.   This
insistence on the absolute and unconditional character of
property rights was heightened in the eighteenth century by
its agreement with several other tendencies, both in the
political thought, and in the economic development, of
the age.

On the one hand, the whole body of political theory which
had found expression in the Revolution of 1688 was of a
kind to lend confirmation to a theory which insisted on the
sanctity of property.   The struggle of the seventeenth
century, as we saw, had from one point of view been a struggle
in defence of the rights of the individual against the encroachments of the Executive.   In the process these rights became,
as it were, canonised and sanctified.   They ended by
becoming almost an end in themselves.   The Bill of Rights
passed in 1689 set limits to the power of the Crown.   The
transfer of the crown to William III. and Mary II. was

1.—*Ibid.*, vol. i., p. 367.
2.—*Ibid.*, vol. i., p. 367.
3.—*A Letter to Sir T. C. Bunbury, M.P., on the Poor Rates and the High
Price of Provisions with some proposals for reducing both*, 1795, (Brit. Mus.
Tracts on Charities, 1787-98), p. 9.

conditional on their observance of parliamentary government, and in general on their safeguarding what was considered the laws, liberties, and religion of the people.[1]   Again, the naturalistic theory of society which the eighteenth century owed partly to Locke, partly also to the scientists and to the Political Arithmeticians whose theory had been influenced by the scientists, exalted the existing order as the Natural Order ; and the Natural Order as the embodiment of the Providential Plan.   Thus Pope whose third epistle of the *Essay on Man* was, in part, but the poetic version of Locke's *Civil Government*, declared " self love and social " to be the " same."   The " natural order " was what remained when the superstructure of State organisation and interference were removed.   It consisted of property rights attaching to individuals and of contracts between individuals.

Another aspect of the same doctrine was the conception of society as a mechanism the smooth working of which depended entirely upon full scope being given to economic interests.   A good insight into the paramount importance which was coming to be attached to the material aspect of life may be obtained from reading the *Proposals for the Reformation of Schools and Universities* addressed to Parliament by a writer in 1704.[2]   The author of this document deplores the practice of encouraging " mechanicks and poorer sort of people   .   .   .   .   to send their sons to schools and universities," while there was such great need for them in the " mechanical employments." [3]   Not less significant was his plea for the adoption of more thorough methods of teaching " natural philosophy " and " mathematicks." [4]   These

1.—See F. W. Maitland, *The Constitutional History of England*, 1919, p. 388.   R. Lodge, *The Political History of England*, 1910, vol. viii., p. 306. The clause in the Act of Settlement of 1700 which made the judges practically independent of the Crown was also of great importance for the economic progress of England.   See W. S. Holdsworth, *History of English Law*, 1903, vol. i., p. 74.   In 1760 an act was passed making the judges' tenure of office unaffected by the demise of the Crown.—*Ibid.*, p. 74.

2.—Printed in *Harleian Miscellany*, vol. i., pp. 500 f.

3.—*Ibid.*, p. 501.   Cf. Mandeville, *Op. cit.*, vol. i., pp. 287-88, and John Bennet, *The National Merchant or Discussion on Commerce and Colonies*, 1736, p. 122.—" Have we not too many People depending on Divinity. Law and Physick ?   .   .   ."

4.—*Harleian Miscellany*, vol. i., p. 501.

were the characteristic sciences of the age. The study of Mathematics, as Mandeville remarked, had become quite " fashionable." Even some ladies were " very expert in Algebra and Sir Isac's Fluxions." [1] It was natural also that the social theory of the age should, in some measure, be influenced by its philosophy which, on the whole, was satisfied with the status of a science, weighing and measuring tangible phenomena and tracing their efficient causes.[2] Thus the idea of purposiveness or teleology disappears also from social theory ; and an atomistic view of society alone remains. Even evils have their place in this view of society ; " private vices " being represented as " public benefits." In a Machiavellian manner Mandeville emphasises the difficulty of individuals or societies attaining to wealth and power without disregarding moral and religious restraints.[3] Not that he wanted men to be vicious ; but to show that some-times virtue was not practised because it did not pay in this life. To expect that virtue, religion and future happiness would ever be sought after by the generality of mankind was " to betray great Ignorance in human affairs." [4] It must also be noted that for Mandeville religion necessarily recedes where knowledge advances ; [5] and moral standards are as variable as the fashions.[6]

Two things, he writes, in one part of his book, are necessary to make a society " strong and powerful " ; security of property and an open road to privileges.[7] But it is quite clear from other passages that he favoured a statute of limitations both with regard to privileges and to property. Learning, for example, should be confined to a few ; [8] the

1.—Mandeville, *A Treatise of the Hypochondriack and Hysterick Diseases in three Dialogues*, 1730,₃ pp. 175-6.
2.—See Windelband, *A History of Philosophy*, 1910, p. 401 *et passim*.
3.—Mandeville, *The Fable of the Bees*, ed. Kaye, vol. i., p. 231.
4.—*The Fable of the Bees*, ed. Kaye, vol. ii., p. 335.
5.—*Ibid.*, vol. i., p. 269.
6.—*Ibid.*, vol. i., p. 331.—There is for him no final or absolute criterion of morality ; " the hunting after this *Pulchrum & Honestum* is not much better than a Wild-Goose-Chase." See, however, vol. ii., pp. 221-2, where he admits that " all men of Midling Capacities " will agree as to the difference between right and wrong. But why, we ask, do they agree ?
7.—*Ibid.*, vol. i., p. 184.—" Let property be inviolably secured, and privileges equal to all men."
8.—*Ibid.*, vol. i., p. 287-8.

happiness of society depends on great numbers being kept " ignorant as well as poor." " If here and there one of the lowest class by uncommon industry "[1] lifts himself above the status in which he was born, he ought not to be interfered with. No organised or institutional attempt at levelling up should, however, be made.[2] His views were thus in accord with, if they did not influence, that conception of society as a joint-stock company in which control rightly belongs to those who hold the most numerous shares, that is, have the most property. Society is not regarded as an organism, but as an economic concern ; established for the convenience of the shareholders, namely property owners. "A Government, in every country," said Lord Braxfield to the reformers in 1794, " should be just like a corporation."[3]

On the other hand, the practical facts of social organisation and economic development strengthened the same attitude towards property. The grosser abuses of feudal property, for example, were unknown in England. " The only resemblance we have in England of the *corvées* of France, and the monstrous personal service which is so destructive to the agriculture of Germany and Poland," wrote Arthur Young,[4] is the " six days work " devoted to repairing the roads, which is " performed at a leisure time of the year." In France the peasant paid innumerable dues—*quints, banalités, lods et ventes*, etc.—to an absentee *seigneur*. In England, landlords might be tyrannical, but the commercialising of land-tenure had swept away most of the more extravagant incidents of feudal land-tenure. To French observers, like Voltaire,[5] the English peasant seemed a free man. In England, at least in the first half of the eighteenth century, there were still numerous small freeholders or " yeomen " To emphasize the sanctity of property, therefore, was to protect a rural middle-class, and not merely the great land-owner.

1.—*Ibid.*, vol. i., pp. 193-4.
2.—*Ibid.*, vol. i., p. 289.
3.—*State Trials*, ed. Howell, 1817, xxiii. 231.
4.—*Political Arithmetic*, 1774, p. 10. In another part of the book, p. 202, he refers to the " absolute slavery of the peasants in some parts of Germany, in Denmark, in Poland, and in Russia."
5.—Voltaire, *Lettres Philosophiques*, ed. Lanson, 1909, vol. i., Lettre x.

Moreover, the rapid economic expansion of the eighteenth century both encouraged a materialistic view of society, and led naturally to a worship of property as the reward of industry. People felt that it was the security of property in England [1] which caused economic development to take place there more rapidly than in France. New and more mobile forms of property were rapidly extending. The economic progress of the century preceding the advent of steam-power is sometimes underestimated in popular histories. The abolition of customs' barriers between Scotland and England, following the union of the two countries, promoted the growth of internal trade. The improvement effected in bills of exchange and promissory notes by legislation, in the early part of the century, was also of the greatest importance for the development of commerce.

Great security was given to the bill of exchange when the person to whom it was assigned was given the right, if necessary, " to maintain an action against the person who first made or assigned it." [2] If the roads in the early part of the century were in a bad condition, that was due to the great traffic consequent on a growing volume of business rather than to the economic passivity of the age. Great coast towns like Liverpool became wealthy by their entrepôt trade, and much of that money flowed back to irrigate the country. Much capital was devoted to the improvement of canals and to the development of mining and textile industries. Many new industries, unknown to previous centuries, were springing up. [3] The establishment of the Bank of England towards the end of the seventeenth century provided greater credit facilities, and this, in part, was responsible for that speculative spirit which found its most dramatic though least reputable expression in the South Sea Bubble collapse in 1720. The broad lines on which the industrial organisation of the second half of the nineteenth century were mainly to develop were thus laid early in the

1.—Cf. A. Smith, *Wealth of Nations*, ed. Cannan, vol. ii., bk. iv., ch. v., pp. 42-3.
2.—R. B. Westerfield, *Middlemen in English Business*, 1915, p. 391.
3.—See Ch. Davenant, *Political and Commercial Works*, ed. Sir C. Whitworth, 1771, vol. i., pp. 375-377.

previous century. But the scandals associated with joint-
stock enterprise, and particularly the legislation of 1719,
prohibiting the formation of companies with transferable
shares unless authorised by Parliament or the Crown, gave
a set back to impersonal capitalism until the changes in
company law of 1844, 1855 and 1862. Thus capital, on the
whole, remained personal and economic enterprise individualistic throughout the eighteenth century. That fact,
coupled with the considerations noted above, helps to explain
why a highly individualistic conception of property bulked
so large in the social theory of the age.

(2.) THE PRACTICAL APPLICATIONS OF

LOCKE'S THEORY.

The influence of the dominant conception of property can
be illustrated by several different examples drawn from the
political practice and social policy of the eighteenth century.
The most general, and in some ways the most significant
example, is supplied by the obvious predominance of property
as the basis of political organisation. Had Cromwell's
government departed a little more from tradition—for in all
ages men of slender means have never had much of a voice
in the councils of the nation—and extended the franchise,
the centre of political gravity might not have reposed in a
class who were less interested in contracting " regal power "
than in stretching their own. From the Revolution, political
power was regarded more and more as a piece of property.
The passing of a special statute in 1710, disqualifying for
Parliamentary membership all those who were not in receipt
of landed incomes, obviously aimed at raising the existing
property barrier.[1] The landed gentry became omnipotent
in central and local government. Indeed their interest in

1.—For details see Edward Porritt, *The Unreformed House of Commons*,
1903, vol. i., ch. ix., p. 152. This law was frequently evaded. At the end
of the century, however, hundreds of towns, some very rich, were
unrepresented in Parliament.

local government was merely a mask to protect their Parliamentary preserves.   Local government was, in reality, atrophied or totally inadequate to the needs of the age. Many of the landed gentry were of course interested in commerce, but that only aggravated the monopoly of political power which they enjoyed.   If the French nobles had privileges without power,[1] the English gentry had power, not without privileges.   They enjoyed the privilege of restricting the rights of many to complete citizenship.

The right to vote, it is true, was still in the hands of the 40/- freeholders and burgesses, or holders of municipal franchises based on property.   But the practical reality went far beyond legal theory.   Very often freeholders, through fear, were unwilling to exercise their political rights, and sold their votes to wealthy landlords.[2]   The position in the towns or " boroughs " was much worse than in the rural districts.   Many wealthy towns were unrepresented in Parliament ; and in those which enjoyed the right to elect two members, the voters were often insignificant in number and sometimes non-existent.   Custom rather than law determined the method of election ; and custom sanctioned methods which were frequently corrupt.   The owner of a borough or site claimed the right to return a member to Parliament just as he would claim his right to a piece of private property. There was a regular market for " rotten boroughs."   The " interests of elections," wrote Defoe in 1719, " were jobb'd upon exchange for money, and transferr'd like East-India stock, for those who bid most." [3]   The nearest analogy to this eighteenth century practice was the mediaeval English custom of buying and selling the right to present to ecclesiastical benefices—*advocatio ecclesiae*.   This right, which at one time was frequently exercised by the lord of the manor, proved to be so profitable that the royal courts made good their claim to exclusive control of it by the twelfth

1.—See Alexis de Tocqueville, *L'Ancien Régime*, trans. G. W. Headlam, 1904, p. 148.
2.—Rev. Sydney Smith, *Works*, 1850, one vol., p. 652, tells us that " instances, in every election, are numerous where tenants have been dismissed for voting contrary to the wishes of their landlords."
3.— *The Anatomy of Exchange Alley*, 1719, p. 48.

century.[1] In the eighteenth century so firmly was the conception established that the right to return a member to Parliament was a piece of private property, that we find Pitt in 1785 actually agreeing to raise a fund to buy out the owners of "rotten boroughs."[2] A majority of the House of Commons, however, refused to have Pitt's Reform Bill even introduced.[3]

Similarly local government was largely based on the ownership of property. The borough or manor was regarded as a community not of residents but of property owners. Harrington's dictum that property is political power was regarded as expressing a precept in the imperative mood. For Burke the right of the landed gentry to exclusive political power was axiomatic.[4] He invoked Harrington's authority to fortify his prejudices, and conveniently omitted any reference to the main idea which gave rise to the *Oceana*.[5] The landed gentry were the repository of the accumulated wisdom of the ages ; the centre of every movement for national greatness. The reasonableness of their right to rule lay in their uniqueness ; they were *sui generis ;* having, "at all times, been in close connexion and union with the other great interests of the country."[6]

Not only was political organisation based on property, but the policy of the age showed a special tenderness for the interests of property-owners. A conspicuous example is afforded by policy as to taxation. In the sixteenth and early seventeenth centuries there is some trace of an attempt to let the poor off lightly.[7] In the eighteenth century it is

1.—See W. F. Maitland, *The Constitutional History of England,* 1919, p. 510.

2.—For details see George Stead Veitch, *The Genesis of Parliamentary Reform,* 1913, p. 102.

3.—*Parliamentary History,* vol. xxv., p. 475.

4.—"Regicide Peace," Letter iii. in *Select Works,* ed. Payne, 1904, vol. i., pp. 243-244.

5.—*Select Works,* ed. Payne, 1904, vol. i., p. 132.

6.—*Select Works,* Payne, 1904, vol. i., pp. 243-244.

7.—See W. Kennedy, *English Taxation, 1641-1799,* 1913, ch. ii., p. 22 *et passim.* Mr. Kennedy thinks that for the century preceding 1640 the tradition was to exempt the poor from taxation. Unfortunately he gives no evidence to show how far exactly they were, in practice, accorded special consideration. An attempt was made to increase the revenue of the Crown by taxing commodities of general consumption both under Elizabeth and the first two Stuarts. See Meredith, *Economic History of England,* p. 217.

usually property for which most consideration is shown.

In the second half of the seventeenth century the theory that all should contribute towards the upkeep of the State in payment for the protection which it afforded was held by many influential writers, including Locke.[1] But while Locke admitted that the duty of paying taxes was binding on all citizens, the emphasis which he laid on the idea that the consent of the people or their Parliamentary representatives was necessary to legitimise taxation tended to undermine the compulsory character of such contributions. Josiah Tucker [2] and Lord Kames pointed out the danger of stressing that aspect of taxation. Those who had no voice in electing Parliamentary representatives,[3] a large number in the eighteenth century, might be disposed to invoke Locke's authority for exemption from taxation. The implications of the theory of taxation by consent, which caused anxiety to Dean Tucker, were a source of a joy to his contemporary Dr. Price,[4] as they were to William Molyneux [5] in the seventeenth century. The latter thought that if the doctrine, popularised by Locke,[6] were true, the sphere of its operation might be extended to Ireland. Dr. Price, when pleading the cause of the revolting American colonists, observed that they were merely insisting on some of the privileges which Englishmen claimed for themselves. " You are taxed by yourselves. They insist on the same privilege." [7] The principle of taxation by consent, however, received but a nominal recognition in the eighteenth century, the golden age of indirect taxation.

The financial exigencies of the second half of the seventeenth century compelled Parliament to broaden the basis of taxation. The imposition of excise duties from the

1.—Locke, *Civil Government*, Morley, 1884, bk. ii., ch. xi., § 140, p. 266. Sir Wm. Petty, *Works*, ed. Hull, vol. i., p. 114.

2.—Josiah Tucker, Dean of Gloucester, *A Treatise concerning Civil Government in three parts*, 1781, p. 13 ; p. 49.

3.—Lord Kames, *Sketches of the History of Man*, 1819 ed., vol. ii., p. 108.

4.—Richard Price, *Observations on the Nature of Civil Liberty*, 1776.

5.—*Case of Ireland being bound by Acts of Parliament in England*, 1698.

6.—The idea that a tax ought to be a voluntary gift was of very long standing in England. See Maitland, *The Constitutional History of England*, 1919, p. 95.

7.—Price, *Op. cit.*, p. 99.

Civil War onwards, however much it might be opposed in practice, appeared defensible on theoretical grounds. These duties were mostly imposed on necessaries. Writers, like Locke, argued that such taxes, even if paid by the poor, were not borne by the poor. Having but a mere subsistence wage, the latter could not really bear the tax. It was shifted on to the shoulders of the manufacturers in the form of higher wages, as Mun thought ; [1] or it was borne, like all other taxes, by the landed proprietors as Locke fancied.[2] The reliance placed on indirect taxation in the eighteenth century contrasts strangely with modern views as to the proper distribution of the burden of taxation ; and with the modern practice of utilising direct taxation to ameliorate the condition of the poorer classes. The great advantage of indirect taxation—that by it the individual may be said to tax himself—was supposed to cover all its practical inconveniences. Luxuries were an ideal target for such taxation ; but the difficulty of defining a luxury was not resolved with any great liberality when it was a question of taxing the articles used by the poor. Mandeville's negative definition of a luxury, as anything that is not " immediately necessary to make Man subsist as a living Creature," [3] was regarded less as a cynical comment on an age that devoted all its energies to the production of wealth and yet affected to condemn the extravagances of which that wealth was the occasion, than as a cold justification for a harsh policy towards the poor. The payment of taxes by the poor, even if it involved great hardship to them, was considered something good for society. It would discourage laziness and promote industry. So Houghton thought in the seventeenth,[4] and Sir James Steuart in the eighteenth century.

The latter thought that in " bad years " the labourers or " manufacturing classes," as he calls them, live better and

---

1.—Thomas Mun, *England's Treasure by Foreign Trade*, 1644, Economic Classics, ed. Ashley, p. 85.

2.—Locke, " Consideration of the lowering of interest and Raising the value of Money," 1691, in *Works*, 1714, vol. iii., pp. 27-28. Cf. A. Smith *Wealth of Nations*, ed. Cannan, vol. ii., pp. 354-5.

3.—*Fable of the Bees*, ed. Kaye, vol. i., p. 107.

4.—John Houghton, *Loc. cit.*

are more assiduous in their work.[1]   And he asks, " Why should a tax laid on by the hands of nature prove such a spur to industry ; and another, similar to it in its effects, laid on by the hand of man, produce such hurtful consequences." [2]   Some writers, like Lord Kames, took a more humane view.   While holding that all should pay something for the protection which the State afforded, he considered a tax on " man's food, or the subject that affords him bare necessaries " as worse than denying him protection. It starves him.[3]   Indeed, the taxation of the poor was frequently opposed on commercial or sentimental grounds throughout the eighteenth century.[4]   But the growth of expenditure caused by war ; the distrust of direct taxation owing to the difficulty of collecting such taxes ;—a difficulty which the weakening of the bonds between the central and local authorities after the Civil War had intensified—the natural inclination of statesmen to follow the line of least resistance with regard to taxation ; and, above all, the special regard in which property owners were held led the governing class to sacrifice equity to productivity in the fiscal system of the country.

Thus one finds the revenue from property taxes in the eighteenth century, as compared with the previous century, falling ;   while the revenue from taxing commodities of general consumption steadily rose.[5]   Not only were the excise duties imposed at the Restoration, in lieu of the feudal dues lost to the Crown by the abolition of the Court of Wards and Liveries, mainly borne by " the lower tenantry and labouring poor," [6] but the health and efficiency of the latter were consistently taxed by duties on salt and soap in the eighteenth century.   Sydney Smith's description of the

1.—*An Inquiry into the principles of Political Economy*, 1767, vol. ii., bk. v., ch. v., p. 504.

2.—*Ibid.*

3.—Lord Kames, *Sketches*, vol. ii., p. 106.

4.—See Cobbett, *Parliamentary History*, vol. viii., pp. 947, 1020, 1051, and A. Boyer, *Animadversions and Observations* (Brit. Mus., Political and Financial Tracts, 1695-1761), p. 46.

5.—See S. Dowell, *History of Taxation and Taxes in England*, vol. ii., p. 34, p. 127.

6.—Thomas Percival, *An Inquiry into the Principles of Taxation*, 1785, p. 11.

condition of things in the early nineteenth century not only exhibits the consequences of a nation " being too fond of glory," but portrays the effects of a country being too attached to its property. In a famous passage he warns America against following England's example which resulted in " Taxes upon every article which enters into the mouth or covers the back or is placed under the foot. . . . Taxes upon everything which is pleasant to see, hear, feel, smell, or taste. Taxes upon warmth, light, and locomotion, taxes on the poor man's salt, . . . on the brass nails of the coffin." [1]

One can form some idea of the extent to which the dominant theory of property influenced thought and policy with regard to taxation from the criticism to which Pitt's income-tax of 1799 gave rise. That income-tax, as is well known, was due to the extraordinary financial situation created by the war with France rather than to any new ideas as to the proper distribution of the burden of taxation. Yet it appeared a revolutionary proceeding to a Commissioner of Taxes. The taxation of income, irrespective of whether it was spent or not, Francis Newbery [2] considered opposed to the " very essence of taxation in a free country," namely " optionality." An impost, which is " inevitable and compulsory," threatens " the dominion of property," and endangers individual freedom.[3] Needless to say Pitt's experimental income-tax was not graduated according to modern notions of " ability to pay "; much less did it embody the socio-political idea of taxation which did not clearly emerge until the nineteenth century. The idea of using taxation to effect a more equitable distribution of wealth, though partially accepted by Smith,[4] was either not generally considered, or was denounced as leading to " an arbitrary levelling of situations." [5]

1.—Rev. Sydney Smith, *Works* (complete in one vol., 1850), pp. 282-3.
2.—*Thoughts on Taxation* (Income Tax Tracts), 1799, pp. 9 f.
3.—*Ibid.*
4.—*Wealth of Nations*, ed. Cannan, vol. ii., pp. 328-9.—Smith advocated the taxation of " ground rents."
5.—George Rose, *A Brief Examination into the Increase of the Revenue, Commerce and Manufactures of Great Britain from 1782-99* (1799), p. 33.

An even better illustration is given by the treatment of the land question. The instrument principally used—Private Bill legislation—was itself an illustration of the extreme individualism of the age which found expression in the theory of property. The essence of Private Bill legislation was that Parliament avoided laying down a *general* policy, but legislated *ad hoc* in response to a request.[1] The initiative was left to the individual, place, or trade concerned. Whatever *motif* inspired Private Bill legislation,[2] the results were not always very happy.

Of this procedure by Private Bill legislation, enclosure policy was one of the leading instances. The whole treatment of the land question shows the way in which the governing classes regarded the liberation of property, from restrictions which impeded its full use and development, as an unquestioned axiom of public policy. This is shown by the principles on which the policy rested. The social doctrine underlying the organisation of the open-field village implied the supremacy of the community over individual self-interest ; that property was a means of service ; and that property owners were trustees. The principles underlying the enclosure acts form a striking contrast to this doctrine. These acts aimed at sweeping away communal restrictions. The commons were to be divided up ; and each man allowed to cultivate as he please. Property owners were actually compelled to use their property for their individual gain, even if they preferred the older system of communal organisation ; the supreme example of " forcing " men to be free.

The enclosure movement of the eighteenth century has been dealt with by more than one well-known writer,[3] but

1.—See Josef Redlich and Francis W. Hirst, *Local Government in England*, 1903, vol. i., pp. 40 f.

2.—Redlich and Hirst, *Op. cit.*, p. 132,—" The procedure of private Bill legislation had been designed and developed in order that local government might be built up bit by bit to suit the particular locality." The same writers think that private Bill legislation proved " a most effective instrument of local administration."—p. 40.

3.—See J. L. and Barbara Hammond, *The Village Labourer*, 1920 ; W. Hasbach, *A History of the English Agricultural Labourer*, tr. R. Kenyon, 1908 ; Gilbert Slater, *The English Peasantry and the Enclosure of Common Fields*, 1906 ; Rev. A. H. Johnson, *The Disappearance of the Small Landowner*, 1910. See the article by E. Davies in *Economic History Review*, vol. i., no. 1, p. 86.

its bearing on the development of a highly individualistic conception of property has not been sufficiently emphasised Notwithstanding the earlier enclosure movements, "common rights" survived as an integral part of the system of land tenure of the greater part of England in the eighteenth century. The owner of land in that part of England which had never come under manorial conditions was not handicapped by customs and "rights" which were the growth of centuries. He was free to consolidate his holdings and to adopt the most scientific methods of agriculture. Not so the man who held land under the surviving manorial system. It was inevitable that improvements in the method of cultivation of the open field village should lead to a modification of the system of tenure or ownership; but it was not inevitable that the position of the poor or small landowners should be worse after the change. The characteristic feature of the manor had been the presence, and often the predominance, of copyhold tenure. The eighteenth century landlord was only too willing to utilise the necessity for agricultural progress to convert the copyholder into a leaseholder, and thus both increase his rents and extend his control over the land.[1]

Unless one possesses some of that imagination which is but another name for "reason in its most exalted mood," one may be misled by the views of writers like Dean Tucker[2] and Arthur Young[3] on the open field English village. It had its weak points; the "right of common" sometimes begot lazy habits in the poor in the case of commons bordering on populous towns. These commons or waste lands often formed the rendez-vous of vagrants unwilling to "submit to the confinement of stated labour."[4] The enclosure of "commons," in the sense of arable fields and meadow land in the neighbourhood of towns, was indeed a public service.[5]

1.—See Edward Lawrence, *The Duty of a Steward to his Lord* . . . 1727, (Goldsmiths' Library), Art. xxii., p. 60.
2.—Josiah Tucker, *The Elements of Commerce and Theory of Taxes*, 1755, pp. 48-9.
3.—*Political Arithmetic*, 1774, p. 123.
4.—See *Gentleman's Magazine*, vol. xxx., pp. 172-3 ; Tucker, *Op. cit.*, p. 54.
5.—The term "common" as applied to the eighteenth century open village refers to three different kinds of land—the arable fields, the common meadowland, and the common or waste. See Hammond, *Op. cit.*, p. 4.

Outside the latter case, the enclosure of arable lands, though a private advantage, was not always a public benefit. In the inland counties particularly—according to a contemporary [1]—where the people were much attached to traditional methods, and where "husbandry" was "the chief employment of the poor," few families believed that they stood to gain after "inclosing their lordships." For in the unenclosed village the poverty of the poor man was no "dismal thing." He was not a mere wage-earner; his income was supplemented from other sources; he had his little cottage beside the common on which "his cow or two, a few sheep, a hog grazed," and from which he gathered firewood; and very often his wife and children found employment in the village industries.[2]

The economic case for large scale farming [3] was not so universally obvious that such great numbers of small landowners should have been forced to leave their holdings, even if they did find it more profitable to seek employment in the rising city industries. Though opinions necessarily differ, owing to the lack of statistical evidence,[4] as to the precise effects of the enclosure movement in the eighteenth century, the almost complete disappearance of the old yeomanry or small landowning class which one finds in the early nineteenth century was little short of a social revolution. It is easy, however, to exaggerate the extent to which enclosures were responsible for the disappearance of the small owner and cultivator in England just as it is easy to exaggerate the rate at which he disappeared. The statement that the race of "hardy, brave" and moral men, known as the yeomanry, was "by the influx of riches and a change of manners nearly annihilated in the year 1750," and but "faintly remembered" in

1.—*Gentleman's Magazine*, vol. xxx., p. 174.
2.—See the anonymous work *An Enquiry into the Cause of the Encrease and Miseries of the poor of England*, 1738, p. 39.
3.—See the *Gentleman's Magazine*, 1766, vol. xxxvi., pp. 475 f.
4.—See an interesting article in the *Gentleman's Magazine*, 1780, vol. 50., p. 79. The writer's suggestion that the collection of such evidence should be undertaken by the clergy was not generally adopted; obviously they did not consider such work "an agreeable amusement."

1795,[1] is probably too sweeping. After 1730, as Hasbach has shown, arable land was frequently converted into pasture to form parks for the gentry.[2] The expansion of industry towards the end of the century, and the war with France, also made enclosure a necessity for the production of food supplies.

It is the methods by which enclosures in the eighteenth century were carried out rather than the policy itself which betray "a change of manners" that was not oversensitive to the claims of justice. Enclosure acts originally were simply a statutory sanction of a private agreement reached between landowners. But in the eighteenth century Parliament intervenes to dissolve a partnership which the larger partner desires to break, and in order to do this it is not always very careful of the property rights of the smaller partner. Of course numerous enclosures in the eighteenth century were the outcome of voluntary agreements reached between landlord and copyholders and small owners ; but the application of Private Bill legislation to enclosure made it comparatively easy for the landlord to compel his tenants to accept a redistribution of property by which the interests and "rights" of the latter were sometimes unnecessarily sacrificed. Wherever a majority desired to have their scattered strips form compact holdings and their individual shares of the commons parcelled out, they could petition Parliament, and a private bill was passed compelling the minority to enclose also.[3] Frequently it was the value of the land rather than the number of owners which determined the mind of Parliament with regard to enclosure. Provided the petitioners owned four-fifths of the value of the land, even though they formed but a minority of the total number of owners and holders of various rights and interests, they could get an enclosure Act passed by Parliament. This can be readily understood when one remembers the predominantly landlord composition of Parliament.

1.—*A letter to T. C. Bunbury, M.P., on the Poor Rates and the high price of Provisions with some proposals for reducing both*, 1795, by a Suffolk Gentleman, Brit. Mus., Tracts on Charities, 1787-98, p. 4.

2.—*Op. cit.*, Appendix ii., p. 369.

3.—See Tucker, *Op. cit.*, p. 54.

Needless to say the landlord stood to gain heavily from enclosures. His farm was consolidated, and he helped himself generously to a share of the common lands also. The big tenants gained also ; but the smaller tenants lost much by the change. They were not always able to prove their titles when they appeared before the law courts. Indeed the proceedings in the law courts were so expensive that the poor were practically prevented from vindicating their claim to a fair division of the common fields.[1] The small tenant's right to use the commons—to graze his cow or sheep and to gather firewood—often meant far more to him than the actual property which he obtained in exchange by enclosure.[2] It is not at all certain that they received that " full and ample compensation " to which Tucker, the ardent champion of " discommoning " the commons, considered them entitled.[3] Although the picture of the poor was occasionally overdrawn by contemporary, as it sometimes is by modern writers, there is no doubt that the policy of enclosure by Act of Parliament caused considerable hardship to the small owner, notwithstanding the increased production of food which the new agricultural methods made possible, and the alternative modes of earning a livelihood which the spreading factory system offered. " The poor," wrote Arthur Young[4] towards the end of the century, " look to facts, not meanings : and the fact is that by nineteen enclosure bills in twenty they are injured, in some grossly injured . . . What is it to the poor man to be told that the Houses of Parliament are extremely tender of property, while the father of the family is forced to sell his cow and his land because the one is not competent to the other ; and being deprived of the only motive to industry, squanders the money, contracts bad habits, enlists for a soldier and leaves the wife and children to the parish."

It is probable that the enclosure movement was a contributory cause of the rise in the poor rate in the eighteenth

1.—See the anonymous work *An Enquiry into the Cause of the Encrease and Miseries of the Poor of England*, 1738, pp. 38-40.

2.—David Davies, *The Case of Labourers in Husbandry*, 1795, p. 37.

3.—*Op. cit.*, p. 47 ; p. 52.

4.—*An Enquiry into the propriety of applying Wastes to the better maintenance of the Poor*, 1801, p. 42.

century. And the theory of property which formed the driving force of enclosures, as well as other movements for economic freedom, made the relief of the poor appear less a question of justice than of charity. Arthur Young's solicitude for the poor, like that of many others, was based on considerations of expediency or "political humanity"[1] rather than on any specifically moral theory of ownership.[2] Though, in Cartesian fashion, he viewed the past as a museum of errors rather than as a storehouse of wisdom from which to draw guidance for the present, one must be grateful for his recognition of the intimate connection sometimes existing between the absence of property and the presence of crime and dishonesty.[3]

(3.) SIGNS OF CHANGE : THE REACTION AGAINST THE INDIVIDUALISTIC THEORY OF PROPERTY.

Partly owing to the evils connected with the enclosure movement, and partly owing to the influence of French writers like Rousseau and Brissot de Warville, the theory of property associated with Locke was subjected to a keener criticism in the latter half of the century. Robert Wallace's *Various Prospects of Mankind, Nature and Providence*, 1758, contains views on property and education which are surprisingly modern. He blamed the individualistic social creed which permitted people to " gratify all their whims and fancies . . . provided only they do not invade property, nor give any disturbance to others, in indulging in the same boasted but dangerous liberty,"[4] for the neglect of education and for the depreciatory attitude adopted towards certain forms of labour. In his ideal society all kinds of useful labour would be considered equally honourable ; or, at least, none of them would be regarded with contempt. Every

1.—Jonas Hanway, *Letters on the importance of the rising generation of the labouring part of our fellow subjects*, 1767, vol. ii., p. 207.
2.—As, for example, William Belsham seemed to hold, *Remarks on the Bill for the better support and maintenance of the Poor*, 1797, p. 20.
3.—Young, *An Enquiry . . .* p. 49.
4.—*Various Prospects*, 1758, p. 94.

individual would be afforded both time and opportunity to cultivate his mind.[1] Wallace, however, knew that his ideas were born out of due season ; he had no illusions as to the practical difficulties in the way of establishing his " perfect constitution."[2]

With the details of his system we are not concerned here. It is his merit, however, to have emphasised the public character of education, and thus by implication the social character of property. If every citizen has a right to at least an elementary education, and if parents are economically unfitted to discharge one of their natural duties to their children, the State should step in and provide some of the necessary training for citizenship by establishing schools from taxes levied on property owners. It is difficult to explain the attitude of eighteenth century statesmen towards education unless one bears in mind their reverence for private property. Private enterprise, it was thought, should prevail in education as in other departments of life. If English State policy in the eighteenth century with regard to education compares unfavourably with that on the continent,[3] it is because English statesmen were reluctant to make the well-to-do hand over some of their wealth for the public good. The keynote to the social policy of the age may be found in Pitt's speech to the House of Commons in 1796.[4] State interference with private property and private enterprise should be the exception ; one " should look to the instances where interference had shackled industry."[5] And of course the poor might not prove so useful or so industrious if they were educated.

Wallace's contemporary, Dr. Joseph Priestly, despite his strong leaning towards individualism,[6] and his opposition to a national system of education as we understand it to-day, denied the right of the individual to use his wealth or property

1.—*Ibid.*, pp. 51-52.
2 —*Ibid.*, p. 58.
3.—See W. E. H. Lecky, *History of England in the Eighteenth Century,* 1887, vol. vi., p. 277.
4.—*Parliamentary History,* vol. xxxii., p. 705.
5.—*Ibid.*
6.—*Essay on the first principles of Government,* 1768.

in an anti-social manner. Like many eighteenth century writers he was alarmed at the amount of money which the poor spent on drink. He suggested that manufacturing towns should be empowered to make bye-laws compelling the poor to save.[1] Although he seems to limit his remarks on the anti-social use of wealth to the poor, one must be grateful for this statement of principle ; " every society has a right to apply whatever property is found, or acquired, within itself, to any purposes which the good of society at large really requires." [2] Needless to say Priestly was too much affected by the temper of his age to expend some of his great intellectual energy in developing more fully the implications of that proposition.   He appears, however, to have been less inconsistent, or more careful, than Dr. Paley who was inclined to view the " law of the land," rather than the needs of society, as the foundation of property rights.

In his treatise on *The Principles of Moral and Political Philosophy*,[3] which passed through fifteen impressions between 1785 and 1804, he considered Locke's account of the origin of the right of property in land unsatisfactory as an explanation of " our present claims of property in land." [4] The real foundation of our right to landed property is " the law of the land." [5] Paley was a confused thinker.   The State's function of regulating the exercise of the right of private property in land is made to appear the sole basis and justification of existing property claims.   That portion of land which the law allows one to possess ;   the division sanctioned by the State is consistent with the " will of God " or " right." [6]   But this statement is no sooner made than it is qualified.   We are told that a man has not always a " right to keep and take everything which the law will allow him to keep and take " ;   for example, he may be morally bound to pay his debts although he is legally absolved from doing so.[7]

1.—*An Account of a Society for encouraging the Industrious Poor*, **1787**, pp. 4-5 ; p. 13.
2.—*Ibid.*, pp. 13-14.
3.—Edition quoted 1804.
4.—W. Paley, *Op. cit.*, vol. i., ch. iv., pp. 130-133.
5.—*Ibid.*, vol. i., p. 134.
6.—*Ibid.*, vol. i., p. 134.
7.—*Ibid.*, vol. i., p. 136.

Paley held that the doctrine of natural rights applied to property only in so far as that property represented the product of personal labour.[1] Land, however, belonged to a different category. An individual might, in the beginning, appropriate as much of it as was requisite for his own use, or was necessary to make " competent provision " for his " natural exigencies " without obtaining the consent of others ;[2] but beyond that, the State's sanction was required to legitimise unequal shares of land. The division of landed property established by law appeared to him something sacred ; a reflection of the Divine will. Thus Paley, like Locke, tended to regard the established order as the natural order sanctioned by Heaven. And yet he was fully aware that some existing property rights were historically modified. The right or " privilege " to make a will with regard to land, he reminds us, was lost at the Conquest and was not restored to the individual until the end of Henry VIII.'s reign.[3] The right to dispose by will of property due to personal labour he regarded as natural and absolute ; " but every other species of property, especially property in land, stands upon a different foundation."[4]

Paley condemned in unmeasured language the mal-distribution of wealth in his time. The words which he employed to describe some of the " paradoxical and unnatural " results of the system of private property of his day[5] would appear quite indiscreet in a twentieth century churchman. "Among men you see the ninety and nine toiling and scraping together a heap of superfluities for one ; (and this one too, oftentimes the feeblest and worst of the whole set, a child, a woman, a madman, or a fool) ; getting nothing for themselves all the while, but a little of the coarsest of the provision which their own industry produces ; looking quietly on, while they see the fruits of all their labour spent or spoiled ; and if one of the number take or touch a particle of the hoard, the others joining against him, and

1.—*Ibid.*, vol. i., p. 98.
2.—*Ibid.*, vol. i., pp. 132-133.
3.—*Ibid.*, vol. i., p. 250.
4.—*Ibid.*, vol. i., pp. 248-249.
5.—*Ibid.*, vol. i., p. 122.

hanging him for the theft." [1] Paley doubted whether the quantity or quality of human life in England had benefited by " foreign commerce." [2] He ignores the important fact that, by the end of the century, commerce in England was organised for popular consumption. Despite the inconsistencies which we have noted, he struck a truly Christain note when he declared that the " partition of property " must not be " rigidly maintained against the claims of indigence and distress." [3] To do so was to sin against the " Supreme Proprietor," and to defeat the purpose for which property exists.

Other writers, like Spence,[4] Ogilvie, Paine, and Godwin,[5] exhibited the latent radicalism of Locke's labour theory of property ; and advocated the appropriation by the State of all property incomes which were not clearly the reward of labour. Ogilvie criticised Locke and his followers for countenancing the theory of the divine right of landlords ; a theory which was similar in its baneful effects to the theory of the divine right of kings, which Locke had combated.[6] He emphasised the fact that land was on a different plane from other forms of property ; and he maintained that no matter how much labour was expended on land by some, it could never supersede the " natural rights " of others to their share of land also.[7] A person who improves the produce or increases the value of land by his labour has a right to the resulting produce or value. He fully recognised the practical difficulty of distinguishing between the original and

1.—*Ibid.*, vol. i., p. 120.
2.—*Ibid.*, vol. ii., p. 409 . . . . " I believe," he writes, " it may be affirmed of Great Britain, what Bishop Berkeley said of a neighbouring island, that, if it were encompassed with a wall of brass fifty cubits high, the country might maintain the same number of inhabitants that find subsistence in it at present ; and that every necessary, and even every real comfort and accommodation of human life might be supplied in as great abundance as they now are."
3.—*Ibid.*, vol. i., p. 276.
4.—T. Spence (1750-1814), *The Real Rights of Man*, 1775 ; W. Ogilvie (1736-1813), *An Essay on the Right of Property in Land* ; T. Paine (1737-1819), *Agrarian Justice*, 1795-6. References to these works are taken from the reprint by Max Beer, *The Pioneers of Land Reform*, Bohn's Lbrary, 1920.
5.—Wm. Godwin, *Political Justice*, ed. 1796.
6.—Beer, *Op. cit.*, pp. 39-40.
7.—Beer, *Op. cit.*, p. 40.

" accessory value " of land.[1]   He appealed to England's common sense and to the enlightened policy which she, as contrasted with other countries, had always pursued towards the cultivators of the soil.[2]   Much had been done.   Why not do more ?   Why not curb that property power which takes toll from poor manufacturing labourers, who are constantly forced to seek new homes according as new branches of manufacture spring up throughout the country ?   Why should " landholders' rents have been doubled within fifty years "? [3] They have less right to their swollen rent rolls than the clergy have to their tithes ; for the latter perform some useful service.[4]

Spence held that the rents derived from land would be sufficient to defray the cost of central and local government. Existing landlords were to be expropriated ; the inhabitants of each parish should, on an appointed day, " form themselves into corporations," and let the land to farmers at a moderate rent.[5]   This rent, he said, would form the only tax in the future.   Both his single-tax theory, as well as his view that the right to land was of the same nature as the right to life,[6] were put forward with little show of argument.

Paine held that private property in land arose with the cultivation of land.   Men found it impossible to separate the improvement made by cultivating the earth from the earth itself on which the improvement was made, and thus they erroneously concluded that they had an equal right to both.[7] But custom, he thinks, cannot abrogate natural right ; and by natural right a man may only " occupy " land, and not " locate " it " as his property in perpetuity." [8]   " The Creator of the earth " did not " open a land-office from whence the first title-deeds " were issued.[9]   Riches to-day

1.—*Ibid.*, p. 45.
2.—*Ibid.*, p. 56.
3.—*Ibid.*, p. 64.
4.—*Ibid.*, p. 68.   Cf.   John Gray, *A plan for finally settling the Government of Ireland upon Constitutional Principles*, 1785.
5.—Beer, *Op. cit.*, p. 10.
6.—*Ibid.*, p. 7.
7.—"Agrarian Justice " in Beer, *Op. cit.*, p. 185.
8.—*Ibid.*, p. 184.
9.—*Ibid.*, p. 184.

are largely an "effect of society."[1]   Since most of the
property which men possess is due to living in society rather
than to personal labour, it is but just that "a part of that
accumulation"[2] shoud revert to society, by means of a
steeply graded income tax, to benefit the propertyless or
poorer members.[3]

It is an easy matter to criticise Paine's exaggerated
antithesis between property due to personal labour and
property which is an effect of society. For as personal
labour can only be effectively performed in society, the
property which it produces may also be viewed as an effect
of social organisation.   The economic value, if not the moral
worth, of an individual's labour, depends upon a variety of
causes over which he has little control ; it depends upon that
organised existence known as society.   If 'influences from
the remotest star converge to make us what we are,' a greater
number still contribute to what we have.   Although it is a
matter of some difficulty to know how much precisely of
one's property is due to personal effort, and how much is
due to broader causes, the distinction is not without value
for ministers of finance.   Had Paine and the other "agrarian
reformers" done nothing more than re-assert the social
character of wealth, as implied in the concept of "unearned
income," they deserve a place in the history of social
thought.

The reaction against the individualistic theory of Locke in
our period culminated in William Godwin's *Political Justice*,
(1793).   "Few things," wrote Godwin, "have contributed
more to undermine the energy and virtue of the human
species than the supposition that we have a right, as it has
been phrased, to do what we will with our own."[4]   Like
some other writers in the nineteenth century Godwin's
influence was largely due to the lucidity of his style rather
than to the originality or profundity of his thought.   He was
much indebted to French writers like Rousseau, d'Holbach,

1.—*Ibid.*, p. 200.
2.—*Ibid.*, p. 200.
3.—*The Rights of Man*, part ii., 1792, ch. v., pp. 142 f, in Brit. Museum,
Tracts relating to Thomas Paine.
4.—*Political Justice*, 1796,[2] vol. i., p. 162.

Helvetius, Condillac,[1] and Brissot de Warville.   The last
writer anticipated many of Godwin's ideas as to private
property.   He thundered against social institutions which
canonised what he said nature called a crime ; the appropriation of more things than one can use.[2]

Godwin, however, was more than a mere compiler ; he was
a keen observer of men and manners.   He pointed out that
people desire less to be rich than to be richer than their
neighbours ;[3] that the " ostentation of the rich " makes the
lot of the poor less easy to endure.   Unfortunately he had
no place in his system for those spiritual forces which curb,
if they do not cast out, the evil spirit that sometimes
accompanies the growth of wealth.   If the " love of distinction " is to be diverted into more useful channels than
those offered by the mere " exhibition of wealth,"[4] one must
not despise a philosophy that leans on heaven or a religion
that threatens hell.   Although he commended that view of
wealth, as a trust, which Christianity had inculcated,[5] he
doubted the social value of religious convictions.   Religion,
according to Godwin, who in this matter was influenced by
Mandeville and Rousseau, was the enemy of progress ;
because, forsooth, it aimed at the extirpation of the
passions.[6]   Reason rather than religion was a sufficient guide
to enable man to go on improving his condition.   Like
Mr. Gradgrind in Dickens' *Hard Times* Godwin, in the
eighteenth century fashion, believed that reason is " the only
faculty to which education should be addressed."[7]   Probably
practice has always been better than theory with regard to
education.   To neglect the training of the will is to render
the individual incapable of discharging either the duties of
property or of citizenship.

Godwin, however, recognised that the real difficulty with

1.—See Ford K. Brown, *The Life of W. Godwin*, 1926, p. 15 ; p. 76.
2.—Brissot de Warville, *Recherches philosophiques sur le droit de propriété &
sur le vol, considérés dans la nature & dans la société* in *Bibliothèque Philosophique du Législateur*, 1782, t. vi., p. 324 ; p. 329.
3.—*Political Justice*, 1796, vol. i., p. 21 ; p. 17.
4.—*Op. cit.*, vol. ii., p. 420.
5.—*Op. cit.*, vol. ii., pp. 422-423.
6.—*Op. cit.*, vol. ii., p. 448.
7.—*Op. cit.*, vol. i., p. 46.   Cf.   Dickens, *Works*, vol. xvi., pp. 259-60.

regard to social reform was the moral one ; of getting people to " change " their " dispositions and sentiments." [1] If society would but estimate wealth at its true value, and regard accumulation and monopoly as the cause of mischief, injustice, and dishonour, then the accommodations of human life would tend to their level ; and the inequality of conditions would be abolished. "A revolution of opinions is the only means of attaining to this inestimable benefit." [2] Believing, as he did, that the idea of private property was rooted in the right of private judgement—the " palladium of all that ought to be dear to us," [3] and the protection of which is the first object of government—it seems rather illogical to expect men to agree to any restrictions on their capacity to accumulate wealth.

Unlike the " agrarian reformers," Godwin's main interest in property was limited to those things which " cannot be obtained without the labour of man." [4] Whether one regards him as the father of Socialism, or of Anarchism, or of both, [5] it is clear that he was not opposed to all forms of private property. Two kinds of property were "highly beneficial," [6] and should be protected by " some species of law or practice " ; the right to those things necessary for our personal use, and the right to the produce of our own industry. But the right to either form of property did not seem to him natural or absolute. With regard to the former, the consent of the community was regarded as a necessary condition ; [7] and the right to property founded on labour was always subordinate to the needs of others. [8] Herein he differs from Locke and from all those who consider property founded on personal industry as conferring an absolute right. Although the individual is only a steward of his wealth, his stewardship may not be arbitrarily interfered with. It is

1.—*Op. cit.*, vol. ii., pp. 430-31.
2.—*Op. cit.*, vol. ii., p. 434.
3.—*Ibid.*, vol. ii., p. 443.
4.—*Ibid.*, vol. ii., pp. 424-25.
5.—Cf. Prof. Nicholson's article in *Cambridge Modern History,* vol. x., p. 778.
6.—Godwin, *Op. cit.*, vol. ii., p. 432.
7.—*Op. cit.*, vol. ii., p. 425.
8.—*Op. cit.*, vol. ii., p. 426.

only " by the censorial power that is vested in the general
sense " of the people among whom he lives that his superfluous property may be utilised to relieve the necessities
of others.[1]

The third species or degree of property—the system " by
which one man enters into the faculty of disposing of another
man's industry " [2]—was, he thought, directly opposed to the
right which every man has to the produce of his own
industry. But surely the power which large property confers
on its owner need not, and does not, necessarily lead to the
exploitation of those whose labour it sets in motion and
whose wants, among those of others, it may help to supply.
Probably what Godwin wanted to draw attention to was
that the owner of large capital, by virtue of his power to
finance production, can obtain an income without any
personal effort beyond that involved in investing his money.
He ignored the risk element in industrial enterprise ;
and the fact that part of the income which the owner
of capital receives merely represents what society is
willing to pay to those who take its risks. It was a
narrow view of the capitalist's function to regard all the
return to his capital as an encroachment upon the rights
of those who were more immediately connected with the
industrial process.

One is less tempted to read too much into Godwin's
views when one remembers that the age in which he
wrote his book was one of industrial awakening ; that
he lived in a country noted for " less wretchedness and
distress " than other countries ; [3] and that the machinery
of impersonal capitalism had not yet reached that perfection
which, in the nineteenth century, was to prove a menace
to, as well as a bulwark of, the small property owner.
The concentration of capital in large scale enterprises,
which the company system of conducting business rendered
possible, has often forced the small producer out of
business ; but, on the other hand, the same limited liability

1.—*Op. cit.*, vol. ii., p. 427.
2.—*Op. cit.*, vol. ii., p. 427-28.
3.—Godwin, *Op. cit.*, vol. i., p. 16.

joint-stock system of production tended to multiply rather than to diminish the number of shareholders. Marx and others have not allowed for the fact that concentration of capital does not necessarily imply concentration of ownership.[1]

With all its imperfections, Godwin's theory of property came as a healthy, though violent, breeze to the unruffled atmosphere of eighteenth century social thought. Ever since Harrington wrote his *Oceana* the idea that property is power was a commonplace of political writers. Economists, however, while admitting its political significance were slow to perceive its full social consequences. They did not visualise the social power of capital to the same extent that they did that of property in land.[2] Locke recognised that money was "an universal commodity";[3] and Steuart described it as but another name for "property, of one kind or other, thrown into circulation,"[4] but both writers, as well as Smith,[5] did not consider social control of the capitalists' activities desirable or necessary except in special circumstances. Steuart, for example, would limit the statutory regulation of interest to the case of loans to the prodigal, bent on having money at any rate to gratify his passions, and to loans to the necessitous poor, whose condition exposed them to the tender mercies of usurious creditors.[6]

Economists, on the whole, were less interested in defining a moral or social ideal than in explaining economic and social facts. The rights of property, sanctioned by custom or by law, were accepted. The duties of property and the moral

1.—See Vladimir G. Simkhovitch, *Marxism versus Socialism* (no date ? 1913), p. 92 ; and the present writer's *Marxian Socialism*, 1917, ch. iv.

2.—See Sir James Steuart, *An Inquiry into the Principles of Political Economy*, 1767, vol. ii., bk. v., ch. iv., p. 500.

3.—Locke, *Considerations of the Lowering of Interest and Raising the value of Money*, 1691, in Works, 1714, vol. ii., p. 5.

4.—Steuart, *Op. cit.*, vol. ii., bk. iv., ch. vii., p. 131.

5.—In the *Wealth of Nations*, bk. ii., ch. iv., ed. Cannan, vol. i., p. 338, he admitted the necessity of legal regulation of interest, but later, probably owing to Bentham's influence, held that absolute liberty should be the rule. See John Rae, *Life of A. Smith*, p. 423. The last attempt to fix a legal rate of interest in the eighteenth century was in the reign of Queen Anne, 1713. The rate then fixed remained until 1854, when all usury laws were swept away.

6.—Steuart, *Op. cit.*, vol. ii., bk. iv., ch. v., p. 121.

aspect of business transactions were considered beyond their province. The rôle of the economist was thus limited to an empirical study of the principles governing the maximum of wealth production with the minimum of effort, unhampered by considerations as to whether that wealth was distributed according to justice, or consumed according to reason. Indeed for Smith the moral aspect of property or economic activities could not arise ; because, according to his religious theory of society, man's self-interest was God's providence. Sir James Steuart's standpoint was more intelligible though not less harmful in its practical results. " My subject," he writes, " is too extensive of itself to admit of being confounded with the doctrine either of morals, or of government, however closely these may appear connected with it ; and did I not begin by simplifying ideas as much as possible, ... I should . . . . involve myself in perplexities inextricable." [1]

Thus the theory that one can do what one likes with one's property, within the limits imposed by the State, became an integral part of the modern science of Economics. The mediaeval theory of property which made the King the ultimate owner of all landed property did not, as we saw, except in legal form, survive the Civil War. By the end of our period the rival conception of private property as an absolute individual right has triumphed. Such eighteenth century books as dealt professedly with the history of property connected the growth of the idea of its free use and disposal with " the progress of society." [2] It must not be inferred that the idea of utilising property or riches as an instrument of social service was dead in the eighteenth century. The very freedom which the individual enjoyed with regard to his property enabled him to be of greater service to his fellow man than his ancestors in the seventeenth century. Though the number of rich men who availed of this opportunity of social service was probably small, owing, perhaps, to the fact that " that independence Britons prize

1.—*Op. cit.*, vol. i., p. 32, (note).
2.—John Dalrymple, *An Essay towards a general history of feudal property in Great Britain,* 1758, p. 75.

too high " may have kept man from man and severed "the social tie,"[1] it is well to remember that the eighteenth century had its Rockefellers and Carnegies.   Thomas Guy, who made a large fortune by speculating in South Sea stock, was spoken of as the friend of the poor and founded the famous hospital which "bears his name."[2]   Joseph Paice spent all his fortune in "charitable ways."[3]   But many used or abused property in such a way as to prevent others from enjoying the means of livelihood.   Defoe has described for us with unsparing irony the "honest methods"[4] by which men like Sir Josiah Child exploited the credulity of an otherwise incredulous generation, by spreading false rumours of lost ships and lost causes, to reap for themselves colossal fortunes on the exchange.   Pretenders and threatened invasions were born and buried in exchange-alley.   Thus money was obtained by methods which in reality constituted an invasion of property, and a form of robbery which was not less reprehensible because connived at by some of the governing classes of the day.   But this abuse of the right of property, or rather this power to injure the property rights of others, is better known in our day and is too big a subject to be dealt with here.   It may, however, be observed that every capitalist, small or large, assumes a moral responsibility in the investment and use of his money.   He is obliged, therefore, to see that his capital is not employed in the production of morally undesirable articles.

1.—Cf.   Goldsmith, " The Traveller," in *Poems, Plays and Essays,* ed. J. Aikin, 1835, p. 19.

2.—G. E. Cunningham, *The English Nation or, A history of England in the Lives of Englishmen,* 1853, vol. iv., pp. 120-21.

3.—H. R. Fox-Bourne, *English Merchants,* 1866, vol. ii., p. 241.

4.—D. Defoe, *The Anatomy of Exchange Alley,* 1719, p. 10, pp. 13-15.   For a criticism of Defoe's account of some of the industrial crises of the seventeenth century see W. R. Scott, *The Constitution and Finance of English, Scottish and Irish Joint-stock Companies,* 1912, vol. i., pp. 357-60.

CHAPTER V.

LOCKE AND AMERICA.

MORE than one well known writer has discussed the connection between Locke's theory of natural rights and the rise of the United States as an independent political power.[1] The application of Locke's political philosophy to America gave rise to great fears and great hopes in the eighteenth century. Dean Tucker,[2] no enemy of the colonists, viewed with scepticism prophecies of the future greatness of America. Price and Paine hailed with enthusiasm the extension to the New World of a doctrine the full significance of which, in their opinion, was obscured by those English writers who saw in it little more than an apologia for the political events culminating in the Revolution of 1688. While much has been written on the relation of Locke's political philosophy to the constitutional struggles which preceded the Declaration of Independence, little attention has hitherto been focussed on the problem as to how far his writings have been responsible for the social theory which triumphed when the constitutional and military issues were no longer in doubt.

It is not possible in this essay to give, even in outline, a picture of the influences which went to form the American people. But in order to estimate Locke's influence on American social theory, particularly in regard to the view of property rights which existed during, and after, the formative period of the Union, a brief sketch of the economic, political

1.—See C. E. Merriam, *A History of American Political Theories*, 1903, p. 47, *et passim*.
2.—Josiah Tucker, *A Treatise concerning Civil Government*, 1781, pp. 103-5.

and intellectual background of pre-Revolutionary America seems to offer, perhaps, the necessary introduction.

(1.) THE HISTORICAL BACKGROUND OF THE AMERICAN REVOLUTION.

It was not until 1577 that England made any serious attempt to claim her share of the New World.   Her right to do so was based on the re-discovery of America in 1497 by John Cabot, an Italian merchant, who resided at Bristol for some years.   The fall of Constantinople in the middle of the fifteenth century, which shut off the East from European traders, did not make British merchants look to the West until all hopes of European expansion were finally abandoned by the loss of Calais in 1557.   From the sixteenth century onwards, religious strifes in England caused many to seek abroad that freedom which they could not enjoy at home. And in the first half of the seventeenth century the economic as well as the religious causes of emigration became more and more operative.   Some pessimistic Puritans like John White [1] maintained that England was over-populated ; it contained more inhabitants than it could " profitably employ."   In reality, what existed was local unemployment due to market variations caused by the decline in the clothing industry, or to actual overcrowding of particular professions.

The motives which led many to emigrate then, as now, were of course very mixed.   Few will take the high view of colonisation with which White and Mather credited the majority of New England immigrants.[2]   It is also difficult to prove that the majority of Puritan emigrants lived up to White's ideal of loving service to one's neighbour " in some profitable and useful calling." [3]   Indeed colonisation in every age, pagan or puritan, is meant primarily to be a convenient

---

1.—*The Planter's Plea*, 1630 (printed in Old South Leaflets, Boston, no. 154), p. 5.   See Robert Reyce, *Suffolk in the XVIIth century : The Breviary of Suffolk*, 1618, London, 1902 edn., p. 58.

2.—White, *Op. cit.*, p. 18.   Rev. Cotton Mather, *Magnalia Christi Americana*, London, 1702.

3.—*Op. cit.*, p. 5.

outlet for what White calls "greedy appetites."[1]   Probably
John Cotton's advice to the colonists, to "offend not the
poore Natives,"[2] was never regarded as conveying much
more than a counsel of perfection.[3]   If the observations of
some eighteenth century travellers are to be credited there
is reason for believing that, outside the State of Pennsylvania,
the interests of the natives were frequently sacrificed to those
of the colonists.[4]   If the Indians, as it was said, were lazy
and fond of "spirituous liquors,"[5] one can easily imagine
how they must have shocked the Puritan conscience ; and
how natural it would be for the severe settlers to make them
feel the discipline of poverty.   William Penn was, probably,
unique amongst colonial governors.   He was a "true friend"
of the Indians, and insisted that they should not be deprived
of their lands without adequate compensation.[6]

In the group of colonies, known as the New England
States, the Puritans displayed that love of industry for which
they were noted in the Old World, and that rigorism which
practically outlawed reasonable recreation.   These qualities,
as is well known, exercised a profound influence both for
good and evil on the American character.[7]   The New
England colonies—Massachusetts, Maine, New Hampshire,
Rhode Island and Connecticut—differed in many respects
from what historians usually refer to as the "proprietary"
colonies of the Southern and Middle states.[8]

At an early period New England showed signs of a decided

1.—*Op. cit.*, p. 4.
2.—*God's Promise to His Plantations*, 1630, O.S.L., no. 53, p. 14.
3.—See Mather, *Op. cit.*, bk. vii., Appendix, p. 61, for an account of the
reasons given by the Indians for the long war of 1688-1698. See, however,
bk. i., ch. vi., p. 25.
4.—Major Robert Rogers, *A Concise Account of North America*, Dublin,
1770, p. 87 ; p. 95.
5.—*Ibid.*, pp. 211-13.
6.—Rogers, *Op. cit.*, p. 87. Robert Proud, *History of Pennsylvania*, Phila.,
1797, vol. ii., p. 128. Cf. James Sullivan, *The History of Land Titles in
Massachusetts*, Boston, 1801, p. 29.—" We do not find, in the memoirs of the
first adventurers to this part of America, any suggestion . . . to justify
their intrusion on the peaceable people who had long been in the uninterrupted
possession of the soil."
7.—See James Truslow Adams, *The Founding of New England*, 1921,
p. 111. Cecil Chesterton, *A History of the U.S.A.*, 1919, p. 6.
8.—See *The History of North America*, ed. Guy Carlton Lee, 1904, vol. vi.,
chapters i., ii.

preference for industrial and commercial pursuits. This love of commerce was not so much promoted by Puritan prejudice as dictated by climatic and geographical conditions. Land in the Eastern colonies was less productive than land in the Southern or Middle states. It was zeal for colonisation, rather than extensive knowledge, which led Captain John Smith to say that the soil of New England was so fertile as to be "capable of producing any Grain, Fruits, or Seeds you will sow or plant."[1] Whether he was ignorant of the law of diminishing returns or not, the colonists acted in accordance with its requirements. Small holdings were the rule in the East, whereas they were the exception in colonies like Virginia. Again, agriculture in the East demanded a degree of intelligence which made slave labour there uneconomic. But despite that fact, and despite the moral disapprobation of slavery by many Puritan writers, slavery became a commercial institution in New England. The monied classes bought and sold human beings to supply the demands of the landed aristocracy of the South.

The land system of the New England colonies, however, contrasted favourably with that of Europe generally; and even with that of England in the seventeenth century. Certainly in the first half of the century the colonists enjoyed a system of land tenure far less feudal than that under which their brethren in England lived. Indeed one might say that feudalism never got a real footing in America. Most of the charters from 1606 to 1732 granted lands in free and common soccage, that is, free tenure without military service. The tenth article of the famous *Body of Liberties* (1641), of the Massachusetts colony declared that all "lands and heritages shall be free from all fines."[2] The eighth article of the same document, while conceding freedom of testamentary disposition to all persons of twenty-one years of age, stated that the eldest son was only entitled to a "double portion" in case of intestacy.[3] The most striking feature of the land

1.—*A Description of New England*, 1616, O.S.L., no. 121, p. 10.   See, however, p. 13, where he is less dogmatic.
2.—*The Body of Liberties*, 1641, O.S.L., no. 164, p. 3.
3.—*Ibid.*, p. 11.

system of the colonists generally was the departure from the English system of primogeniture.

Though the eldest son was not regarded as having a right to the entire property, he was, as in the case of Massachusetts, generally accorded special consideration. Thus the Pennsylvania Act of 1683, (which lasted until 1794) abolishing primogeniture, gave the eldest son a double share of the inheritance. The Massachusetts Act of 1692 also gave the eldest son preferential treatment, but equal division was substituted in 1836. In 1715, Maryland, and in 1770, Rhode Island substituted equal division for primogeniture. In New York and the Southern States, however, promogeniture was the rule. During the Revolutionary period Virginia abolished primogeniture. The War of Independence gave a new impetus to the abolition of English customs. In about two decades after the Declaration of Independence the prevailing custom of giving the eldest son a double portion, or the whole property, was abolished in favour of equal division of property amongst all the children.[1] Although there is no law in the United States prescribing compulsory division of landed property, custom has operated with the force of law restraining Americans from leaving all their land to their eldest sons. The spirit of Jefferson still prevails. His famous reply to the suggestion that the eldest son should have a double portion was : " that if the eldest son could eat twice as much, or do double the work, it might be a natural evidence of his right to a double portion." [2]

During the first half of the eighteenth century we find the agrarian relationships of New England becoming increasingly commercialised. This was partly due to the pressure of population in particular places ; and, may also, perhaps, have been prompted by the enclosure movement proceeding in England. Thus communal rights began to disappear as the result of the speculative land policy consciously promoted

1.—See Alexis de Tocqueville, *Democracy in America*, tr. Henry Reeve, 1838, vol. i., p. 44. Evelyn Cecil, *Primogeniture, a short history of its developments in various countries and its practical effects*, 1895, pp. 74-77. Shosuke Sato, *History of the Land Question in the United States*, Baltimore, 1886, p. 18.

2.—*The Jeffersonian Cyclopedia*, edited by John P. Foley, New York, 1900, p. 719.

by colonial governments.   Large tracts of land were granted
to speculators who resold them to emigrants lately arrived.
The distinction between the farming class and the merchant
and manufacturing class, as well as the division between the
agricultural labourer and the town craftsman, were becoming
more sharply defined.   In the East the economic disparity
which existed between the rich landowner and the agricultural
labourer, on the one hand, and between the capitalist and
the artisan, on the other, often gave rise to bitter complaint.
The selfishness and lack of honour which sometimes
characterised the economic relations of the farmers and
merchants with the poor were depicted in the pamphlets and
newspapers of the day.[1]

Business relations and credit connections tended, as a rule,
to make the colonial merchant look on England in a more
friendly light than the ordinary farmer.   The popular view,
which regarded the country as possessing peace as well as
prosperity until England passed the unfortunate Stamp Act
of 1765, was exploded by John Adams when he declared that
America, like all other countries, had been " a theatre of
parties and feuds for near two hundred years."[2]   In the
first half of the eighteenth century New England displayed
all the qualities of a rudimentary capitalist civilisation :
ship-building, iron mining, saw and grist mills, tanneries
and distilleries, linen, woollen and paper manufacture—all
were taking root in American soil.   The paper mills of
Pennsylvania, as well as its glass and cloth manufactures,
were widely known.   Philadelphia in those days was
materially and intellectually ahead of New York.   And
Boston had merchants who died leaving estates valued
at £20,000.[3]

About the time John Bennet was extolling the " Goodness
of God "[4] for giving Britain so many colonies and plantations,

1.—T. R. Cooper, "A letter to the Common People of the colony of Rhode
Island," 1763, *Boston Evening Post*, Oct. 21, 1764, quoted in J. T. Adams,
Revolutionary New England, 1923, p. 254.

2.—*Works*, ed. C. F. Adams, 1850-6, vol. x., pp. 241-42.

3.—*Belcher Papers*, vol. i., p. 315, *apud* James Truslow Adams, *Revolutionary
New England*, 1923, p. 115.

4.—*The National Merchant or Discussion on Commerce and Colonies*, London,
1736, p. 9.

a silent and, at times, a strong sentiment against the economic tutelage of England was developing amongst the colonists. The decade following 1730 was one of disordered currency in New England. The less wealthy merchants, as well as many private individuals, wanted to issue their own currency. They favoured the establishment of a land bank, with the right to issue paper money based on land. The Massachusetts Assembly refused to consider these proposals. The movement met with the strong opposition of the monied classes, who used their influence to have the English Privy Council suppress it. Accordingly the British Parliament declared that the Bubble Act of 1720 applied to America, and that the proposal for bank notes, secured by land, came within its scope. The Act was also made retroactive by twenty years.[1] This aroused the indignation of the parties affected. Up to that time there was no law preventing the issue of circulating notes by associations, or private persons. Moreover, it was not the intention of the promoters of the Bubble Act of 1720 to apply it to the colonies. This marked the first important stage in the economic discontent which preceded the Declaration of Independence.

From the Restoration onwards Parliament devoted more and more attention to regulating the economic life of the colonies in the interest of the mother country. Laws were passed restricting their navigation, trade, and manufactures in the interest of the English mercantile and manufacturing classes. These laws, as is well known, brought little or no revenue to the home parliament or to the colonies. The evil effects of the industrial and commercial restrictions imposed on the colonies have often been exaggerated. The restrictions placed on American exports were largely a dead letter until the middle of the eighteenth century. The disregard shown for these laws by Americans was relatively as universal, though not quite so lucrative, as the violation of prohibitionist legislation is to-day in the States. Notwithstanding the numerous devices by which the colonists evaded the trade

1.—Adams, *Revolutionary New England*, 1923, pp. 158f.

restrictions imposed by England, the facts brought to light
in a work published by an unknown merchant in 1769,[1]
concerning the treatment of the American colonies by English
companies, were deemed so formidable that great efforts
were made to prevent the circulation of the book.

It was not until the middle of the eighteenth century that
really serious methods were employed to enforce the
Navigation Laws. The first Navigation Act (1660) enacted
that none but English or colonial ships might carry goods to
or from the colonies. The Act of 1663 was more stringent.
It decreed that the colonists must buy in English markets
and import in English ships. This helped to discourage ship-
building in a country abounding in woods.[2] In the
eighteenth century a new view of the function of colonies
had developed in England to suit the interests of the manufacturing classes. The colonies were now to serve as a shel-
tered market for British manufactures rather than as suppliers
of raw material. The colonists naturally resented the efforts
made to crush such nascent industries as iron and steel; and,
towards the middle of the century, they had sufficient hope
in their own economic future, born of the results produced
by the investment of English capital in American industries,
that their severance from England was inevitable.

If Voltaire was surprised in his day to see maps engraven
which referred to America as "the Atlantic Island,"[3]
posterity has not been less puzzled by the paradox of England
viewing with an optimism, bordering on folly, the future of
its colonies while sacrificing their economic interests to those
of its own on every possible occasion. The colonists were
not without their spokesmen in England. Dean Tucker and
Adam Smith, for example, condemned the colonial system.
The *Wealth of Nations*, which appeared the year of the
Declaration of Independence, referred to it as "a manifest
violation of the most sacred rights of mankind."[4]

1.—*The American Traveller*. A French translation of the book appeared
in 1782, *Le Voyageur Américain*, Amsterdam. See p. 6 of the French version.
2.—John Smith, *Description of New England*, loc. cit., p. 13.   J. Winsor,
Narrative and Critical History of America, Lond., 1888, vol. vi., pp. 7-8.
3.—*The Philosophy of History*, tr. 1766, p. 46.
4.—Bk. iv., ch. vii., pt. ii., ed. Cannan 1920, vol. ii., p. 83.

Although the part played by the Puritan element in the commercial and political life of the colonial population was very great, it is a significant fact that the revolutionary movement in America received its chief impetus not from the Eastern but from the Middle and Southern colonies. The minute regulations of the New England theocracies were, in many ways, a menace rather than an inspiration to real democracy or individualism.[1] It was the example set by the Virginia Convention which supplied the driving force of the American Revolution. Like all great historical innovations the movement for independence owed more to practical necessities than to theoretical systems. But when the Virginia Convention on June 12, 1776, declared that all men, having a permanent interest in the community, " cannot be taxed or deprived of their property for publick uses, without their own consent, or that of their representatives " . . . ,[2] it was converting into a text for the American Revolution a doctrine which formed the prologue of the English Revolution. It was the language of Locke.

(2.) AMERICAN THOUGHT ON PROPERTY AND THE FEDERAL CONSTITUTION.

The first article of *The Virginia Bill of Rights* has all the appearance of a paragraph from Locke's *Civil Government*. "All men," it states, " are by nature equally free and independent and have certain inherent rights, of which, when they enter into a state of society, they cannot by any compact deprive or divest their posterity ; namely, the enjoyment of life and liberty, with the means of acquiring and possessing property, and pursuing and obtaining happiness and safety."[3]

Carlyle's statement that " man's philosophies are usually the supplement of his practice ; . . . some outerskin of

1.—See, however, De Tocqueville, *Democracy in America*, tr. H. Reeve, 1838, vol. i., pp. 29f.

2.—*Sources and Documents illustrating the American Revolution*, ed. S. E. Morison, 1923, p. 150.

3.—*Ibid.*, p. 149.

articulate intelligence, with which he strives to render his
dumb instinctive doings presentable when they are done," [1]
is partly true of the life of nations as it is of that of
individuals.   It does not, however, furnish a complete
explanation of that mysterious leavening of the classes, as
well as of the masses, which bursts forth, at times, in the
form of a Revolution.   While fully conceding the part played
by environment, frontier life, the opportunity for adventure
and economic expansion, in fashioning American political
and social individualism, one cannot afford to neglect the
purely intellectual forces which acted on that environment.

Intellectually, America's handicap was necessarily very
great.   As Sydney Smith remarked in the early nineteenth
century it had but few " historical recollections," or " classical
associations." [2]   Indeed its civilisation began only with the
Renaissance.   These cultural disadvantages, however, were
partially compensated for by " the absence of all feudal
nonsence, inveterate abuses and profligate debts of an old
country," [3]   The almost complete intellectual dependence of
the colonists on English writers probably made a first hand
knowledge of past civilisations appear unnecessary.   Thus
for John Adams, the canon and feudal law represented a
system of tyranny [4] from the taint of which Americans had
happily escaped.   Yet he himself was influenced by the
language of feudalism when he used such an expression as
"the common people," [5] and he was guilty of more than
mediaeval credulity in maintaining that an illiterate native
American was as rare a phenomenon as " a Roman Catholic "
or " a comet." [6]   Certainly the evidence furnished by some
writers,[7] who knew eighteenth century America well, does
not support Adam's contention as to the widespread diffusion
of elementary education.   The early law providing for
the establishment of a grammar school in " every town,

1.—" Past and Present " in *Works*, 1870, vol. xiii., p. 235.
2.—*Works*, 1850, p. 404.
3.—*Ibid.*, p. 404.
4.—*An Essay on Canon and Feudal Law*, London edn. 1782, p. 84, Brit.
Mus., 116, g.63.
5.—*Op. cit.*, p. 91.
6.—*Op. cit.*, p. 91.
7.—Major R. Rogers, *Op. cit.*, pp. 59-66.

consisting of so many families,"[1] seems to have been in abeyance, at least when Rogers wrote. The education of the poor was neglected even in those states renowned for their riches. In a wealthy state like New Hampshire there were " very few schools regularly kept up, or well supplied with masters." In Rhode Island, "the garden of the colony," the education of children was "generally shamefully neglected."[2] Noah Webster also thought that education was more widely diffused in America than in any other country, but he seems to limit it to a " knowledge of the rights of men and the principles of government."[3] That knowledge, as *The Virginia Bill of Rights* shows, was not indigenous.

There is a sense in which it is true to say that the Declaration of Independence was "an expression of the American mind";[4] but there is also much truth in Henry Lee's observation that it was "copied from Locke's treatise on *Civil Government*."[5] Locke, of course, was not read by the general public in America. His political philosophy, however, was not unknown to some university graduates and publicists. As early as 1714 the Yale authorities thought it necessary to warn their students against his works, as well as those of Sidney and Cumberland.[6] It would be interesting to know whether the lives of all, or any, of the fifty or sixty " young gentlemen," who annually graduated at Harvard,[7] were really influenced by Cumberland's view, " that *Acts* promoting the *public universal Good* are the *only Acts* which, in themselves, sufficiently and powerfully can promote the full, complete private happiness of each and every individual."[8] If the "law of nature"—requiring, according to Cumberland,[9] that private interest be subordinated to the public good—

1.—John Adams, *Op. cit.*, p. 91.
2.—Rogers, *Op. cit.*, pp. 64-66.
3.—*Pamphlets on the Constitution of the United States*, ed. Paul L. Ford, Brooklyn, 1888, p. 60.
4.—*The Jeffersonian Cyclopedia*, ed. John P. Foley, 1900, p. 243.
5.—*Ibid.*, p. 244.
6.—See J. T. Adams, *Revolutionary New England*, 1923, pp. 98-99.
7.—Rogers, *Op. cit.*, p. 54.
8.—Richard Cumberland, *A Philosophical Inquiry into the Law of Nature*, tr. Towers, Dublin, 1750, pt. ii., ch. v., § 10, p. 312,
9.—*Op. cit.*, p. 312,

influenced the political and social theory of some Americans, that was due to Harrington rather than to Locke.

William Penn, one of the greatest seventeenth century American statesmen, was well acquainted with Harrington's political and social views. Penn studied at Oxford during the year 1660-'61, and Harrington's *Oceana*, which was published in 1656, attracted much attention then. Penn's secretary of state in America had a copy of the *Oceana*.[1] While governor of Pennslyvania, Penn endeavoured to give concrete expression to many of Harrington's ideas. His treatment of the land question, for example, showed traces of Harrington's humanity and social sense. The modifications of the English law of primogeniture, adopted by Massachusetts as well as by Pennslyvania, were in conformity with the spirit of the *Oceana*. Harrington held that in the ideal commonwealth no one should possess landed property exceeding the value of £2,000.[2]

Locke had also criticised the English law of primogeniture and provided a philosophical basis for its abolition in so far as he held a labour theory of property. That aspect of his theory was, as we saw, passed over quietly in England. But to men like Thomas Jefferson, Locke's *Civil Government* was probably valued more for that principle than it was for furnishing phrases for the Declaration of Independence. The theory that property is the reward of industry appealed so much to Jefferson that he was prepared to tolerate any inequality in the distribution of property arising from a man's personal effort, or that of his father.[3]

The works of Locke, Harrington, and Montesquieu were well known in pre-Revolutionary America. Most of the political and social writings which appeared prior to James Otis's *Rights of Colonies* were probably little more than a *rechauffé* of their ideas. Otis's book, however, was a veritable voice from the past. Considered from the standpoint either of political or of social theory it cannot be described as an

1.—For a full discussion of Harrington's political influence in America see H. F. Russell-Smith, *Harrington and his Oceana*, 1914, p. 179 *et passim*.
2.—*Oceana*, ed. H. Morley, 1887, p. 7, p. 104.
3.—*The Jeffersonian Cyclopedia*, edited Foley, 1900, p. 727.

American edition of Locke's *Civil Government*. The protection of property is not the sole reason why men enter into civil society.[1] Government is not an accidental affair. " It has an everlasting foundation in the unchangeable will of God, the author of nature " . . .[2] Political society is as natural and necessary as family society ; it is, in fact, but an outgrowth of the latter. In thus connecting the family with society, and recognising God as the Author of both institutions, Otis was implicitly giving expression to a social theory which the progress of commerce, amongst other causes, had long since thrust into the background in England. Property, as the " incomparable Harrington " had shown, conferred power, but it did not bestow wisdom. " The possessor of it may not have much more wit than a mole or a musquash." [3] He regretted that riches were sought after " without the least concern about the right application of them." [4] When people pursue wealth for the power or superiority which it confers, they have not the time, even if they had the inclination, to consider the rights of others. It was the old theory that the due harmony of society, as well as the true happiness of the home, consisted less in the assertion of individual rights than in the faithful discharge of duties.

But the tide of American social and political thought was destined to sweep Otis's ideas away.[5] The question of taxation was to play a similar part to what it did in seventeenth century England in creating an atmosphere favourable to the development of an extremely individualistic conception of property rights. George III. of England was the American Charles I. Amongst the examples of his " tyranny " set forth in the Declaration of Independence, prominence was given to the fact that he imposed taxes on

1.—James Otis, *The Rights of the British Colonies asserted and proved,* Boston, 1764, p. 8. Extracts printed in *Sources and Documents*, ed. Morison, pp. 4f.

2.—*Ibid.*

3.—Otis, *Op. cit.,* p. 8.

4.—*Ibid.,* p. 8.

5.—He was one of those who definitely admitted England's right to rule the colonies, provided it respected the natural rights of the latter. See *Op. cit.,* p. 32.

the colonists without their consent.[1] But long before that impressive declaration was signed the Miltons and Hampdens of America had ceased to be mute. Like Locke's Irish friend, Molyneux, many of the colonists thought that if a principle is true, its application to countries other than that in which it was supposed to be discovered should benefit rather than injure mankind.

The first important application of Locke's doctrine of natural rights to the American colonies was made in a pamphlet by John Wise in 1717.[2] In 1772 Samuel Adams[3] took Locke as literally as Molyneux[4] who declared that he had " no other notion of property but a Power of disposing of my Goods *as I please*, and not as another shall command," and that, therefore, " to tax me without consent is little better, if at all, than down right robbing me." Samuel Adams, like Molyneux in the case of Ireland, applied Locke's principles to the actual circumstances of the colonists. But if Adams may be justly considered " the Father of the American Revolution," he has no claim to be regarded as the founder of a new theory of property. The view of property which he took was that current in England and attributed to Locke : that property was one of the " absolute rights of Englishmen."[5] The same view applied to the colonists, he thought, since England was the custodian of their rights. Not only did Locke's theory of property suffer by Samuel Adams's abridgement of it, but it also lost by the heated atmosphere surrounding the commercial treatment of the colonies by England. To make the case against England as formidable as possible the absolute character of property, as well as other rights, was placed in the strongest relief. And so another Adams was led to define a freeman as " one who is bound by no law to which he has not consented."[6]

1.—*Sources and Documents illustrating the American Revolution*, ed. Morison, 1923, p. 159.

2.—*The Law of Nature in Government*, O.S.L., no. 165.

3.—*The Rights of Colonists*, O.S.L., no. 173.

4.—William Molyneux, *Case of Ireland being bound by Acts of Parliament in England*, Almon edition, Dublin, 1698, p. 170.

5.—*The Rights of Colonists*, O.S.L., no. 173, p. 4.

6.—John Adams, *Works*, ed. C. F. Adams, vol. iv., p. 28.

Though John Adams realised that a master of metaphysics might be guilty of a " signal absurdity " when entrusted with " legislative proposals," he had no qualms in accepting Locke as a social philosopher while rejecting him as a legislator.[1] While Adams erred in taking Locke's association with *The Fundamental Constitutions of Carolina* (1669) for authorship, and while his criticisms of that academic constitution have the air of true democracy, he apparently did not realise how much his own views on property and its right to rule tended towards the setting up of an " oligarchical sovereignity." [2] He placed too much reliance on popular elections ; [3] and seemed to be unaware of the extent to which liberty and free government are dependent upon a just distribution of property in modern communities. He knew as well as Harrington—whom he quotes—that property is power, but he accepted that formula in an aristocratic and fatalistic sense. " Riches," he writes, " will hold the place in civilised societies at least, among the principles of power, and will often prevail, not only over all the principles of authority, but over all the advantages of birth, knowledge and fame." [4]

These words, written after the Federal Constitution was drawn up, formed, however, the working creed of many writers and publicists during the anxious years leading up to the Federal Convention.

During the War of Independence the various States were so concentrated on the supreme problem of winning their collective freedom, that little time was left for them to consider their particular interests as individual entities. When, however, England had agreed to recognise American independence in the famous treaty of Versailles (1783), each State grew more conscious of its sovereignty, and viewed with suspicion any movement which might diminish the power it had wrested from the English Crown. The Continental Congress, which came into existence during the war,

1.—*A Defence of the Constitutions of Government of the U.S.A.*, Phila. 1787, p. 365.
2.—*Ibid.*, p. 365.
3.—*Ibid.*, p. 369.
4.—*Ibid.*, p. 158.

was, constitutionally speaking, little more than a council of war accepted by the thirteen States. The Articles of Confederation, agreed on in 1777 and ratified in 1781, left many important problems still unsolved. The articles were too loose to secure unanimity in the event of external troubles, while they were inadequate to compose the internal differences which menaced the Union as a whole. Many States had refused to pay the levies imposed on them by Congress ; commercial jealousy between different States was rife ; and, even within the same State, there were social and financial troubles which were a danger to organised government.

Like all wars, the struggle with England had left its aftermath of economic problems. Farmers in the inland States who had contracted heavy debts to the merchants were crying out for " cheap money." One State, Rhode Island, had, with disastrous consequences, yielded to that demand ; others, like Massachusetts, had dealt firmly with the situation by refusing to listen to petitions like those of the towns-people of Greenwich, Mass., in 1786.[1] The inhabitants of that town complained that they were weighed down with heavy taxation ; their property was being eaten away by lawyer's justice ; and that government was little more than a conspiracy of rich men intent on making the people poorer. Why should his Excellency the Governor enjoy " eleven hundred a year " while many are starving ? How can existing inequalities be reconciled with " the principles of our Constitution (viz.) piety, justice, moderation, temperance."? [2]

Owing to the want of sufficient currency, ran another petition, may industrious members of the community are are confined to gaol for non-payment of debts.[3] To the government's order urging the practice of economy, the people, as is their wont at all times, replied that example speaks louder than words. " It is with indignation," said the convention of the county of Worcester, Mass., in 1786,

1.—See MSS., printed in *Sources and Documents*, ed. Morison, pp. 208 f.
2.—*Ibid.*, p. 209.
3.—*Ibid.*, p. 211. The English practice of imprisoning a " Debtor for ever, tho' not worth one Farthing in the World "—in order to safeguard " credit "—was denounced by John Bennet in 1736—*The National Merchant,* 1736, pp. 139-141.

" that the good people of this county have seen more money lavished by a single grant of the General Court on one officer of government who has rendered himself generally disagreeable to the people than can be obtained by a long life of industrious labour." [1]

An interesting account of the economic factors and conflicts leading up to the establishment of the Federal Convention in May, 1787, is contained in the letters written in 1786 by the French Ambassador at New York to the Minister of Foreign Affairs in France.[2] The absence of diplomatic language in his description of the unhappy victims of famine and finance was not unnatural at that period, even for a Frenchman.[3]

If men like Dan Shays entertained communistic ideas, and sought to give effect to them, one must remember—what John Jay apparently overlooked—that such movements usually originate as a protest against that " private rage for property," [4] which is insensible to considerations of the public good. One may, however, appreciate Jay's alarm at the " insecurity of property " even though his sympathies were confined to those who enjoyed the blessings of ownership. The insecurity, of which Shays' rebellion was a portent, might easily lead those who were " content with their situations, and not uneasy in their circumstances," [5] to think that America's hard won political liberty was a very shadowy affair. The number of such people was, of course, considerable. It was natural, therefore, that those who held great property, and who had given generously of their resources in the hour of their country's need, should desire what Hamilton called " greater energy of government." [6]

Important economic groups, like the holders of securities, manufacturers, traders, and shippers felt that financial ruin was imminent, unless some national solution of debt payments, coinage, and other problems was arrived at. The United States had no national system of coinage until 1785, and new

---

1.—*Sources and Documents*, ed. Morison, p. 211.
2.—*Ibid.*, pp. 219-225.
3.—*Ibid.*, p. 220.
4.—*Letter to Washington*, June 27, 1786, in Morison, *Sources*, p. 214.
5.—*Ibid.*, p. 215.
6.—*The Federalist*, n. 26, Everyman's Library edition, p. 125.

coins were not actually issued until 1793. Various European coins—English, French and Spanish—circulated in the country, and the fluctuations in the value of these had a depressing effect on business. Though ostensibly the Convention was convened for the purpose of amending the Articles of Confederation, it was obvious from the beginning that the solution of the above problems lay in the adoption of a Federal or National Constitution. The Federal Constitution of 1787 was the outcome. Some of the States were slow to recognise what Pendleton [1] called the " imbecillity " of the Confederation, or to ratify the Constitution. North Carolina and Rhode Island, for example, did not join the Union until George Washington was inaugurated President in 1789.

Broadly speaking, the Southern States represented the landed interest, and were suspicious of the financial and commercial interests of the North who were urging the adoption of the Constitution.[2] From the debates of the Federal Convention, and from the discussions to which the Constitution gave rise when submitted to the various State assemblies for ratification, one can obtain a fair idea of the different currents of thought both with regard to property, and to political and social theory, in America. It is important, however, to remember that the excitement and fear of anarchy which prevailed led men, who in calmer times would probably have espoused more liberal social and political views, to adopt a rather conservative attitude. The Federal Constitution was largely a *pièce de circonstance*. If, in some of its features, it was less democratic than one would be inclined to expect, that, perhaps, may have been due to a genuine fear of an untried democracy rather than to any conscious adoption of European ideas.[3]

1.—Morison, *Sources and Documents*, p. 316.
2.—See *Essays on the Constitution of the United States, 1787-8*, edited by Paul L. Ford, 1892.
3.—Cf. however, John Adams, *A Defence of the Constitutions of Government of the U.S.A.*, Phila., 1787, p. 5. Replying to Turgot, who complained that the " customs of England are imitated in most of the new constitutions in America," Adams said, " Why should one reject customs or institutions which were good just because they happen to be English " For a similar protest against the prejudice which was sometimes shown against English institutions, see James Sullivan, *Op. cit.*, pp. 13-14.

Some, influenced by Montesquieu's writings, believed that a Republican form of government could only be a success in the case of a small territory. A Federal Constitution and a Federal Government would, in their opinion, endanger private property and put an end to Republican rule.[1] If one of the principal reasons why men enter into political society declared Clinton, quoting Locke, is the preservation of their property, the larger the area under a government the less easy will it be to protect the property of its subjects.[2] Other pamphleteers, while distinguishing more carefully between union and consolidation, were anxious to see individualism written large into the Constitution. Voicing the commercial interests of Massachusetts, James Winthrop advocated the insertion in the Constitution of a " restraining clause " against the granting of exclusive trading privileges and monopolies, which had led to so many abuses in the Old World.[3] Free competition was essential not only to the commercial supremacy of Massachusetts, but to the welfare of the United States. The ideas of others were pitched in a still more individualistic key. The welfare of the people was largely independent of the State. " Good government " was, in fact, a consequence rather than a cause of the people's virtue, industry and economy.[4] If the people work they can become as rich as they are free.[5]

The views of these essayists, it seems to us, cannot be wholly explained as a psychological product of America's newly attained political freedom. They are, in addition, an attempt to popularise Locke's social philosophy. These writers would reduce the State to the level of a partnership

1.—*Essays on the Constitution of the United States, 1787-8*, ed. Ford, 1892, pp. 255f.

2.—*Ibid.*, p. 255.

3.—*Ibid.*, p. 70-71.

4.—*Essays on the Constitution of the United States published during its discussion by the people, 1787-1788*, ed. Paul L. Ford, 1892, p. 201.

5.—*Ibid.*, p. 202. George Clinton was opposed to the Constitution because he thought that the liberty as well as the property of the individual could not be adequately safeguarded under a federal government. " For the security of the property of the community, in which expressive term Mr. Locke makes life, liberty and estate to consist, the wheels of a republic are necessarily slow in their operation " ; and, therefore, the larger the territory the more difficult to protect property.—See *Essays on the Constitution of the United States*, ed. Ford, 1892, p. 257.

based upon property. They would interweave into the Constitution a " veneration for wealth " ;[1] and make property almost entirely immune from State supervision. The wisdom of that policy was doubted by sincere democrats like Franklin, who thought that " a veneration for property and virtue " ought to form the object of " republican encouragement." [2] Some of the leading promoters of the Constitution, however, believed that in protecting property the Constitution was protecting labour.

" Property as well as personal rights," said Madison, " is an essential object of the laws, which encourage industry by securing the enjoyment of its fruits : that industry from which property results, and that enjoyment which consists not merely in its immediate use, but in its posthumous destination to objects of choice and of kindred affection." [3] Thus whatever was sacred or absolute about property rights appeared to Madison to be due to their labour origin. That was how he understood Locke. Property rights should never over-rule personal rights. Thanks to the wide diffusion of property in the United States, the power of property to oppress liberty, at least on a large scale, was, he thought, a remote contingency. " The United States," said Madison in 1787, " have a precious advantage also in the actual distribution of property, particularly the landed property ; and in the universal hope of acquiring property." The latter " peculiarity " constitutes one of the " happiest contrasts in their situation to that of the old world, where no anticipated change in this respect can generally inspire a like sympathy with the rights of property." [4]

Although we have no precise data as to the distribution of landed property when the Constitution was framed, one may readily accept Madison's opinion that the majority of the nation were " freeholders, or the heirs, or aspirants to

1.—*The Records of the Federal Convention of 1787*, ed. Max Farrand, 1911, vol. ii., p. 123, Cf. T. Ford, *The Constitutionalist*, 1794, p. 21.

2.—*The Records of the Federal Convention of 1787*, vol. ii., p. 123.

3.—*The Records of the Federal Convention of 1787*, ed. Max Farrand, 1911, vol. iii., p. 450.

4.—*Ibid.*, vol. iii., p. 451.

Freeholds." [1] But Madison foresaw the day when property owners—particularly the landed proprietors—would cease to form the predominant element in the community. [2] He trembled to think of the situation of a country the majority of whose inhabitants were without landed or other property, and who were deprived of the " means or hope of acquiring it." [3] With prophetic insight he saw the proportion of commercial and manufacturing classes increasing [4] in the future; the majority of citizens becoming dependent on the " wealth of a few," and society dividing into a large number of indigent labourers and a few " wealthy capitalists." [5]

That his prophecy, like that of Marx much later, has not yet been literally fulfilled does not impair the soundness of his judgement as to the broad sweep of economic development in the United States. He is surer of his ground, however, when he comes to analyse existing conditions. Society is viewed as a complexus of conflicting economic interests. His economic interpretation of politics is not marred by the unrealistic theory of social dichotomy one finds in Marx. Society is composed of a landed, a manufacturing, a mercantile and a monied interest, " with many lesser interests." [6] But he does not say that social harmony will result from allowing each of the separate classes to pursue its own interests unfettered by the State. On the contrary his social philosophy was summed up in the memorable words : " the regulation of these various and interfering interests forms the principal task of modern legislation." [7]

Like Jefferson he had a special predilection for the landed interest. Both writers were obviously greatly influenced by Harrington's views. Thus, for Madison, the " obvious and permanent division of every people is into the owners of the soil and the other inhabitants. In a certain sense the country

1.—*Ibid.*, vol. iii., p. 451.
2.—*Ibid.*, vol. iii., p. 451.   Cf. vol. ii., pp. 203-4.
3.—*Ibid.*, vol. iii., p. 452.
4.—*Ibid.*, vol. ii., p. 124.
5.—*Ibid.*, vol. iii., p. 452.
6.—*The Federalist*, n. 10, Everyman's Library, p. 43.
7.—*The Federalist*, n. 10, Everyman's Library, p. 43.

may be said to belong to the former."[1]   Should the non-landed interests ever " become the majority," they ought not to pass legislation " without the consent of the landed proprietors."[2]   The landed interest, though entitled to great respect, ought not, however, to have a monopoly of political power ;   the mass of the citizens should have a voice in making the laws " they are to obey."[3]   Though political power in the hands of a propertyless people might lead to " agrarian laws, and other levelling schemes,"[4] that was not a decisive argument against democracy as he conceived it. In all forms of government there is a power which is capable of being abused.   A democratic franchise was only just.   The poor have been so often oppressed by the rich in the past that they ought to have some defence against a like danger recurring in the future.[5]

Madison's solicitude for the property owner was, as we saw, based on the conviction that property is the reward of industry.   He seemed to forget that landed property, to which he was so partial, was a free gift of nature ; and that there is no necessary correlation between inequality in the distribution of property generally and the diversity of men's faculties.[6]   While admitting that the regulation of conflicting economic interests forms the main task of legislation, he seems ro reduce the State's function with regard to property to the mere protection of the different kinds of property arising from unequal faculties of acquiring them.[7] In short, he did not distinguish clearly between the moral and the legal aspects of ownership.

The social views of Thomas Jefferson and John Taylor were more radical.   The social philosophy of the former was neither an expression of Locke's mind nor of the American mind.   His practical distrust of commerce in a commercial age is quite surprising.   In answer to a letter asking his

1.—*Records of the Federal Convention of 1787*, Farrand, vol. iii., p. 452.
2.—*Ibid.*, vol. iii., p. 452.
3.—*Ibid.*, vol. iii., p. 454.   That was his mature view.   For a more conservative attitude see vol. ii., pp. 203-4.
4.—*Ibid.*, vol. iii., p. 451.
5.—*Ibid.*, vol. iii., p. 451.
6.—*The Federalist*, no. 10, Everyman's Library edn., p. 42.
7.—*Ibid.*, pp. 42-43.

opinion as to the " expediency " of encouraging the " States to be commercial," he replied, in 1785, as follows : " Were I to indulge my own theory, I should wish them to practise neither commerce nor navigation, but to stand with respect to Europe precisely on the footing of China. We should thus avoid wars, and all our citizens would be husbandmen . . . But this is theory only, and a theory which the servants of America are not at liberty to follow. Our people have a decided taste for navigation and commerce." [1] But he continued to warn his country against the evils of a commercial civilisation. Those evils, he thought, found their most tragic illustration in England. Wars for commerce had impoverished the labouring class there and made millionaires of the few.[2] Equal division of property was impracticable ; but " legislators cannot invent too many devices for subdividing property, only taking care to let their subdivisions go hand in hand with the natural affections of the human mind." [3] In 1785 he made some interesting suggestions for lessening the inequalities of property in France as, for example, " to exempt all from taxation below a certain point, and to tax the higher portions of property in geometrical progression." [4]

While sharing Jefferson's regard for landed property, John Taylor [5] differed from him in opposing the Constitution. Unlike Noah Webster,[6] Taylor believed that " the inequalities produced by commerce " were a greater menace to society than inequalities arising from the distribution of landed property. Despite the extreme and superficial character of much of his writings, Taylor was, perhaps, unique amongst eighteenth century American writers in pointing out the social power of capitalism, and in emphasising the dangers associated with the growth of intangible forms of property.

1.—*The Jeffersonian Cyclopedia*, ed. John P. Foley, 1900, p. 160.

2.—*Ibid.*, p. 158.

3.—*Ibid.*, p. 727. But the property due to a man's " own industry, or that of his father's " should be maintained.

4.—*Ibid.*, p. 727.

5.—*An Inquiry into the Principles and Policy of the Government of the United States*, Fredericksburg, 1814.

6.—For Webster's views see *Pamphlets on the Constitution of the United States*, ed. Paul L. Ford, 1888, p. 59.

The latter, unlike landed property, could not be " measured or limited,"[1] and hence they made it almost impossible to preserve that balance of property which Harrington had shown to be essential to the preservation of liberty.[2]   He did not, however, approve of levelling property by law.[3] His chief object seems to be to ridicule the rising " aristocracy of paper " whose hands are in every purse, and at every heart.[4]

In his denunciation of interest as the deprivation of the fruits of labour, as well as in his characterisation of Banking as " a paper feudal system,"[5] he was more mediaeval than the mediaevalists.   His inability to grasp the real nature of the modern credit system was as great as his insight into the evils which often accompany it was profound.   Though he failed to distinguish between what is essential and what is accidental in the credit system, the emphasis he laid on the relations between inequality in the distribution of purchasing power and the distribution of property is something for which economists, peaceful as well as militant,[6] may be grateful.   While he seemed to view with complacency existing property rights in land, as well as in slaves,[7] he was sincere in his desire to adjust the balance created by the growth of new forms of property.

If Taylor's writings had been less occupied with furthering the interests of a party, his denunciation of avarice as one of the greatest vices of the age[8] might have given a new direction to social thought.   But his opposition to the Federal Constitution, and to the commercial and financial interests urging its necessity, must have appeared infantile to men of such sane social views as Madison, and an abomination to economic realists like John Adams and

1.—*Op. cit.*, p. 23.
2.—*Ibid.*, p. 51.
3.—*Op. cit.*, p. 404.
4.—*Ibid.*, p. 23.
5.—*Ibid.*, p. 291.   It is interesting to note that he practically uses the same words as Gerard de Malynes who objected to Banking in 1603.   See his *England's View*, 1603, Goldsmiths' Library, pp. 191-2 and Cf. Taylor, *Op. cit.*, p. 272.
6.—Cf.   Major Douglas, *Credit Power and Democracy*.
7.—*Arator*, 1813, p. 62.
8.—*An Inquiry*, 1814, p. 529.

Alexander Hamilton. Though Franklin deplored the undue importance attached to the mere possession of wealth by the members of the Federal Convention, and Jefferson regretted their "ignorance of the value of public discussions," [1] both realised that a national solution of the problems confronting the country could only be arrived at by the adoption of some form of Federal Government. But it was Alexander Hamilton who dealt a death blow to the prejudices of Taylor, and to the social views which the latter shared in common with Jefferson.

Both in the *Federalist* and in his famous *Report on the Subject of Manufactures* (London, 1793), he showed that the manufacturing and agricultural interests were not really opposed.[2] When he presented that Report in 1791 the question of encouraging manufactures in the United States had passed out of the debating stage. In masterly style he demolished the physiocratic prejudices which had taken hold of some American minds. For example, to the objection that the labour employed on land was more productive than labour devoted to manufacture, he replied that in manufacture labour can be employed more constantly than in agriculture which is subject to seasonable influences ; and that among the cultivators of the soil there is probably " more remissness than among artificers." [3]

When Hamilton declared that the Federal Constitution was " in every rational sense, and to every useful purpose, a Bill of Rights," [4] he was obviously thinking of the rights of States rather than of the rights of individuals. Indeed the remarkable fact about the Constitution is the absence of any declaration of individual rights such as that contained in the Declaration of Independence. That document was prefaced by a declaration of the " unalienable rights " of man to " life, liberty and the pursuit of happiness." [5] The American

1.—*Records of the Federal Convention*, vol. iii., p. 76. In a letter from Paris to John Adams, Aug. 30, 1787.
2.—*Report of the Secretary of the Treasury of the United States on the Subject of Manufactures*, London, 1793, p. 69 *et passim*.
3.—*Ibid.*, p. 9.
4.—*The Federalist*, n. 84, Everyman's Library, p. 440.
5.—*Sources and Documents*, ed. Morison, p. 157.

Constitution framers were more prudent than the French "Constitution mongers" of 1791, 1793 and 1795, who placed a statement of the rights of man at the head of their constitutions because they regarded these rights as also the rights of citizens. There was reason, as we saw, for this caution. The economic and social disturbance following the close of the War of Independence made men with a good stake in the country, as Ireton would have said, suspicious of abstract discussions on the rights of man.

If, for example, the Federal Constitution contained a clause similar to that quoted from the Declaration of Independence, one can imagine what doubts might arise in the minds of some as to how far existing property rights prevented them from pursuing their natural right to happiness. Above all, the right of property in human beings could not be reconciled with such a Constitution. The same reasons which prevented a denunciation of slavery in the Declaration of Independence, the fear of alienating the powerful proprietary interests of the South and of thus wrecking American unity,[1] operated also when it came to framing the Federal Constitution. In vain did Col. Mason in the Convention debates inveigh against the "infernal traffic" which "originated in the avarice of British Merchants";[2] in vain did Butler insist on the essential value of all human labour. Butler thought that as "the labour of a slave in South Carolina was as productive and valuable as that of a freeman in Massachusetts," both should enjoy equal political rights in a "government which was instituted principally for the protection of property."[3]

The Constitution, however, was really favourable to slavery. It perpetuated the distinction between freemen and slaves, though it employed such euphemisms as "those bound to service for a term of years" to describe the

1.—*Records of the Federal Convention,* ed. Max Farrand, vol. ii., p. 371. Because some "Southern gentlemen" disapproved of the strictures passed on George III. for negativing the "repeated repeals of the law which permitted the importation of slaves," they were omitted from the catalogue of grievances in the Declaration of Independence. See *The Jeffersonian Cyclopedia,* ed. Foley, 1900, p. 243.

2.—*Records,* vol. ii., p. 370.

3.—*Sources and Documents,* ed. Morison, p. 268.

latter.[1] The provision in the first article of the Constitution giving three fifths of the negroes representation was, as Gouverneur Morris pointed out in the Convention debates, a direct encouragement to the slave trade.[2] Again, section nine of the first Article,[3] declaring that "no capitation, or other direct tax shall be laid, unless in proportion to the census or enumeration hereinbefore directed to be taken," favoured slavery, because according to section two of the first Article, five negroes were regarded as only equivalent to three whites.

If the framers of the Constitution refrained from calling things by their names, it may be that they felt that the Constitution would outlive slavery ; and that its toleration, as Lord Bacon said of interest-taking, was a concession to men on account of the hardness of their hearts. But that toleration lasted too long. The new inventions and the development of English manufactures gave a fresh impetus to the demand for cheap labour in America, which American capitalists were determined to exploit to the fullest. So that even after the slave trade was abolished in 1808, Virginia found it profitable " to raise a large number of slaves to be sold to the people further South." [4]

The approval of slavery in the middle of the nineteenth century is less easily condoned. When the United States was about to receive the territories of New Mexico and Utah into the Union, it allowed them to join the Union " with or without slavery, as their constitutions should at the time prescribe." [5] It is regrettable that for the continuation of slavery until 19 June, 1862, many Christian bodies must accept some responsibility. The Society of Friends was

---

1.—*Ibid.*, p. 293.

2.—*Sources and Documents*, ed. Morison, p. 274. Art. 1, § ii., § 3, reads : " Representatives and direct taxes shall be apportioned among the several States which may be included within this Union, according to their respective numbers, which shall be determined by adding to the whole number of the free persons, including those bound to service for a term of years, and excluding Indians not taxed, three-fifths of all other persons."—*Sources and Documents*, p. 293.

3.—*Sources and Documents*, p. 298.

4.—*History of North America*, ed. Guy Carlton Lee, vol. vii., p. 44.

5.—Max Farrand, *The Legislation of Congress for the Government of the Organised Territories of the United States, 1789-1895*, 1896, p. 43.

exceptional ; it excluded slaveholders from its membership.
The Rev. James Smylie of Mississippi, who wrote in favour
of negro slavery in the early nineteenth century, gives some
idea of the extent to which slavery was approved by the
members of various denominations. " If slavery," he writes,
" be a sin, and advertising and apprehending slaves with a
view to restore them to their masters, is a direct violation
of the Divine law . . . then three fourths of all the Epis-
copalians, Methodists, Baptists and Presbyterians in Eleven
States of the Union, are of the devil. They hold, if they do
not buy and sell, slaves." [1]

The Constitution not only assumed that property in
human beings is lawful, but it helped to convert the
presumption that property is the reward of industry into a
prejudice against State interference with property, how-
soever acquired.

(3.) THE CONSTITUTION AND SOCIAL POLICY.

The development in the nineteenth century of the
conception of property held when the American Constitution
took shape falls outside the scope of this essay. But theories
must be judged by their application, and the vitality shown
by the philosophy of the eighteenth century is so remarkable
that a few illustrations of it, derived from that period, may
be permitted. The idea that political power was a natural
adjunct of property, particularly of landed property, had
taken deep root in American soil since the seventeenth
century.[2] It was embodied in many of the State constitutions before the Federal Constitution was framed. In
most of the State constitutions in 1787 a man could not vote
unless he possessed a certain amount of real property ; other
States restricted the franchise to tax-payers.[3] To hold office
in the senate or legislature of the various States the property

1.—Cited in *The American Churches, the Bulwarks of American Slavery*, by
an American (E. Habich ?), Newburyport, 1842, p. 29, Brit. Mus., 8156, aa. 8.
2.—See C. Edward Merriam, *A history of American Political Theories*,
1903, p. 193.
3.—*Sources and Documents*, ed. Morison, p. 165.

qualification was naturally much greater. On the whole, owing to the wide distribution of landed property, these restrictions did not prevent government from having a large democratic basis.

The Constitution omitted all reference to property qualifications, either for the exercise of the franchise, or for the holding of office. Gouverneur Morris's suggestion that " if qualifications are proper, he would prefer them in the electors rather than the elected "[1] was unnecessary. Only one branch of the Federal Government, the House of Representatives, could be elected by popular vote, and thus the existing property qualifications demanded by the various State constitutions were a sufficient restriction of the franchise.[2] Thus when the people were asked to express their approbation or disapprobation of Hamilton's " Bill of Rights," many of them were disfranchised by property qualifications. Many of course abstained from voting through lack of interest. Prof. Beard is of the opinion that the Constitution was ratified by a vote of probably not more than one sixth of the adult males of the country.[3]

The Constitution made no contribution to the theory of property. It contained no provision whereby the growth of anti-social property rights might be checked. Congress is not permitted to employ readily equitable methods of taxation. Ardent advocates of the Constitution like Hamilton, while conceding that the Federal Government should have the power of imposing direct taxes, believed that that power ought not to be exercised except as an emergency measure, and then only after taking a new census of the population of each State.[4] " No capitation or other direct

1.—*Records of the Federal Convention*, ed. Max Farrand, vol. ii., p. 121. Morris thought that if votes were given to people without property they would sell them to the rich. We must look to the future. " The time is not distant when this country will abound with mechanics and manufacturers who will receive their bread from their employers. Will such men be the secure and faithful guardians of liberty "? Such " ignorant " and " dependent " people " can be as little trusted with the public interest " as children.—*Sources and Documents*, ed. Morison, p. 276.

2.—See Charles A. Beard, *An Economic Interpretation of the Constitution of the United States*, New York, 1913, p. 168.

3.—*Op. cit.*, pp. 324-5.

4.—*The Federalist*, n. 36, Everyman's Library, pp. 172-175.

tax shall be laid unless in proportion to the census or enumeration herein before directed to be taken."[1]

Hamilton was merely giving expression to a pious wish when he wrote : "Happy it is when the interest which the government has in the preservation of its own power coincides with a proper distribution of the public burdens, and tends to guard the least wealthy part of the community from oppression."[2] The cast iron character of the Constitution, however, really impeded the adoption of methods of taxation which would reduce, if not remove, such "oppression." An Income Tax, which had actually become law in 1894, was declared unconstitutional by the Supreme Court on the grounds that it exempted incomes below a certain point, and because such an exemption was believed to be a contravention of that article in the Constitution stating that no direct tax shall be laid except in proportion to the population of each State. It was not, as is well known, until 1913 that the Federal Constitution was amended to allow the levying of income tax by Congress.

A better illustration of the extreme individualism with regard to property rights which the Constitution fostered may be found in the struggles between Labour and Capital in the nineteenth century. With the exception perhaps of the continuation of negroe slavery, the most striking feature of nineteenth century America is the comparative absence of social legislation. This is all the more remarkable when one remembers that from the middle of the century it was becoming far more industrialised and politically democratic. Frontier conditions of life in the Western and Southern states, combined with the growth of industrial classes, gave rise to a wave of democratic individualism in the first half of the century which enabled Andrew Jackson[3] to carry out important reforms.

Whatever democracy exists in the United States to-day, though some see in it little more than a " nebulous political

1.—The Federal Constitution, art. 1, § ix., § 4 and Cf. art. 1, § ii., § 3. in *Sources and Documents*, (Morison), p. 298 and p. 293.

2.—*The Federalist*, n. 36, Everyman's Library, p. 174.

3.—For an account of Jackson see De Tocqueville, *Democracy in America*, tr. 1838, vol. ii., p. 294.

liturgy,"[1] is mainly due to the reforms carried out by President Jackson in face of the opposition of typical Federalists like Henry Clay and Daniel Webster, who denounced manhood suffrage and claimed that wealth should rule.[2] It was Jackson who abolished property qualifications for the exercise of the franchise, and, thanks to his influence, property qualifications for holding office disappeared in practically all the States about the middle of the century.[3]

But wealth in all ages is power, and those who possess it can have a big say in the councils of a nation. And so, in a few decades after Jackson's reforms, we find that the forces which were supposed to be dead were but sleeping. Just three years after the emancipation of the negro population an Amendment was added to the Constitution, ostensibly to safeguard the new freedom of the negroes, but in reality to restrict the legislative powers of the various States, particularly with regard to property rights. The famous Fourteenth Amendment of 1868 declared that : " No State shall make or enforce any law which shall abridge the privileges or immunities of the citizens of the United States ; *nor shall any State deprive any person of life, liberty or property, without due process of law.*"[4]

What this eventually meant in practice was that the Supreme Court assumed the right to review all State legislation, including legislation affecting property rights. This Amendment to the Constitution, or rather the interpretation of it which gained ground after 1873, proved a serious obstacle to the growth of social legislation in the United States. One of the best known early illustrations of the Supreme Court's interference with the economic legislation of the States occurred in 1889.[5] The State of Minnesota

1.—See John G. Brooks, *Labor's Challenge to the Social Order*, N.Y., 1920, p. 136.
2.—Cf. *The Life and Letters of Harrison Gray Otis*, ed. Samuel Eliot Morison, 1913, vol. ii., p. 308.
3.—A few States, like Delaware and Massachusetts, retained the property qualification for office until the end of the nineteenth century.
4.—*Sources and Documents*, ed. Morison, p. 365. My italics.
5.—For a detailed account of these facts see Charles A. Beard, *Contemporary American History*, New York, 1920, pp. 73f. For a fuller discussion of the Fourteenth Amendment the reader should consult Rev. Dr. John A. Ryan, *Declining Liberty and Other Papers*, N.Y., 1927, chs. i. and xxi.

had made a law conferring power upon a Railway Commission to fix "reasonable rates." The Commission accordingly fixed a certain price for the transportation of milk between two places. The Chicago, Milwaukee and St. Paul Railway Company refused to put the recommendation of the Commission into effect, protesting that the rate fixed was too low. The Commission applied to the Supreme Court with the result that the majority of the latter decided against the Commission ; declaring its action unconstitutional. The Court held that it was a deprivation of property " without due process of law," and, therefore, in opposition to the Fourteenth Amendment.

The economic anarchy, the disordered currency schemes, and the repudiation of debts which prevailed before the Civil War, may, as some think,[1] have rendered the assumption of some such power by the Supreme Court inevitable. Its exercise, however, was not always conducive to social solidarity. Indeed, it may fairly be doubted whether, on the whole, the action of the Supreme Court in checking social legislation has not diminished rather than increased that reasonable respect for private property rights which is an indispensable condition of any civilised community. The driving forces behind the Fourteenth Amendment, as Roscoe Conkling who served on the committee which drafted it admitted in 1882, were rich individuals and joint-stock companies who felt that their property rights were being too closely scrutinised by State legislatures.[2]

These circumstances, however, might not have so materially affected the working of the Amendment had not the judges of the Supreme Court allowed their decisions to be coloured by their own social philosophy. In all essentials it differed but little from that which the fathers of the American Constitution had learned from Locke ; and it was probably inevitable that the Amendment should have been utilised as a barrier against social legislation and labour organisations

1.—Beard, *Op. cit.*, pp. 86-7.
2.—Beard, *Op. cit.*, p. 57. Taylor, *Origin and Growth of the American Constitution*, p. 355.

when the need for both was becoming more urgent. The consequences of their attitude were, however, extremely unfortunate.

The immense expansion which took place in the agricultural, industrial, and financial life of the United States during the second half of the last century has tended to make people forget the shadows in that picture of progress. In the race for industrial leadership, however, many a home was ruined, and many a property right set at nought. The unscrupulous methods generally employed to convert the proprietors of small and medium-sized businesses into cogs of a mammoth trust machine are features of American industrial development which one might forget, if the evils which they caused did not live after them. Through such devices as " stock-watering " a large amount of fictitious property claims exists in the United States to-day.[1] The consuming public, especially the poorer classes, are thus the victims of a species of forced taxation. They are made to pay millions of dollars annually, in higher prices, to procure dividends on shares which are non-existent, or which represent no objective economic service.[2]

Of course, the Supreme Court, charged as it was with safe-guarding property as well as other rights, frequently and effectively exercised its good offices to check unfair competition. But the evils which it checked in one sphere were, perhaps, of less moment than the good which it prevented in another. America's adaptive genius, so quick to seize on what was valuable in English industrial machinery, was blocked from learning a lesson from the social machinery which England, as the result of a painful experience, had come to regard as essential to social progress. It was not until the Roosevelt administration that the United States began to tread the paths blazed by England and Germany in the realm of social legislation. Audacious and pioneering in economic practice, it was timidly conservative in economic and political thought. In the complex industrial

---

1.—" Stock-watering " of course is not peculiar to the United States. For the moral aspect of it, see John A. Ryan, *Distributive Justice*, 1916, ch. xix.

2.—Cf. Beard, *Op. cit.*, p. 236.

environment of the late nineteenth century it still clung, tenaciously if unconsciously, to political categories which had been forged in the England of the seventeenth century, and which England had long discarded.

Even in the twentieth century examples are not wanting of the arbitrary manner in which the Supreme Court's power of judicial review has blocked social legislation. In 1905 a law passed by the State of New York, prohibiting the manufacture of cigars under unhygienic conditions, was declared null and void by the Court. The same year a Pennslyvania law, prohibiting the payment of wages in "scrip" or store orders, met with a similar fate.[1] These laws, in the opinion of the majority of the Court, were unconstitutional. They deprived the employer of property, and the labourer of liberty, without due process of law. It is obvious that both property and liberty required new definitions ; but the pronouncements of the judges, like the stars, afforded little light because they were too high. For the judges all forms of property were equally sacred ; no attempt was made to distinguish between those property rights which support and those which stifle liberty. They were satisfied with enumerating the fundamental rights of the individual to life, liberty, and property. They assumed that because the right of property normally includes the right to make contracts, the latter should be subject to as little regulation as possible. The labour contract, in particular, was too sacred to be supervised by trade unions, much less by the State.

It is, perhaps, not surprising that in the present century the American worker has had a rude awakening. His hopes of securing some economic independence must be greatly shattered when he sees a few large corporations completely, or partially, controlling the production of a variety of articles ranging from "iron and steel to candy, from locomotives to tin cans, and from beef to buttons."[2] Some Americans are even beginning to doubt whether the existing economic

1.—See Beard, *Op. cit.*, pp. 88f.
2.—Frank T. Carlton, *The History and Problems of Organised Labour,* 1920, p. 70.

dependence of many on the property of a few does not make American democracy a somewhat nebulous affair.

Such developments of American social philosophy and social practice are not, however, the result of accident. On the contrary, however influenced by the economic environment and by political conditions, they spring logically and naturally from the conceptions of property and of social relations which were held in America in the formative period in the closing years of the eighteenth century. The individualistic philosophy which inspired them had received its classical expression in England in the work of Locke. That philosophy, transplanted to America, was crystallized in the Constitution of the United States, and even three quarters of a century later, in spite of the immense economic changes of the intervening period, determined, however unconscious of it they might be, the intellectual attitude of the statesmen who drafted the Fourteenth Amendment and of the judges who interpreted it. Admirably adapted though it was to the requirements of a community of landowners and farmers, master craftsmen and merchants, who formed the majority of the population of the United States in 1800, its appropriateness to the conditions of an industrial civilisation is less evident. Looking back on the history of America in the past half century, one is inclined to think that the fears entertained by Henry in the Virginia Ratifying Convention, as to the probable effect of the working of the Constitution on " the middling and lower class,"[1] have not been unjustified.

It is hardly possible, indeed, to study the social history of America since the Revolution without being impressed by the extent to which Locke's individualism, his glorification of property rights and his love of commerce, have been interwoven into the economic and social texture of American life.[2]

1.—*Sources and Documents*, ed. Morison, p. 329. In the course of his speech Henry said, "And yet who knows the dangers that this new system may produce ? They are out of the sight of the common people : . . . . I dread the operation of it on the middling and lower class . . . . ."

2.—The American labour movement shows the effects of the same intellectual influence ; the right wing, A.F. of L. accepting naively the existing order, and the left wing, I.W.W., revolting more or less blindly against it. See *Voice of Labour*, (American), June, 1905; Dr. Paul F. Brissenden, *The I.W.W.*, 1920.

On the question whether this coincidence amounts to a causal connection it is unnecessary to dogmatise, as there were many other factors favourable to the development of a highly individualistic view of property and social relations. Some of the most ardent promoters of the Constitution, as we saw, were men who feared rather than favoured a very unequal distribution of wealth. Certainly in the eighteenth century, Locke's idea that property is the reward of labour appealed as much to the American mind as the view that it was an absolute right. Indeed, one might say that the latter view was largely held as a consequence of the former. Two sets of circumstances, however, tended to make the theory of the absolute character of all property rights prevail : the quarrel with England over taxation and other questions, leading up to the War of Independence ; and the social disturbances which followed on its termination.

It seems, at first, surprising that Harrington's views on the necessity of a well distributed system of property for social welfare, so well known to eighteenth century Americans, did not exercise a more salutary influence in the nineteenth century. The reason, perhaps, was due to the fact that he forgot to emphasise the disadvantages which may arise from inequalities in the distribution of property other than that of land. And so America, that took a leaf out of his book to regulate her land system, neglected the most important lesson which the *Oceana* contained when she set her face towards a capitalist civilisation. Had James Otis's criticism of the undue influence commanded by the mere possession of property been taken to heart, the balance of property might be much different in America from what it is to-day. And some Americans might not be less really great for practising some of that renunciation with which " life properly speaking " not only begins,[1] but continues.

Despite the fact that the leeway in social legislation has been made up in recent years and despite the high standard of comfort enjoyed by many of its people, America tends to-day, probably more than in the time when Otis or De Tocqueville

1. —Cf. Carlyle, " Sartor Resartus " in *Works*, 1870, vol. i., p. 184.

lived, to be a land where "riches are sought after" without much "concern about the right application of them." [1] America is still "a land of wonders" where every movement seems an improvement.[2] But the reign of social peace there, to which some early nineteenth century writers looked forward, is still far from realisation. Yet that fact does not discourage numerous Europeans from gladly exchanging the certainties of home life for the "excellent uncertainties" of American skies.

1.—Otis, *Op. cit.*, p. 8. De Tocqueville writes : "I know no country indeed where the love of money has taken stronger hold on the affections of men."—*Democracy in America*, tr. H. Reeve, 1838, vol. i., p. 45. It must, however, be admitted that many American business men love business for its own sake. And Europeans, as well as Americans, are greatly indebted to some millionares of the New World who have utilised their vast fortunes to promote knowledge, peace, and charity. Again the generous manner in which the American public responds to charitable appeals from any quarter of the globe is too well known to need extended notice.

2.—See De Tocqueville, *Op. cit.*, vol. ii., p. 309.

CHAPTER VI.

THE FRENCH CONTRAST.

THE outlook and institutions of the French people in the eighteenth century offer many interesting points of contrast to those of England during the same period. Calvinistic Protestantism, while exercising a powerful influence in many directions on English life, had left the practical optimism of its people untouched.[1] Despite, or as a result of, the religious and constitutional struggles of the previous century, England, in the eighteenth century, presents the spectacle of a country satisfied with its lot and confident in its future. Broadly viewed, its philosophy is one of repose while that of its French neighbours is one of restlessness and, at times, of pessimism. Intellectually, though not politically, one might almost say that France suffered from an "inferiority complex." Voltaire who had travelled in order to laugh at men, and Montesquieu who had travelled in order to instruct them, were both eloquent in their praise of English thought and English institutions.[2]

The two subjects, religion and government, which mainly occupied the attention of French writers in the eighteenth century, were, as practical problems, settled in England at the Revolution. For France, however, these questions had far more than the academic interest which was taken in them in England. However abstract and fantastic the garb it assumed at times, French thought was directed primarily to practical objects. Its philosophy was highly polemical.

1.—Cf. Charles de Rémusat, *L'Angleterre au xviiie siècle*, 1856, vol. i., p. 55.
2.—For Montesquieu's comments on the English character, see J. Churton Collins, *Voltaire, Montesquieu and Rousseau in England*, 1908, p. 138. An interesting account of the influence which the reports of French travellers in the seventeenth century had on the critical spirit of French writers in the eighteenth century is given in G. Atkinson, *Les relations de voyages du xviie siècle et l'évolution des idées*, (Paris, no date).

Political despotism was attacked in the name of individual liberty and democratic government, and supernatural religion was opposed by systems of natural morality. The unsettled character of speculative philosophy, resulting from the difficulties suggested by the systems of Descartes and Locke, gave a new impetus to the study of the practical sciences like Ethics, Politics and Physics.[1] Voltaire pronounced the study of metaphysics worthless. Man cannot know the ultimate nature of things ; he can only " calculate, measure, weigh, and expand." [2] Locke's empiricism and Descartes's rationalism, however, left their impress on political and social philosophy as well. If Montesquieu and Rousseau represent the eighteenth century in so far as political and social ideas in France are concerned,[3] it must not be forgotten that they are, in many respects, representative of two rival schools of thought. In Montesquieu we find some of Locke's realism, whereas in Rousseau it is Descartes's disregard of history and tradition which is, perhaps, most manifest.

Montesquieu, Voltaire, and Rousseau were the three great intellectual forces which contributed to that break with history known as the French Revolution. Each of these writers, however, contributed in an utterly different way to that result, and the influence of all three was strengthened immensely by the religious and economic conditions of France in the eighteenth century. History, which at all times is an object lesson, becomes at certain stages a judgement. Frenchmen, having before them Montesquieu's account of the political institutions of other countries in various epochs, were naturally led to pass judgement on their own. His great work *L'Esprit des Lois*, published anonymously in 1748, was far more than a collection of essays on the English Constitution.[4] Like Voltaire he was impressed by the respect

1.—Although Physics deals with material objects rather than human actions, one may regard it as a practical science in the sense that the progress of human society is bound up with man's knowledge of the secrets of nature.

2.—Voltaire, *Candide ou l'Optimisme*, ed. André Morize, Paris, 1913, p. xxi.

3.—See Ad. Franck, *Réformateurs et Publicistes de l'Europe : dix-huitième siècle*, Paris, 1893, p. xv.

4.—See Joseph Dedieu, *Montesquieu et la tradition politique anglaise en France*, 1909. Jules Barni, *Histoire des idées morales et politiques en France au dix-huitième siècle*, Paris, 1865, vol. i., pp. 17f.

for liberty and property which obtained in England.[1]   Both
writers were anxious to see the cultivators of the soil in France
enjoy some of that security which property owners enjoyed
in England.   They were, however, conservative critics of
private property rather than standard bearers of a radical
social theory.   Voltaire liked to point out the conditions
under which the establishment of peasant proprietorship
might prove beneficial to the crown, namely, if it led to the
creation of a more powerful army, and to an increase in the
revenues of the State.   But, he adds, a " firm and wise
government " ought " to fix the extent of lands which wealthy
plebeians may be allowed to purchase." [2]

The object of this chapter is to give a short account of
social thought in France in the eighteenth century, with
special reference to the influence of Locke's views on property.
And as the agrarian privileges of feudalism were one of the
driving forces of the Revolution, and the occasion of most
of the discussions on property which arose, some account of
the land question, however brief, must be included.   The
parliamentary debates of the French Revolution, and the
legislation of 1789, will also be examined briefly with a view
to illustrating the various strands of opinion with regard to
the right of private property.

(1.) THE MAIN CURRENTS OF THOUGHT.

If Locke may justly be regarded as one of the principal
writers who influenced political thought in eighteenth century
France, a corresponding position cannot be attributed to him
in the sphere of social theory.   It was not until the French
Revolution, in its social aspect, threatened to become something more than a movement for the abolition of feudal
privileges that his theory of property, at least, may be said
to have commanded attention.   Up to that time his theory

1.—Voltaire, *A Philosophical Dictionary*, 1764, English tr. 1843, " ' Liberty
and Property ' is the great national cry of the English .   .   . it is the cry of
Nature."—vol. ii., p. 362.   See also his *Lettres Philosophiques*, ed. Gustave
Lanson, 1909, vol. i., Letter x., pp. 120f.

2.—*A Philosophical Dictionary*, vol. ii., p. 364.

of property was hardly discussed in France, though from about the middle of the century the Physiocrats were giving firm but uninfluential expression to the absolute aspect of individual property rights which English writers, on the whole, had accepted as the proper interpretation of Locke's theory. If one excepts a few like Barbeyrac, who in a note on Puffendorf's theory of property quoted and accepted Locke's labour theory,[1] one finds very little mention of Locke's name in connection with property theories in the first half of the century. Indeed, up to the time of the appearance of Rousseau's *Discours sur l'inégalité*[2] and Morelly's *Code de la Nature*[3] in 1755, French writers seemed more interested in the metaphysical than in the social and political elements of Locke's philosophy. The *Essay on the Human Understanding*, translated by the Frenchman Pierre Coste under Locke's own supervision, had a considerable vogue on the continent even in Locke's lifetime. That book raised issues which dwarfed into insignificance such mundane topics as property. Even Voltaire, who boasted that he had introduced Locke to the French public, appears to have been more interested in Locke's views on the question as to whether matter could be brought to think than he was in his theory of property.[4] Although Locke's second treatise on *Civil*

1.—See Puffendorf, *Law of Nature and Nations*, English tr. Kennet, 1749, bk. iv., ch. iv., sec. 13, p. 376 note. For the differences between Quesnay and Locke see the important article " Les fondements philosophiques de l'économie politique de Quesnay et de Smith," by W. Hasbach, in *Revue d'Economie Politique*, Sept.-Oct., 1893, pp. 747f. Hasbach thinks that Quesnay's views on property and economic and social theory owed more to Bishop Cumberland, and to the German philosopher Wolff, than to Locke.— *Loc. cit.*, pp. 764-5.

2.—See *The Political Writings of J. J. Rousseau*, ed. C. E. Vaughan, 1915, vol. i., p. 169.

3.—Édition quoted Edouard Dolléans, Paris, 1910. André Lichtenberger, *Le Socialisme au xviiie siècle*, Paris, 1895, ch. iv., p. 114, styles Morelly's work " the great socialistic book of the eighteenth century." I desire to acknowledge my indebtedness to M. Lichtenberger's book, particularly for the valuable bibliography which it contains. The proposal to establish the *vingtième* and the State's claim to tax the property of the clergy about 1750 gave rise to new discussions on the nature and extent of individual property rights. See Lichtenberger, *Op. cit.*, p. 14.

4.—*Lettres Philosophiques*, ed. Lanson, vol. i., Lettre xiii., p. 170. It was through Bolingbroke's residence in France early in the century that France first became acquainted with English ideas. See E. J. B. Rathery, *Des relations sociales et intellectuelles entre la France et l'Angleterre depuis la conquête des Normands jusqu' à la Révolution française*, Paris, 1856, pp. 92-95.

Government, containing the chapter on property, was published
in French at Amsterdam [1] before the close of the seventeenth
century, it does not seem to have been generally known in
France judging by Linguet's confession in 1767 that he had
not read Locke and that he was unaware of the existence
of a French translation of the book.[2]   A century before
Linguet wrote, the most exclusive intellectual body in
France, the Academy of Sciences, regretted its inability to
find a man sufficiently acquainted with English to review
the scientific books which poured steadily from its younger
but more prolific sister foundation, the Royal Society.[3]   And
Abbé Le Blanc in 1747 was implicitly condemning the
linguistic lethargy of his countrymen when he stated that
" the English translate all that is published in French." [4]   In
the latter half of the century the balance was redressed.   The
effects of Voltaire's propaganda work for English ideas were
manifest in the economic and political sphere by the translation of Hume's *Essays* in 1752, and Josiah Child's treatise
on *Commerce* in 1754.

The latter treatise had a special significance for many
French writers, because it raised the question of the extent
of the rights of property in capital.   Child was one of those
seventeenth century English writers who urged the government to reduce by statute the rate of interest in England in
order that its merchants might compete successfully with
those of Holland.   He failed to see that the low rate of
interest in Holland was an effect rather than a cause of the
prosperity of that country.   The controversy about usury
in France forms not the least interesting illustration of the
collisions between the survivals of the past and the thought

1.—Jean Le Clerc, *Bibliothèque Choisie*, Amsterdam, 1705, t. vi., art. v.,
p. 380.   See the *Avertissement* to apparently the first translation of
Locke's *Civil Government* published in France by D. Mazel in 1795.   Cf.
Henri Marion, *J. Locke, sa vie, son oeuvre*, 1893, p. ii.
2.—Simon N. H. Linguet, *Théorie des Loix Civiles*, London, 1767, vol. ii.,
ch. xv., p. 83.
3.—See Rathery, *Op. cit.*, p. 51.   Cf.   Charles Bastide, *The Anglo-French
Entente in the Seventeenth Century*, London, 1914, ch. ii., p. 19.
4.—*Letters on the English and French Nations*, Dublin, 1747, vol. ii., Letter
lxvii., p. 78.   The Abbé says that the French books he saw in London
" dishonour our nation."   Frenchmen had become " philosophers in trifles
and triflers in philosophy."—*Ibid.*, vol. ii., Letter xc., p. 254.

of the eighteenth century. It was re-opened by Holden's contention in the seventeenth century that the interest contract was not opposed to the natural law.[1] The animated discussion, to which the question of interest-taking gave rise, forms a striking contrast to England where the problem was settled for over a century in favour of the practice.

The strict mediaeval teaching on usury was stated with great vigour by Du Tertre in 1673 [2] in reply to Chaduc's qualified approval of interest.[3] And the eloquent Bossuet,[4] despite his admiration for the new Cartesian philosophy, was a sturdy champion of the old philosophy of property also. Fundamentally, the question of the lawfulness of interest-taking is a question of the 'limits of the right of private property.[5] To his Catholic brethren, no less than to his Protestant neighbours, he must have appeared reaction incarnate. The conflict between the old and the new, the strict and the liberal views, are illustrated by the works of Thornentier and Le Correur.[6] The former quotes St. Chrysostom's saying that " in the case of money, it is impossible for one person to get rich without making another poor," [7] while the latter refers to St. Antonino's broad

1.—For a history of the controversy see Jules Favre, *Le prêt à intérêt dans l'ancienne France*, Paris, 1900, pp. 154f. The starting point of the seventeenth century controversy was the publication in 1546 of Molinaeus (Dumoulin), *Tractatus Commerciorum et Usurarum*. See *Op. cit.*, p. 31.

2.—Du Tertre, pseud. for Le P. Jacques Thornentier, *L'Usure Expliquée et condamnée*, Paris, 1673. An echo of this controversy in England was found in John Dormer, S.J., *Usury explained ; or Conscience quieted in the case of putting out money at Interest*, London, 1695-6, by Philopones. Reprint in 1699 as *A Vindication of the practice of England in putting out money at use*, and also in 1817, under the original title, *Usury Explained*. See *The Pamphleteer*, 1818, vol. xi., n. 21, pp. 165f. It was translated into Latin by Dr. Hawarden in 1701, and was condemned by the Holy Office in Rome on October 11th, 1703. See *Index Librorum*, Romae, 1925, p. 408.

3.—P. Chaduc, *Lettre d'un Théologien*, 1671. See preface to Thornentier, *Op. cit.*, p. iii. Chaduc held that interest was lawful in the case of loans to the rich and, generally, as long as charity is observed.

4.—*Traité de l'Usure*, 1682.

5.—See the article by Rev. Dr. John A. Ryan, " The Unilluminated Interest Question " in *America*, N. York, June 18, 1921, pp. 203f.

6.—*Traité de la pratique des Billets entre les Négocians*, Louvain, 1682.

7.—*Op. cit.*, Paris, 1673, p. 165. Du Tertre, wrote Dormer in 1695, " pretends with a scrap or two of a holy father to block up the way to heaven, and to exclude all merchants and tradesmen from eternal bliss."—*The Pamphleteer*, vol. xi., n. 21, p. 211.

definition of usury with approval.[1]   Le Correur points out
that St. Thomas's ideas on usury were formulated in an age
when the opportunities for the profitable or productive
employment of money were the exception rather than the
rule.[2]   Le Correur was merely restating the liberal doctrine
on usury which was held by sixteenth century writers like
Molina, Cajetan, and Sylvius.[3]   Both he and they agreed,
however, that to exact anything over and above the principal
of a loan, solely on account of the act of lending, was unlawful
and opposed to the teaching of the Church.[4]

In France we find laymen as well as clerics participating
in the debate.   Towards the end of the seventeenth century

1.—Le Correur, *Op. cit.*, p. 17, " L'usure," says Le Correur, " est un profit,
que l'on prétend tirer d'une chose, principalement parcequ' on l'a prestée."—
Op. cit., p. 27.

2.—When St. Thomas described usury as the price paid for the use of money,
the use of money then meant the "usage de consomption & de destruction,"
and not the " usage d'emploi & d'accroissement."—*Op. cit.*, pp. 18-19.

3.—The best study of this subject from the Catholic standpoint is that
by Dr., now Cardinal, van Roey, *De Justo Auctario ex Contractu Crediti*,
Louvain, 1903. See *Op. cit.*, pp. 4, 208 *et passim*.   For a good account in
English of the theological aspects of money-lending see Rev. Dr. Patrick
Cleary, *The Church and Usury*, Dublin, 1914.

4.—It is only on account of the existence of so many extrinsic titles and the
State's recognition of these titles that the Church to-day lays down the general
rule that those who take interest for loans are not to be disquieted.   The
modern mind tends to get impatient with a theory which historically seems
to have been overladen with cumbrous distinctions, and was often boldly
ignored in practice.   The nature of money was tolerably well understood by
Aristotle.—" By wealth we mean all the things whose value is measured by
money."—Aristotle, *Ethic., Nic.*, iv., 1, 1119b-26 ; cited and adopted by
St. Thomas in *Summa* 2.2, q. 78, *a* 2.   If money, as Sigismund Scaccia, the
Italian jurist, stated in the sixteenth century (*Tractatus de Commerciis et
Cambio*, Cologne, 1620, q. vii., part ii., p. 314), virtually includes everything,
being a generic name for all forms of property on account of its general
purchasing power, it seems unreasonable to discriminate morally between the
incomes derived from loans and the rents derived from letting a house or a
piece of land.   Had a Marshall or Böhm-Bawerk lived in those ages of controversy, they would have shown that some interest is founded on the nature
of things, and on the nature of man, because the element of time affects the
value of money or capital quite apart from the risk which may be involved
in lending it.   While the controversies waged over interest have often been
more conspicuous for heat than for light, it must not be forgotten that, even
in this age of " progress," the number of people who often require money to
meet pressing wants—the normal function of loans in the Middle Ages—is
much greater than even six centuries ago.   For such people the productivity
of capital, so much elaborated by economists and so little understood, at
times, by socialists and moralists, has no practical meaning.   The case
against the modern practice of tolerating interest is ably stated by Dr. Henri
Savatier, *La théorie moderne du Capital et la Justice*, Paris, 1898, p. 13,
et passim.

Domat, the jurist, declared usury "naturally unlawful" and destructive of social order.[1] In our period Montesquieu and others attempted to secularise the discussion. The influence of the traditional theory of the unlawfulness of interest was so great, however, that the Civil law prohibiting it was not abolished in France until 1795.[2] Montesquieu, in words similar to those employed by Bacon and Locke, stated that "the affairs of society" will always make lending a necessity, and that, therefore, the lending of money without interest must be regarded as a "counsel of religion" rather than as a matter for legal compulsion.[3] On the other hand, some writers condemned interest-taking on social as well as on religious grounds. Thus Étienne Souchet[4] in 1776 maintained that interest was not only against the natural and divine law, but opposed to the welfare of society. It promoted idleness ; increased the cost of production of commodities ; and raised the prices of goods consumed by the workers.[5] He thought that the connection between the payment of interest and the volume of accumulation was exaggerated.[6] Savings would not be diminished by the abolition of interest, and capital would not emigrate from France because the French people are slow to invest their money abroad, particularly in Protestant countries.[7]

1.—*The Civil Law in its natural order together with the Publick Law*, English tr. Wm. Strahan, London, 1722, vol. i., p. 123. The punishments for usury in France, he tells us, were, for the first offence, " a publick acknowledgement of the offence, in an ignominious manner ; which in France is called *L'Amende Honorable*, and Banishment moreover. And the second offence is Death."— vol. i., p. 127. Cf. Count de Boulainvilliers, *Mémoires présentés à Monseigneur le Duc d'Orléans*, Hague & Amsterdam, 1727, vol. i., p. 15, " Usury is not one of the legitimate ways by which to acquire riches."

2.—Favre, *Op. cit.*, p. 265. The law of 25th April, 1795, gave full liberty to contract for interest. An attempt to fix a legal rate of interest for commercial loans was made in 1807, but was abolished in 1886.

3.—*Works*, English tr. 1777, vol. ii., bk. xxii., ch. xix., p. 111. Cf. Bacon, *Essays*, " Chandos Classics," 1888, p. 75. . . . " For since there must be borrowing and lending, and men are so hard of heart as they will not lend freely usury must be permitted."

4.—*Traité de l'Usure*, Paris, 1776, Bibl. Nat. Souchet was an "Avocat en Parlement." The treatise was meant to serve as " a reply to a letter on this subject published in 1770 under the name of M. Prost de Royer . . .; and to an anonymous treatise on the same subject published at Cologne, 1769."

5.—*Op. cit.*, p. 6, p. 136.

6.—*Op. cit.*, ch. vii., p. 134.

7.—*Ibid*, p. 135. Cf. Abbé de La Porte, *Principes théologiques et civiles sur l'usure*, Paris, 1769, vol. i., p. 157.

One of the most interesting features of the *vis inertiae* of French social theory, so to speak, is afforded by the attitude of even the Physiocrats, as a whole, towards the question of usury. With the exception of Turgot, who rather resented being classed with the "sect," most Physiocratic writers adopted a very vague and halting attitude towards interest-taking. The Marquis de Mirabeau is as much opposed to interest as Turgot is in favour of it. Mirabeau quoted scriptural texts to re-enforce his arguments against interest-taking, which were based mostly on social grounds.[1] He seems to have accepted the full logical consequences of the doctrine, admitted by most of the Physiocrats, that labour is the only real title to property, and land the basis of all wealth.[2] If the cultivators of the soil feed all other classes, the latter must not be permitted to live on money obtained without personal effort. The *rentier* class is his *bête-noire.*[3] There should be no "fortunes steriles" or, as some modern writers would have said, "functionless property." All classes must perform certain duties.[4] Social Justice demands that the real wealth producers, those who labour on the land, should be supplied with free credit.[5]

Another Physiocratic writer, Clicquot-Blervaché,[6] notwithstanding his advocacy of freedom of labour and freedom of contract, and his opposition to the artificial regulations of the eighteenth century generally, also held rather uncertain views about interest. Labour for him was the fundamental fact in society, and property and wealth were its reward. His book *Le taux de l'intérêt de l'argent* (1755)[7] was the outcome of the renewed interest in the question of usury which the translation of Hume's and Child's works on the

1.—*Philosophie Rurale*, Amsterdam, 1766, vol. i., pp. 268f.
2.—*Ibid.*, vol. i., p. 128.
3.—*Ibid.*, vol. i., p. 259.
4.—*Ibid.*, vol. i., pp. 133-134.
5.—*Ibid.*, vol. i., p. 268. M. Gide in Gide-Rist, *History of Economic Doctrines,* 1919, p. 32, thinks that Mirabeau would admit "that whenever a real increase of wealth resulted from the use of capital, as in agriculture, the payment of interest was only just." M. Gide, however, does not furnish any evidence or reference in support of this statement.
6.—Extracts from his work are printed in Jules de Vroil, *Etude sur Clicquot-Blervaché, économiste du xviii⁰ siècle*, Paris, 1870.
7.—See Jules de Vroil, *Op. cit.*, ch. i., for extracts.

subject occasioned. The subject of the book was suggested by the Academy of Amiens which, like the modern " Pollak Foundation," believed that good research work needed the stimulus of a prize. He set out to prove that all interest is " an impost which the idle levy on industry," [1] but he assumes rather than proves that all lenders are parasites. Finally, he seems to confine his attack to *haut intérêt* rather than to *tout intérêt*.[2] Legislative interference with the rate of interest has often been inopportune, but he thinks the time is ripe in France for the State to reduce, by statute, the existing rate of interest. Long before Turgot's plea for freedom with regard to interest, Bouché de Pavillon [3] pointed out that the rate of interest, like the price of everything else, was governed by the natural laws of demand and supply, and that State regulation could never permanently override these laws.

Turgot was definitely in favour of interest ; [4] and in this he differs from Quesnay who extended only a very qualified approval to it. For Quesnay interest is justified when the owner of capital foregoes, by lending it, the profit which he could procure from investing it in land.[5] Provided, therefore, that the money lent for industrial or commercial purposes led to an increase in the net product (*produi net*), interest was legitimate. But incomes or interest derived from loans to the State he classed as " *fortunes steriles*," and that species of loan which led to " tax-farming " [6] was particularly abominable. Turgot's characterisation of usury legislation as proper only to the " centuries of ignorance " [7] betrays,

---

1.—*Loc. cit.*, p. 4.

2.—*Loc. cit.*, p. 8.

3.—*L'Essai sur les causes de la diversité des taux d'intérêt de l'argent chez les peuples*, 1757, extracts printed in Jules de Vroil, *Loc. cit.*, pp. 19-24.

4.—" Mémoire sur les prêts d'argent," 1769, printed in *Oeuvres de Bentham*, 1828, vol. xii., pp. 202f. See also his *Reflections on the Production and Distribution of Wealth*, 1766, in Economic Classics, ed. Ashley, pp. 74f.

5.—Quesnay, " Observations sur l'intérêt de l'argent," 1766, in *Oeuvres Economiques et Philosophiques de F. Quesnay*, ed. Auguste Oncken, Paris, 1888, pp. 401f.—" Nothing except land and water can really produce an income. . . . Hence the excuse for lending money at interest can, in the order of nature and justice, be based only on the conformity of this interest with the income which can be acquired by purchasing land. For it is impossible to imagine any other income which one can acquire for money without unjustly taking from another what belongs to him."

6.—*Maximes*, ed. Oncken, p. 337.

7.—*Mémoire*, in *Loc. cit.*, p. 220.

however, a very unhistorical mind. The divergency of opinion on the question of interest even amongst writers who, in the main, believed that the unhampered pursuit of individual self-interest involved in some mysterious way the realisation of justice for all, illustrates the strong hold which the traditional theory of property, taught by the Church, had on the French mind.

That theory was opposed alike to the pretensions of the legists, who exalted the King's right over all property,[1] and to the extravagant doctrine of Morelly,[2] and others, who asserted that the right of private property ought not to extend to anything beyond what is " actually being used " by the individual.   Thus the Church taught that the individual had a right to private property quite independent of the *beneplacitum* of the King or the State.   Its doctrine differed, therefore, from that held by Grotius and Puffendorf which had many adherents in France during the eighteenth century.   But while denying that the right of private property was a mere social convention, the Church continued to emphasise the social character of wealth ; the right of the poor to succour from the rich ; and the unlawfulness of excessive wealth accumulation.[3]   However much the lives of individual ecclesiastics might at times contradict that Christian philosophy of property, the Church, as a body, continued to teach the duties of ownership and to warn the rich that their wealth might easily prove an occasion of sin. Thus in the *Catéchisme des Riches*,[4] published with

1.—See Charles Gérin, *Recherches Historiques sur l'Assemblée du Clergé de France de 1682*, Paris, 1868, p. 80 *et passim*.   *Oeuvres de Louis XIV.*, 1806, Paris, vol. ii., pp. 121f.

2.—*Code de la Nature*, ed. E. Dolléans, 1910, p. 85.   Jean Meslier, (the Curé ?), 1664-1729 ? in his alleged *Testament*.   See edition by Ch. Rudolf, *Le Testament de Jean Meslier*, 3 vols., Amsterdam, 1864.   This " Testament " was referred to by Voltaire and D'Holbach, but the existence of the said Curé is contested.   See *Le Dictionnaire des Dictionnaires*, ed. Paul Guérin, Paris, 1892, vol. v., p. 150.   See, however, a recent article "An atheist Curé of the Eighteenth Century," by J. M. Thompson in *The Hibbert Journal*, Jan., 1928, pp. 284f.

3.—See Jean Gerard de Ville-Thierri, *Vie des riches et des pauvres*, Paris, 1700, p. 362.   Cf.   Joseph-Aignan Sigaud de La Fond, *De l'école du bonheur*, Paris, 1782.   See Lichtenberger, *Op. cit.*, pp. 349f. for details of other writers.

4.—The author, Remi Breyer, 1669-1749, was a canon of Troyes.

ecclesiastical approbation at Troyes in 1711 and taught universally in France, the first question asked is : " Quels sont les pechez des Riches ? " The answer which follows is given in the words of St. Paul : Riches usually beget an inordinate love for the things of this world, forgetfulness of God, and contempt for the poor. The *Catéchisme* stresses the obligation of giving alms in common necessity, and states that the poor are ordinarily in such circumstances and have a claim on our superfluous wealth.[1]

Laymen, as well as ecclesiastics, in the seventeenth century were mostly content with renewing the mediaeval warning that there is no profession " more exposed to avarice and to injustice " than commerce. Thus Domat considered it " the first duty of those who exercise this profession " to " propose to themselves other views than that barely to make gain by it . . . ., to confine themselves to an honest profit . . ., and to sell at a reasonable price." [2] But in the eighteenth century it is an ecclesiastic who essayed to infuse new spirit and life into these glittering generalities of tradition. Abbé Méry's treatise, *L'Ami de ceux qui n'en ont point*,[3] which appeared about the time of the Physiocrats' rise to power (1767), is at once a masterly comment on their individualistic social philosophy and a refutation of Rousseau's insinuation that a Christian could not be practical.

Referring to the contemporary custom of publishing books with the title of " L'Ami," as, for example, " The Friend of Men," " The Friend of the Young," etc., the Abbé humorously remarks that hitherto writers have called everybody their friend except "those who have nothing." [4] And, he observes, if writers had devoted more of their time to devising means for the employment of the poor than to suggesting methods

1.—*Catéchisme des Riches*, Troyes, 1711, p. 21. In Bibl. Nationale, Paris.

2.—Jean Domat, (1625-1695), *The Civil Law in its natural order together with the Publick Law*, London, 1722, tr. W. Strahan, vol. ii., pp. 462-463. Domat restates the old functional view of society and supports it with scriptural texts, as, for example, " Everyone according to their office and burdens." Numbers iv.49 and St. Paul i. Cor., ch. xii., 18.—*Op. cit.*, vol. ii., p. 406.

3.—The sub-title of the book is also significant : *Système économique, politique et morale*, Paris, 1767. I am indebted to Prof. H. J. Laski for drawing my attention to this book and for kindly lending it to me.

4.—*Op. cit.*, Preface p. 3.

for their punishment, there would be fewer poor and fewer beggars in France to-day.[1]   It is not possible to consider in detail here the points raised by the Abbé, and particularly his interesting contribution to social therapeutics.   If he had no love for the " new philosophy," armed with an impure and fanatical zeal to destroy all religion,[2] he had almost equal contempt for barren speculative discussions such, for example, as whether the earth is flat or round.[3]   For him the important point is that the earth is a fact, and many of its inhabitants are suffering unnecessarily.   Intellectual energy, therefore, ought to be directed to perfecting the things that are " useful and necessary " ; and, above all, to improving the labourers' *métier*.[4]   His suggestion for making the Academies of Agriculture in France less academic ;[5] his emphasis on the right of the poor to a decent subsistence ; to proper education, religious and secular ;[6] his plans for the rationalisation and co-ordination of charity ; the establishment of *Monts de Piété*, such as had been successfully established in Italy and other European states, offering cheap loans to those on the verge of poverty and thus preventing them from becoming actually poor ;[7] his insistence on the poor man's right of access to all trades ; his condemnation of a system which compelled men not only to pay for the right to work, but also for the right to sell the products of their industry ;[8] these and many other practical suggestions show how thoroughly the Abbé understood one of the greatest problems of the age, and, indeed, of every age, the problem of creating conditions in which the poor can work out their own economic salvation.

His proposal that the State should tax luxuries in order to furnish funds for putting the poor to useful work is interesting, not only because it illustrates his conception of the State's duty with regard to property, but because the question of

1.—*Ibid.*, p. 5.
2.—*Ibid.*, p. 225.
3.—*Ibid.*, p. 97.
4.—*Ibid.*, p. 96.
5.—*Op. cit.*, p. 77.
6.—*Ibid.*, p. 9, pp. 27f.
7.—*Ibid.*, pp. 34-35.
8.—*Ibid.*, pp. 38-44.

luxury was the *pièce de résistance* of French writers in the eighteenth century. Méry pointed out, what other writers have elaborated in more modern phraseology, that the imitative instinct and the spirit of rivalry are sometimes harmful from the individual, and costly from the social point of view. The successful business man, " l'homme de fortune " of those days, was apparently surrounded with a more brilliant equipage than that of a duke.[1] A simple *bourgeois* wore garments embroidered with gold. Méry thought that sumptuary laws should be re-enacted. Dress was no longer an index of social status : the robes worn by the business classes then would be considered almost a profanation in the time of Louis XIV.[2] To put an end to this useless display of vanity and to keep the various social classes differentiated, he would like to see a heavy tax put on superfluities, and the proceeds administered in a business like manner for the relief of the poor.[3]

He wisely refrains from defining a " luxury," the content of which is constantly changing, as Mélon observed in 1734.[4] Although Méry does not discuss the practical difficulties involved in enforcing sumptuary legislation, he relies on what he knows of its operation in Sweden to assert its probable success in France. Thus he believed that if only half the articles of luxury taxed in Sweden were taxed in France, they would produce a sum sufficient to feed all the poor in the latter country.[5]

His condemnation of luxury, at least if luxury is defined as " a taste for superfluous things," would not, however, commend itself to his fellow countryman, Abbé Le

1.—Méry, *Op. cit.*, pp. 50.—" In fact you there see a man of fortune in a more brilliant equipage than that of a duke or peer. . . . The wife of a manager or agent wears more superb clothes and more diamonds than a countess or marchioness."

2.—Since the death of Louis XIV. the laws regulating the dress to be worn by different classes had fallen into abeyance, and, indeed, luxury legislation generally. See *Collection des Meilleurs Dissertations, Notices et Traités particuliers relatifs à l'histoire de France composeé en grande partie de pièces rares,* par C. Leber, J. B. Salgues et J. Cohen, Paris, 1826, vol. x., pp. 466f., vol. xix., pp. 512-27.

3.—Méry, *Op. cit.*, pp. 54-60.

4.—*A Political Essay upon Commerce*, English tr. David Bindon, Dublin, 1738, ch. ix., pp. 182-183.—Sumptuary laws " are relative to Commerce."

5.—Mery, *Op. cit.*, p. 55.

Blanc.[1]   Twenty years before, Abbé Le Blanc declared that luxury, in the sense of a desire to procure more of the amenities of life, was a refining influence.[2]   It had helped to banish " drunkness " from France.[3]   " It seems in many respects to be the father of labour and industry."[4]   Luxury has its disadvantages and riches may disorder men's heads, but if you confine people " to necessaries only, you discourage industry, you ruin arts, you change their manners ; in short, you reduce them almost to the condition of savages."[5]   The Abbé failed to understand the psychology of the English who railed at luxury despite " the close connexion there is between that commerce which is so advantageous to them, and the luxury they so severely condemn."[6]   The debate on luxury is interesting as an illustration of the growth of opinion as to the right of the individual to make the most of his property.

The subject of luxury, as Mélon observed, had given rise to " many wild declamations."[7]   Le Blanc, who was obviously influenced by Melon, had expressed the common sense view of the question.   Melon himself held that the State was bound to prohibit " whatever is in itself pernicious "[8] since men are " very rarely guided by the Rules of Religion."[9] If men were so happy as to regulate their actions " according to the pure maxims of Religion, they would not have occasion for Laws."[10]   It is the business of the State, therefore, to turn to wise account man's passion for wealth and other

1.—*Letters on the English and French Nations*, Dublin, 1747, vol. ii., Letter lx., p. 40.
2.—*Ibid.*, p. 46.
3.—*Ibid.*, and Cf. Mélon, *Op. cit.*, p. 178.
4.—Abbé le Blanc, *Op. cit.*, p. 41.   Cf. Mélon, *Op. cit.*, p. 178.—Luxury is " the destroyer of sloth and idleness."
5.—Abbé le Blanc, *Op. cit.*, p. 42.
6.—*Ibid.*, p. 42.
7.—Melon, *Op. cit.*, p. 173.
8.—*Ibid.*, p. 192.
9.—*Ibid.*, p. 194.   " It is," he writes, " the part of Religion to endeavour to destroy Luxury, and it is the business of the State to make an advantage of it."   This statement is misleading.   If the State, as he admits, is bound to prohibit whatever is pernicious the antithesis is not justified.   Mr. F. B. Kaye, in the introduction to his edition of Mandeville's *Fable of the Bees*, 1924, vol. i., p. cxxxvi, seems to underestimate Melon's belief in the practical efficacy of religion.
10.—Melon, *Op. cit.*, p. 173.

things, rather than to give full rein to them.[1]

The controversy about luxury in eighteenth century France gave rise to an immense literature of attack and defence.[2] This was largely due to Mandeville's *Fable of the Bees* of which a French translation appeared in 1740. Even in 1725, as Mr. Kaye has shown, leading French periodicals were discussing Mandeville's defence of luxury.[3] With the enemies of the Church, like Voltaire, Mandeville's defence of luxury was turned into a weapon to discredit the Christian ideal of life.[4] If "civilisation," as Mandeville suggested, involved the granting of free scope to self-interest, the fostering of the acquisitive instinct, and the arousing of new wants in man, a doctrine which urged the necessity of charity and restraint in social relations and put in the foreground the evils attending wealth accumulation could easily be represented as the enemy of progress. Christianity was, therefore, arraigned for its restrictions on individual liberty. Its theory of rights, it was said, had not kept pace with its elaborate theory of duties. For Rousseau true Christianity is incompatible with good citizenship. "We are told," he writes, "that a nation of true Christians would form the most perfect society conceivable. In this supposition I see only one great difficulty—that a society of true Christians would be no longer a society of men."[5] His hatred of Christianity, and especially his confusion of its counsels with its precepts, were mainly due to Pierre Bayle's influence,[6] and to the caricature of Christianity which he witnessed in Calvinistic Geneva.

1.—*Op. cit.*, pp. 173-4.

2.—For a list of books dealing with the subject in its various aspects see Lichtenberger, *Op. cit.*, pp. 400f. See Abbé Francois André-Adrien Pluquet, *Traité Philosophique et Politique sur le luxe*, Paris, 1786, vol. i., p. 12. Since Mandeville, he says, people have not ceased to discusss luxury in its philosophical and political aspects. For the Abbé, luxury does not consist in superfluities or their use, but in *attachment* to them.

3.—Kaye's Introduction to Mandeville, *Fable of the Bees*, 1924, vol. i. p. cxxxvi.

4.—Voltaire, *Défense du Mondian ou l'apologie du luxe*, ed. A. Morize, 1909.

5.—*The Social Contract*, ed. Henry J. Tozer, 1905, bk. iv., ch. viii., p. 225. "Christianity is an entirely spiritual religion, concerned solely with heavenly things ; the Christian's country is not of this world. He does his duty, it is true ; but he does it with a profound indifference as to the good or ill success of his endeavours. Provided that he has nothing to reproach himself with, it matters little to him whether all goes well or ill here below."—*Ibid.*, p. 225.

6.—Bayle's *Dictionary* was the "bible of the eighteenth century" says Émile Faguet, *Dix-huitième siècle*, Paris, 1890, p. 1.

Yet with all his contempt for tradition, Rousseau's attitude towards some features of modern civilisation, as, for example, the growth of commerce,[1] appears quite reactionary compared with that of some of the writers whose religion he

1.—*The Social Contract*, ed. Tozer, bk. ii., ch. xi., p. 146.—" Foreign commerce," he thinks, " diffuses merely a deceptive utility through the kingdom generally." It " enriches a few individuals " but " the nation as a whole gains nothing." This is quite in keeping with Rousseau's hankering after individual equality. Here we may see interesting traces of Mandeville's thought to which Rousseau gave a new direction. Mandeville's *Fable of the Bees* was, in one sense, an apologia for civilisation, or rather for the evils with which its actual development was accompanied. Rousseau's thought is an indictment of civilisation, and all the conventionalities and restrictions which it implies. Mandeville's views are sometimes set in a false perspective. His approbation of unrestricted self-interest and commerce was hypothetical. His object was to show " the unreasonableness and folly of those, that desirous of being an opulent and flourishing people, . . . are yet always murmuring at and exclaiming against those Vices and Inconveniences, that from the beginning of the world to this present day, have been inseparable from all Kingdoms and States that ever were fam'd for Strength, Riches and Politeness at the same time."—*Fable of the Bees*, 1714 edn., Preface p. 4. " The main design of the Fable," he says again, " is to show the impossibility of enjoying all the most elegant comforts of life that are to be met with in an industrious, wealthy and powerful Nation, and at the same time to be bless'd with all the Virtue and Innocence that can be wished for in a Golden Age."—*Ibid.*, p. 4. " If I were asked," he writes, " What place I thought most pleasant to walk in ? Nobody can doubt but before the stinking streets of London I would esteem a fragrant garden, or a shady grove in the country. In the same manner, *if laying aside all worldly greatness and vain glory, I should be ask'd where I thought it was probable that men might enjoy true happiness, I would prefer a small peaceable society, in which men neither envy'd nor esteem'd by Neighbours should be contented to live upon the natural product of the spot they inhabit*, to a vast multitude abounding in Wealth and Power, that should always be conquering others by their Arms Abroad, and debauching themselves by Foreign Luxury at Home."—*Ibid.*, pp. 11-12. My italics. Mandeville's view that the knowledge of the " working poor " should be confined to those things which relate " to their Calling " was a mild criticism of civilisation in the sense of " intellectual improvement."—*Fable*, ed. Kaye, vol. i., pp. 287-288. For an interesting discussion of Mandeville's relation to Rousseau see W. Windelband, *A History of Philosophy*, tr. James H. Tufts, N.Y., 1910, pp. 524-525. We think, however, that Dr. Windelband (like many others) over-emphasises Mandeville's cult of individualism. Mandeville seems to doubt very much that the ideal social system or happy nation will result from the interplay of individual interests. " *The great Art then to make a Nation happy and what we call flourishing, consists in giving every Body an Opportunity of being employ'd ; which to compass let a Government's first care be to promote as great a variety of Manufactures, Arts and Handicrafts as Human wit can invent ; and, second, to encourage Agriculture and Fishery in all their branches*."—*Fable*, ed. Kaye, vol. i., p. 197. My italics. Mandeville probably influenced Rousseau's attitude towards the cultivators of the soil and also the Physiocrats' views on land. " Let the Value of Gold and Silver either rise or fall, the Enjoyment of all Societies will ever depend upon the Fruits of the Earth and the Labour of the People."—*Fable*, ed. Kaye, vol. i., p. 198. Mandeville may have been influenced by Locke, but Mandeville's views seem to have been better known in France.

ridiculed. His attitude towards private property is also some-what puzzling. In the *Discours sur l'inégalité*, (1765), he claims that society and all its principal evils are due to the introduction of private property.[1] Private property is the root cause of the self-seeking spirit and degeneration of modern society. But a few months later, in his article *De l'Economie Politique* in the Encyclopedia, private property is referred to as "the most sacred of all the rights of citizens."[2] It is in the *Contrat Social* (1762) that his final views on the question of property are found. Though there are some who see in the opening line of the *Social Contract*— "Man is born free and everywhere he is in chains"—a text to prove that Rousseau was an apostle of individualism,[3] the theory of property outlined in that book does not manifest many traces of individualism.

Rousseau's cardinal principle is that there is no absolute individual right of property or of anything else. All rights are a creation of the State. "The State, with regard to its members, is owner of all their property by the social contract, which in the State, serves as the basis of all rights."[4] In Rousseau's hands the contractual theory of government receives a revolutionary meaning. For Locke it served as the basis of individualism with regard to property and other rights; for Rousseau it becomes the foundation of an unlimited Collectivism.[5] Once it is granted that the State is the source of all rights, who shall set limits to its inter-ference in social life? To style Rousseau a "socialist" or "collectivist" would be to apply terms which had no meaning then. He did, however, lay the theoretical foundation of Collectivism as commonly understood to-day.

But he was no communist or leveller. The equality which he desired to see established was *not* one in which "the

1.—See *The Political Writings of J. J. Rousseau*, ed. C. E. Vaughan, 1915, vol. i., p. 169.
2.—*Ibid.*
3.—As, for example, Émile Faguet, *Op. cit.*, p. 385. For an excellent criticism of Rousseau see Jacques Maritain, *Three Reformers*, Sheed & Ward, pp. 93-164.
4.—*Social Contract*, ed. Tozer, bk. i., ch. ix., p. 115.
5.—Cf. Dr. Vaughan's introduction to *The Political Writings of Rousseau*, vol. i., p. 39.

degrees of power and wealth should be absolutely the same."
With regard to wealth he thought that " no citizen should
be rich enough to be able to buy another, and none poor
enough to be forced to sell himself ; which supposes, on the
part of the great, moderation in property and influence ;
and, on the part of ordinary citizens, repression of avarice
and covetousness." [2] Rousseau's doctrine of equality reduces
itself to this, that all men should at least enjoy the necessaries
of life.[3] Rousseau's plea for moderation in property was a
potent influence in promoting the growth of peasant
proprietorship in France. In the absence of a " legal-title "
to land, the only marks of ownership which he thought
worthy of respect were "labour and cultivation." [4] Thanks
to the current of ideas which he set in motion, the influence
of the Physiocrats which, on the whole, tended towards the
establishment of large farms, was largely counteracted.[5]
From the foregoing it appears that Rousseau's ideas on
property owe very little to Locke. In whatever other
respects the *Social Contract* may resemble Locke's *Civil
Government*, the theory of property contained in the former
is far from being an obvious imitation of that expressed in
the latter.[6] The power which Rousseau vested in the State
forms a striking contrast with Locke's individualism. It
prepared the way not only for large scale interference with
property, but also for the confiscatory policy adopted during
the later stages of the Revolution.

In reality, however, Rousseau's theory was less novel than
the reader might be disposed to suspect. If one substitutes
the State for the King, there is no difference in principle
between it and that contained in Louis XIV.'s instructions
to the Dauphin in 1666 : " In the first place you must be

1.—*Social Contract*, ed. Tozer, bk. ii., ch. xi., p. 145.
2.—*Ibid.*, bk. ii., ch. xi., p. 145.
3.—*Ibid.*, bk. i., ch. ix., p. 115.—" Every man has by nature a right to all
that is necessary to him."
4.—*Social Contract*, ed. Tozer, bk. i., ch. ix., p. 115.
5.—Quesnay, for example, *Maximes*, ed. Oncken, p. 334.—" Que les terres
employées à la culture des grains soient réunies, autant qu'il est possible en
grandes fermes exploitées par de riches laboureurs."
6.—Ad. Franck, *Réformateurs et Publicistes de l' Europe · dix-huitième siècle*,
Paris, 1893, pp. xv., xvi., seems to exaggerate Rousseau's general indebtedness
to Locke.

convinced that kings are absolute lords and have naturally the full and free disposal of all the goods which are possessed by churchmen or by laymen, in order at any time to use them in the manner of wise stewards, that is according to the general needs of their State." [1]

The doctrine that the King is father of his people, and, therefore, responsible for their economic and social welfare, had quite a number of adherents in France even in the eighteenth century.[2] It inspired the spirited protests against unnecessary inequalities which are scattered throughout the diffuse writings of D'Argenson.[3] It seems to have influenced Montesquieu's views as to the State's function with regard to property, though of course he had no love for the political theory which regarded the State and the King as synonymous terms. Montesquieu may be regarded as occupying a middle position between the individualistic tendencies of the Physio-cratic school and the collectivist tendencies of Rousseau. The latter, as was pointed out, regarded the State as the source of all rights, including the right of property. Montesquieu, while denying that private property was a natural right, admitted that there was a natural law or justice anterior and superior to positive laws.[4] Indeed, the function of positive or civil laws was to give effect to the " relations of justice." To maintain " that there is nothing just or unjust, but what is commanded or forbidden by positive laws, is the same as saying that, before the describing of a circle, all the radii were not equal." [5] Laws, in the wide sense, are " the necessary relations arising from the nature of things." [6] Man is led by the laws of his being to seek nourishment, to found a family and to live in society.[7]

Whatever may have been the condition of man in the

1.—*Oeuvres de Louis XIV.*, Paris, 1806, t. ii., pp. 121f.

2.—See Count de Boulainvilliers, *Mémoires présentés à Monseigneur le Duc d'Orléans, Régent de France*, Hague and Amsterdam, 1727, vol. i., p. 70.— The king is father of his people, and in this capacity is obliged " de veiller à leur subsistance."

3.—*Considérations sur le gouvernment ancien et présent de la France,* Amsterdam, 1765, p. 272 ; p. 308 ; pp. 259-63.

4.—*Works*, London, 1777, vol. i., bk. i., ch. i., p. 3.

5.—*Ibid.*, vol. i., p. 2.

6.—*Ibid.*, vol. i., p. 1.

7.—*Ibid.*, vol. i., pp. 5-6.

pre-political state, and he disagrees with Hobbes's view of it, society, as we know it to-day, is composed of individuals with divergent claims and interests.[1] The State ought, therefore, to regulate these conflicting interests so that each individual may enjoy at least " a certain subsistence, a proper nourishment, convenient clothing, and a kind of life not incompatible with health." [2] If private property was introduced by civil law, the civil law ought not to be regarded as its palladium except in so far as that law reflects the relations of justice. Montesquieu, it is true, was inclined to be optimistic with regard to the justice of the legal *status quo* as to property, but the fact of admitting that it was the duty of the State to ensure to every citizen a minimum of subsistence proves that, in the abstract at least, he did not regard property arrangements as inviolable. His conservatism is sometimes over-emphasised.[3]

Like Rousseau he considered real equality of possessions impracticable,[4] but he thought inequalities of wealth could be diminished somewhat by imposing duties on the rich, and by modifying the laws of inheritance. In a " trading republic " the paternal estate should be divided equally among the children.[5] Such a policy would lead the latter to avoid luxury and to work harder. No law of nature is violated by departing from the system of primogeniture. " The law of nature ordains that fathers shall provide for their children, but it does not oblige them to make them their heirs." [6]

Montesquieu's general position with regard to property was attacked by Linguet and others in the second half of the century. Property was not introduced by civil law or social sanction ; its origin must be traced to force ; and laws or prescription have but consecrated that violence.[7] Civil laws, Linguet thinks, are " a conspiracy against the most

1.—*Ibid.*, vol. i., pp. 5-6.
2.—*Works*, vol. ii., bk. xxiii., ch. xxix., p. 156.
3.—For example, Ph. Sagnac *La Législation civile de la Révolution française,* Paris, 1898, p. 26.
4.—Montesquieu, *Works*, vol. i., bk. v., ch. v., pp. 57-8.
5.—*Works*, vol. i., bk. v., ch. vi., p. 59.
6.—*Ibid.*, vol. ii., bk. xxvi., ch. vi., p. 208.
7.—Linguet, *Théorie des Loix Civiles*, London, 1767, t. i., pp. 63-64.

numerous part of the human race." [1] They are fortresses established in favour of wealth in an enemy country ; their spirit is that of property, and it is the rich who principally benefit by them.[2] He bids us consider how the poor are sacrificed to the interests of the rich. They are compelled to work long hours in order that they may have less time to brood over their misery.[3]

Justice, according to the lawyers, consists in the constant desire of rendering to everyone what is his.[4] " But the poor have nothing but their indigence. The laws, therefore, can conserve nothing for them. The principal object of laws is to render the owners of superfluities immune from the attacks of those who lack necessaries." [5] The root of the evil is due to the fact that the law has sanctioned the right to enjoy property without personal labour.[6] The current fashion of advocating a large population is ridiculed. What advantage is it to the State to have a large number of neglected and under-fed children ? [7] Subsistence is very difficult for three quarters of the human race, and sometimes impossible.[8] The unequal distribution of purchasing power which causes labour to be devoted to such frivolous uses as the procuring of " a diamond for a lady without beauty or virtue," and the display of luxury in general, open the door to robberies and the punishment which follows them.[9]

Speculation which enables three quarters of the nation to

1.—*Ibid.*, t. i., p. 195.

2.—*Ibid.*, t. i., pp. 195-6.—Karl Marx was obviously influenced by Linguet's work which he quotes in *Capital*, Kerr edn., vol. i., p. 675, note. Law according to Marx is " a product of the material relations of production." Linguet, he writes, " overthrew Montesquieu's illusory *'Esprit des Lois'* with one word : ' L'esprit des lois, c'est la propriété.' "

3.—Linguet, *Op. cit.*, t. i., p. 189.

4.—*Ibid.*, t. i., p. 196.

5.—*Ibid.*, Linguet, of course, admits that laws do more than protect property ; they preserve peace and control passions.—*Ibid.*, t. i., p. 199. The phrase " the poor have nothing but their indigence " reminds one of Marx's *Communist Manifesto*—" the workers have nothing to lose but their chains."

6.—Linguet, *Op. cit.*, t. i., p. 197.

7.—*Ibid.*, t. i., pp. 205-9.

8.—*Ibid.*, t. i., p. 211.

9.—*Ibid.*, t. i., pp. 217-18 ; p. 220. He was sceptical as to the simple and virtuous life which eighteenth century travellers attributed to the inhabitants of Africa and America.

enjoy property without personal effort is largely responsible for existing inequalities.   And yet the laws framed to protect property when it principally represented the effects of individual industry are now extended to legalise property claims which are, in a large measure, a tax on the really industrious portion of the community.[1]

Some of the principal ideas in Linguet's work were developed in a more philosophical and detailed manner by Brissot de Warville.[2]   Like Linguet he deplored the absence of independent thinking on the subject of property.   Hitherto writers had been content with noting what was said about the right of property in former centuries.   They had valued quotations more than truth.[3]   What was needed was " to carry the torch of reason into this very obscure part of natural right." [4]   That task, he thought, should be undertaken now that the King and the people were trying to elucidate their rights, and he claimed to have accomplished it.

The essence of Brissot's criticism of contemporary thought and policy with regard to property was that they did not distinguish sufficiently between positive and natural property rights.   The legal protection extended to certain forms of property prevented some from enjoying the minimum of property required for civilised existence.[5]   If, therefore, the poor are occasionally driven to rob or steal, they cannot be accused of violating a natural right.   Nor ought they to be

1.—" Now that speculation has become the favourite resource of three quarters of the nation ; now that the nation is composed practically of two kinds of men, borrowers and lenders ; now that the mass of imaginary riches—*rentes* and paper of every kind—is infinitely greater than the mass of real and solid riches, *i.e.* land ; now finally that every power, having voluntarily become subject and tributary to commerce, is merely a colossus with head of gold and feet of clay ; why persist in keeping the same jurisprudence which was appropriate when a head of clay was supported by feet of metal ? "—*Ibid.*, i., 56f.   See also *Ibid.*, ii. 441.

2.—Jean Pierre Brissot de Warville, *Recherches Philosophiques sur le droit de propriété & sur le vol, considérés dans la nature & dans la société*, 1780, printed in his *Bibliothèque philosophique du Législateur*, 1782, Paris, tome vi., pp. 261f. from which we quote in the text.

3.—*Ibid.*, pp. 263-4.   Cf.   Linguet, *Op. cit.*, t. i., p. 146.

4.—Brissot, *Op. cit.*, p. 338.

5.—*Ibid.*, pp. 331-333.   Although he says " If forty crowns are sufficient to preserve our existence, to possess two hundred thousand crowns is a clear robbery, an injustice " (*Ibid.*, p. 293), his meaning is that no one should retain more than he can use if others are in want.

punished severely for doing so.[1] The flaw lies in our social institutions that canonise what nature calls a crime—the appropriation of more things than we can use.[2] His object is not so much to incite to robbery—although for his political opponents "voler" and "brissoter" were synonymous terms [3]—as to offer an apologia for the petty larcenies of the poor. Property is robbery only in so far as it prevents human beings from satisfying their hunger.[4] The satisfaction of human wants is the object and cause of the right of property.[5] One cannot claim to have a natural right to any more property than is requisite for one's essential needs such as food and clothing, etc.[6] Human wants may be divided into essential and capricious ; the former are very few, but the latter are infinite.[7] It is interesting to note that although he refers to the "learned Locke," when discussing the question as to whether plants have a soul,[8] he nowhere mentions Locke's theory of property. Despite its varied assortment of ideas on vegetarianism, the "rights of animals," and cosmic evolution, his book constituted, in the main, a criticism of the philosophy of property rights developed by the Physiocrats.

Abbé Morellet, an ardent disciple of Vincent de Gournay, the man who by conversation rather than by writing initiated Physiocracy, considered Brissot's " dreadful doctrine " subversive of society.[9] Brissot, in reply, insinuated that the Abbé's criticism merely voiced the views of property owners.[10]

1.—*Ibid.*, p. 335.

2.—*Ibid.*, p. 329.

3.—See *Dictionnaire des Dictionnaires*, ed. Paul Guérin, t. ii., p. 303. Brissot became the soul of the Girondin party which was sometimes called Brissotin, and for his moderate policy found himself in opposition to men like Robespierre and Camille Desmoulins. Though he had served his country well, he was, like many others, suspected of royalist tendencies and condemned to death in 1793. See *Nouvelle Biographie Générale*, Paris, 1855, t. vii., p. 443.

4.—Brissot, *Op. cit.*, pp. 332-333. He is not opposed to civil property— that is the extension of legal protection to property not immediately necessary for human existence—for otherwise industry and commerce would stagnate.

5.—*Ibid.*, p. 277.

6.—*Ibid.*, p. 293.

7.—*Ibid.*, p. 279.

8.—*Ibid.*, p. 305.

9.—*Mélanges de littérature et de Philosophie du xviiie siècle*, Paris, 1818, t. iii., p. 308.

10.—Morellet, *Op. cit.*, t. iii., pp. 309-10.

The Abbé was undoubtedly affected by contemporary events such as the confiscation of Church property, for although he moved in the circle of men like Helvetius and Diderot he remained a convinced Catholic all his life.[1]   While he was no enemy to "just and necessary changes,"[2] he feared that Brissot's views on property might assume a dangerous turn in the hands of the Jacobin party.   As he told Lord Shelbourne, his aim was to act as "an apostle of moderation."[3]   Like Locke he held that the right of private property was not a social creation, but a right anterior to society itself.[4]   The primary, or at least the principal, motive which induced men to form political societies was to safeguard the right of private property.[5]   Indeed, an inviolable respect for property and all its rights is the sole basis on which a sound political edifice can be raised.[6]   Like most members of the Physiocratic school, he tended to regard all property rights as equally sacred and made landed property not only the basis of the economic system, but the sole foundation of the right to govern.[7]

Lord Acton's account of the social philosophy of the Physiocrats does not contain the whole truth.   For the Physiocrats, he writes, " Society secures rights ; it neither bestows nor restricts them.   They are the direct consequences of duties . . .   Society is founded, not on the will of man, but on the nature of man and the will of God . . .   Relief of those who suffer is the duty of all men, and the affair of all."[8]   It must be admitted that the Physiocrats were far from holding Rousseau's theory of the conventional character of the State, but it is difficult to accept the opinion that they regarded the relief of the distressed as a " duty," for the

1.—See Auguste Mazure, *Les idées de l'Abbé Morellet*, Paris, 1910. p. 88. The Abbé was not a priest.
2.—*Mélanges*, t. iv., p. 309.
3.—*Lettres de l'Abbé Morellet à Lord Shelbourne, 1772-1803*, Paris, 1898, Lettre lix., p. 275.
4.—*Mémoires sur le xviiie siècle*, Paris, 1821, t. i., p. 190.
5.—*Mémoires*, t. i., p. 190.
6.—*Mélanges*, t. iii., p. 294.
7.—*Mémoires*, t. i., p. 151. Cf. *Lettres . . . à Lord Shelbourne*, Lettre lxii., p. 291.   In this letter, written February, 1791, he promised to write " a large treatise on property," but apparently the work never appeared.
8.—Lord Acton, *Lectures on the French Revolution*, 1910, p. 13.

obvious reason that their social philosophy was too optimistic to contemplate such a condition. The Physiocratic conception of Providence left little room for the problem of evil or suffering.[1] Most of the Physiocrats ignored it, or naively hinted that its existence was due to the fact that people had not yet understood the more excellent way to which Physiocracy pointed. Man was destined to be happy here as well as hereafter. He has only to obey nature to be happy ;[2] and, strange thought, the natural order is a physical rather than a moral order.[3] There are certain physical laws governing social phenomena which, if obeyed, will infallibly secure the welfare of society as a whole. From the economic point of view these laws may be reduced to self-interest. Not only is it man's interest not to interfere with this natural law, but it is also his duty. Thus duty and self-interest could never collide. Moral disorders, according to Mirabeau, being a consequence of physical and economic derangements, it was putting the cart before the horse to maintain that the social problem was primarily a moral one.[4] It was, he thought, a purely economic problem.[5]

The Physiocrats, on the whole, regarded the moulding of a man's fortune as being in his own hands.[6] The evils of society were mainly due to ignorance ;[7] and society itself was envisaged as a mechanism rather than as an organism.

1.—Cf. René Savatier, *La Théorie du commerce chez les Physiocrates*, Paris, 1918, ch. iii., p. 26.
2.—Quesnay, *Le Droit Naturel*, ed. Oncken, p. 368.
3.—Quesnay, *Op. cit.*, pp. 374-5, says natural laws may be physical or moral.
4.—Marquis de Mirabeau, *Philosophie Rurale*, Amsterdam, 1766, t. i., p. 134.—" Les dérangements de l'ordre moral sont une suite des dérangements de l'ordre physique et économique." This sentence is mis-quoted by R. Savatier, *Op. cit.*, ch. iii., who has " *ou* " instead of " *et*."
5.—*Op. cit.*, t. i., 135.—" If the products of property and the reward due to labour are reestablished and secured, men will of themselves replace themselves in the moral order. This is the true foundation of natural law and civil order. If moralists and politicians do not base their sciences on the economic order, on the plough, their speculations will be vain and chimerical ; they will be physicians who perceive only the symptoms and are ignorant of the disease." See *Op. cit.*, pp. xli.-xliv., where he speaks of the necessity of dealing quantitatively with economic phenomena. Statistics are essential if the economist is to reach reliable conclusions.
6.—See Quesnay, *La Liberté*, ed. Oncken, pp. 755-758.
7.—L'Abbé Nicolas Baudeau, *Première introduction à la Philosophie Economique*, 1771, ed. A. Dubois, 1910, p. 8.

The mechanism will work smoothly if men will but follow their enlightened self-interest. Property and liberty, being natural rights, there ought to be as little interference as possible with either. Every individual has a natural right to at least those things which are necessary for his welfare.[1] In that sense all men are equal.[2] Why then are there such inequalities in life ? And what is the function of the State with regard to them ?

Some inequalities are inevitable, due to Divine Providence, to the different talents which God has given to men.[3] But men themselves are largely responsible for their economic condition. Those who are energetic and industrious can always improve their status in society.[4] Those, however, who are unable to work, must rely on the assistance of those who are "attentive to the rules of equity and the precepts of religion."[5] The duty of the State is to protect life, liberty and property.[6] Social order would be endangered if the State outstepped these negative duties. If the State attempted to remedy the inequalities in wealth which continually arise amongst men, that policy would but aggravate the evil by favouring idleness and discouraging individual initiative.[7] Elsewhere Quesnay observes that no class in society should dominate the State so as to interfere with the general interest of all classes, which consists in the vigorous promotion of agriculture.[8] But yet Quesnay was inclined to identify the general interest with the interest of

1.—Quesnay, *Le Droit Naturel*, ed. Oncken, p. 359.—"The Natural right of man can be vaguely defined as the right which man has to the things required for his happiness." On p. 364, *Loc. cit.*, he gives various definitions of natural right. In *La Liberté*, ed. Oncken, p. 754, man's natural rights are said to include the right to light.

2.—*La Liberté*, ed. Oncken, p. 755.

3.—*Ibid.*, p. 757.

4.—*Ibid.*, p. 757.

5.—*Ibid.*, p. 758.

6.—*La Liberté*, ed. Oncken, p. 758.

7.—"Without disturbing the order of society and encouraging the disorder of men who fall into want through their bad conduct, it cannot remedy the disarrangements which continually occur in the distribution of goods."—*Ibid.*, pp. 757f.

8.—*Maximes*, ed. Oncken, p. 331. The sovereign authority should be "unique et supérieure à tous les individus de la société et à toutes les entreprises injustes des intérêts particuliers."—*Maximes*, ed. Oncken, p. 329. Though the King is regarded as the sole and absolute authority in the State, his despotism is justified by the fact that he is the instrument by which the "natural order" can be enforced.

the great landed proprietors. Holding, as he did, that labour is the natural title to property, one might expect that he would consider more fully or more fairly its moral and logical implications. On the contrary, he contents himself with labouring the platitude that the security of property is the essential basis of social order.[1] The " wise " laws of the Emperor of China, particularly with regard to property, are held up as a model for Europeans.[2] The right of property, he observes, is well respected in China ; it extends not only to material objects but to servants.[3]

Agriculture being the only industry which was really productive, according to the Physiocrats, one might expect that they would lay more stress on the rights of those immediately connected with it than on the claims of those who merely owned the land. The lion's share of the net product was considered the rightful portion of the proprietary class for two reasons. Firstly, in agriculture, nature labours with man ; and hence the cultivators of the soil, the farmers, *métayers* and labourers, are less important members of the social hierarchy than would at first sight appear. Their productivity bears no proportion to their personal efforts ; they do not furnish the land on which they work. In the second place, the landed proprietors have in the past, if not in the present, expended labour and money on the improvement of the land. The peculiar sacredness of landed property, and the superior claim of its owner, were based on the supposition that property in land arose from labour.[4] Labour is the natural and legal title to property.[5] Mirabeau justified property in land by the labour and expenditure incurred by the original owners. Thus barren or uncultivated land, such as that found in " new countries," ought to have no value. That is the " natural order." [6] The Physiocratic

1.—*Ibid.*, pp. 331-32.
2.—*Ephémérides du citoyen*, ed. Oncken, p. 564.
3.—*Ibid.*, p. 599.
4.—For a fuller account of the contradictions in the Physiocratic doctrine see Gide-Rist, *A History of Economic Doctrines*, 1919, pp. 22-24.
5.—See L'Abbé Nicolas Baudeau, *Op. cit.*, p. 183. Cf. Quesnay, *Maximes*, Oncken, p. 331.
6. —*Philosophie Rurale*, t. i., p. 128. This book, according to Quesnay *Maximes*, pp. 329-30, note, was but a development of his own *Tableau Economique*.

conception of landed property is analogous to the Marxian view of capital as " congealed labour."

With all its emphasis on labour and land, the social philosophy of the Physiocrats was not very favourable to the agricultural labourer or, indeed, to wage-earners generally.[1] Although Quesnay's doctrine of natural right implied that everyone should at least enjoy a decent subsistence,[2] he seemed to accept as " natural " and inevitable that scale of livelihood to which the wage-earner may be reduced by the action of competition.[3]   The Physiocrats, it is true, demanded that the landed proprietors should shoulder the whole burden of taxation, but nevertheless the position of the landowners was to remain a privileged one.   The emphasis which they laid on direct taxation, however, was prompted more by economic than by moral considerations.   Indirect taxes should be abolished not so much because they involve hardship to the poor as because they impede the progress of agriculture.   For the Physiocrats it was the unequal distribution of the burden of taxation rather than the uneven distribution of property which constituted the social problem. Quesnay, we noted, was inclined to believe that there was a necessary correlation beween differences in natural endowments and unequal possessions.   And Turgot, though he pointed out the influence exercised by inheritance laws on the distribution of property,[4] was a Physiocrat to the extent of maintaining that the " most powerful " principle of inequality was " the contrast between the intelligence, the activity, and, above all, the economy of some and the indolence, inaction and dissipation of others." [5]

The writings of the Physiocrats played an important part in discrediting the agrarian privileges of feudalism, and thus helped to liberate the peasant from the restrictions imposed

1.—See Georges Weulersse, *Le Mouvement physiocratique en France de 1756 à 1770*, 1910, t. ii., 729.

2.—*Le Droit Naturel*, ed. Oncken, p. 359.

3.—Quesnay, " Second Problème économique " in *Oeuvres*, ed. Ocnken, pp. 697f.

4.—*Reflections on the Production and the Distribution of Wealth*, 1776, ed. Ashley, Economic Classics, p. 12.

5.—*Ibid.*, p. 13.   For the differences between Turgot and the Physiocrats see Gide-Rist, *Op. cit.*, p. 25, note and *passim*.

on his liberty and labour. Their social theory, despite its strong individualistic trend, illustrates nevertheless the persistence of feudal ideas as to property in eighteenth century France. It recognised the State's joint ownership of all land. By virtue of its primordial right to a share in the products of the land, the State was entitled to levy taxes on land.[1]

In a sense the main currents of property thought in the eighteenth century are focussed in the writings of the Physiocrats. A fuller insight into the different shades of opinion on the nature of property can be gained by examining the parliamentary debates of the Revolution, but before passing to that some account of feudal restrictions in the eighteenth century seems desirable.

(2.) THE LAND QUESTION.

Although feudal theory was largely discredited in the eighteenth century, the facts of feudal property and, indeed, feudal law itself, survived in France with a completeness unknown in England. Personally, except in one or two remote regions, the peasants were free ; but the tenure by which they held their lands were still burdened with onerous and arbitrary obligations which descended from an age when the mass of the population had been serfs. In the eighteenth century, as Karéiew and other students have shown, the French peasants, generally speaking, were free men rather than serfs, but they were crushed by the weight of fiscal and other burdens.[2]

The number of peasants in 1789 who held land under servile conditions, that is, were so dependent that they could not dispose of any of their property without the consent of their lord, is a matter of conjecture. Clerget in a book dedicated to the States General stated that the King had a

1.—Quesnay, *Maximes*, ed. Oncken, pp. 331-332.
2.—N. Karéiew, *Les paysans et la question paysanne en France dans la dernier quart du xviiie siècle*, 1899, pp. 529-30.

million and a half *mainmortable* subjects in his realm.[1]
Boncerf,[2] a contemporary of Clerget, put the number at
three hundred thousand, but a modern French historian
adopts a rather agnostic attitude towards the question.[3]
M. Aulard, whose knowledge of the published and unpublished
material of the French Revolution is sometimes regarded as
unrivalled,[4] thinks that there is " no certainty as to the
degree of aggravation of feudalism under Louis XVI., if,
indeed, such aggravation took place at all." [5]   He is of opinion
that feudalism gave rise to more complaints in the second
half of the century, because the masses had been leavened by
the ideas of Voltaire and other critics of feudal survivals.
And the fact that the French peasant saw his brethren in
the neighbouring province of Savoy being freed from feudal
exactions naturally intensified the discontent of the former.
While it must be admitted that the picture of poverty of the
French peasants was sometimes overdrawn for political reasons
by French writers,[6] there are some grounds for holding the
view that in the generation preceding the Revolution the feudal
lords began to turn the screw on the peasantry.[7]

The remarkable growth in foreign trade during the decades
immediately preceding the Revolution, the expansion in
the coal, iron, and textile industries, the improvement in

1.—*Le Cri de la Raison, ou examen approfondi des lois et des coutumes qui tiennent dans la servitude mainmortable quinze cent mille sujets du Roi.*   Clerget defines *Mainmorte* as " a right which renders a man so dependent upon another, that he cannot dispose of his property without the consent of his master."—*Op. cit.*, ch. i., p. 1.   The right of mainmorte sometimes included more, but the above distinction, as Karéiew remarks, was common to all forms of mainmorte.—*Op. cit.*, p. 22.

2.—Pierre-Francois Boncerf, *Les Inconvénients des droits féodaux*, 1776. This book was translated into all European languages and served as the basis of the decrees of 4th August, 1789.

3.—Alphonse Aulard, *La Révolution française et le régime féodal*, 1919, pp. 10-11.

4.—Lord Acton, *Op. cit.*, Appendix, p. 372.

5.—Aulard, *Op. cit.*, pp. 69-70.

6.—See M. Roustan, *Pioneers of the French Revolution*, tr. F. Whyte, 1926, ch. vii., p. 227.   It is well known of course that the condition of the French peasant was far superior to that of those in other parts of the continent.

7.—Henri Sée, *La France économique et sociale au xviiie siècle*, 1925. M. Sée has supplied a very valuable bibliography of recent work in French economic history which will be of great service to the English reader.   See *The Economic History Review*, vol. i., no. 1, pp. 137f.

agricultural technique and the rise in prices of agricultural commodities, moved the nobility to take advantage of the general economic situation by raising their rents. And feeling that their social prestige was being menaced by the rising commercial aristocracy, they were driven to revive old claims and to enforce old privileges, which had been largely neglected in the earlier part of the century.[1]

The number of feudal dues, however, which were imposed on the peasants throughout the century were by no means inconsiderable. Although the political power of the nobles was so reduced since the time of Louis XIV. that the *seigneur* was, in theory, but "the first inhabitant of the parish," in practice,[2] he still enjoyed some of the prerogatives of political power. He was allowed to tax the labour and industry of his tenants by enforcing *droits de corvée, de mainmorte, de banalité, de minage* and *de banvin*.[3]

These tenurial burdens were denounced by many contemporary writers, including members of the *noblesse*. Condorcet, for example, referred ironically to them as "fruits of the wisdom of our ancestors," [4] and condemned those who held that because the worst features of feudalism had disappeared existing feudal rights could not be interfered with "without violating property." [5] Inequalities, which are largely due to differences in natural faculties, ought not to be aggravated by bad customs and by bad laws.[6]

Like Boncerf he wanted to see the nobles and peasants live peaceably, and he was in favour of giving them adequate compensation if they surrendered their feudal rights.[7] Even

1.—For evidence to that effect for the Bordeaux district see the important article by M. Marion, " État des classes rurales dans la généralité de Bordeaux," in *Revue des Etudes historiques*, 1902. Some further evidence of a "feudal reaction" seems to be contained in the cahiers or list of grievances drawn up by the third estate in 1789. See Sydney Herbert, *The Fall of Feudalism in France*, 1921, p. 202. *Appendix*.

2.—A. de Tocqueville, *L'Ancien régime et la Révolution*, trans. G. W. Headlam, p. 36.

3.—Condorcet, " Refléxions sur les Corvées," 1775, in *Oeuvres,* ed. Condorcet O'Connor and M. F. Arago, Paris, 1847, t. ii., p. 63.

4.—*Oeuvres*, t. ii., p. 61.

5.—*Ibid.*, p. 63.

6.—*Oeuvres*, t. x., p. 603.

7.—Condorcet, *Op. cit.*, t. ii., p. 83. Cf. Boncerf, *Refléxions sur le rachat des droits féodaux*, 1789.

the King himself showed that he had some regard for the rights of man. His reply to those who magnified the royal power to the extent of saying that the right to work (*droit de travailler*) was a royal right, capable of being bought and sold, is worthy of note.[1] " The right to work," he states in almost Lockeian language, is " the property of every man, and this property is the first, the most sacred and the most imprescriptible of all." [2]   In August 1779, Louis XVI. gave proof of the sincerity of his words by abolishing mortmain and servitude in his own dominions.[3] The King was greatly affected by the number of his subjects who were deprived of the liberty of their persons, treated as feudal possessions and denied the consolation of disposing of their effects or transmitting the fruits of their labour to their children. He was particularly grieved to hear that certain lords had violated the " principles of social justice " to the extent of claiming feudal rights in free territories.[4] Though " respect for the laws of property " prevented him from abolishing, without compensation, the feudal rights of the lord of fiefs, he expressed the hope that they would follow his example as such enfranchisements were only " a return to natural right." [5]

So many contemporary[6] and later writers[7] have pointed out what feudalism meant to the peasantry in the eighteenth century, that only a brief sketch of the obstacles which the feudal régime placed to the acquisition of property, on the one hand, and the uncertainty with which it surrounded its enjoyment, on the other, need be attempted here. It may, perhaps, be necessary to observe that the word

1.—See Jules de Vroil, *Etude sur Clicquot-Blervaché*, 1870, pp. 138-9 for extract.

2.—*Ibid.*, " God, by giving man needs by making work necessary for him, has made the right to work the property of every man ; and this property is the first, the most sacred and the most imprescriptible of all."

3.—A copy of this famous edict was printed in the *Gentleman's Magazine*, 1779, vol. xlix., pp. 543f.

4.—*Loc. cit.*, p. 544.

5.—*Ibid.*, p. 544.

6.—See, for example, Clicquot-Blervaché, *L'Ami du cultivateur*, 1789 extracts from which are printed by Jules de Vroil, *Op. cit.*, p. 300. Condorcet, *Oeuvres*, t. ii., pp. 61f.

7.—Amongst modern writers probably the most philosophic discussion of the problem is by Ph. Sagnac, *La Législation civile de la Révolution française*, Paris, 1898. See especially bk. i., pp. 57f.

" peasant," as applied to agrarian classes in eighteenth century France, has not always been employed in one and the same sense. Sometimes it includes not only those who own and cultivate some land, but also the tenant-farmer or *métayer*; and quite often the term is applied generally to all those connected with the cultivation of the soil.[1] While it is certain that the number of peasants who were full proprietors of their land, at least in the sense of being free from all feudal dues and only bound to pay tithe and royal taxes, was extremely small, it is fairly well established that the peasants in 1789, who enjoyed proprietary rights of varying degrees, formed the most numerous class in a land-owning population of about five million people.[2]

The right of *mainmorte*, generally speaking, prevented the peasant from disposing of his property without the seigneur's permission, and it sometimes involved the reversion of the peasant's land to the lord if the peasant's children did not happen to be living in community with him at the time of his death. There were two classes of *mainmorte :* the so-called ' personal ' which attached to individuals, and the ' real ' which was associated with the land. In other words one form of *mainmorte* was natural, in the sense that the disadvantages attaching to it were due to the fact that a peasant was born of parents of a servile status. " Real " *mainmorte* was an acquired condition ; its disabilities arose from the occupation of a servile tenure for a definite period of time. In practice, however, as Karéiew has shown, there was no great difference between these two conditions with regard to the restrictions which they imposed on the peasant.[3]

1.—See Ph. Sagnac, *La Législation civile de la Révolution française*, 1898, pp. 57f. For a synopsis of the views of French and Russian scholars as to the distribution of landed property amongst the different social classes before the Revolution the reader may consult Sydney Herbert, *Op. cit.*, ch. ii., pp. 53f. Cf. Sagnac, *Op. cit.*, p. 189., note (2).

2.—See J. Leutchisky, *L'Etat des classes agricoles à la veille de la Révolution*, 1911. Leutchisky's statistical studies on property have been confirmed by more recent research. See Jean Donat, *Une Communauté rurale à la fin de l'ancien régime*, 1926.

3.—Karéiew, *Op. cit.*, p. 19. Legally, of course, the peasant who was not born into a servile status and who held land of a servile tenure could become a free man by giving up his holding. Cf. **Herbert,** *Op. cit.*, **p. 5.**

The number of cultivators of the soil who were affected by the condition of *mainmorte*, at least in the extreme form described above, were fortunately few.   But there were other disabilities under which the tillers of the soil generally laboured, and which also deprived society " of the effects of that energy in labour which sentiments of the most free property is alone capable of inspiring."[1]   In the eighteenth century the *corvées*, or labour rents, which the tenant paid to the feudal lord were less burdensome than those which the tenant was compelled to render in former ages.   In many parts of the country also these *corvées* were being commuted into fixed payments in produce or money.   When the payment took the form of a certain amount of the tenant's crops, it was called *champart, terrage (tierce)*.   The term *cens (censives)* denoted payments in money and in kind which appears to have been the prevailing custom.   The *champart*, being a fixed amount of produce, was particularly odious to the peasant.   Its real incidence was much greater whenever the price of food increased, as happened, for example, in the second half of the century.   The severity of these feudal dues seemed to have varied from province to province.   But, on the whole, they not only discouraged individual effort but impeded agricultural progress.   The real hardship which they caused was frequently due less to the amount levied on the peasant than to the delay and expense involved in its collection.   The peasant could not interfere with the produce of that part of his land subject to *champart* until the tax-gatherer came to claim the *seigneur's* portion.   Delays being dangerous, especially in agricultural industry subject to influences such as weather over which the individual has no control, the peasant not infrequently found his crops injured and thus greatly reduced in value.   The most odious feature of many of these regular feudal rents was the absence of what one might call limited liability.   The peasants were collectively responsible for their payment, and thus the industrious villager was penalised for the indolent.[2]

1.—Edict of Louis XVI., in *Gents. Magazine*, vol. lxix., pp. 543-4.
2.—See Professor H. Sée, *Les Classes rurales en Bretagne du XVIe siècle à la Révolution*, 1906, p. 91.

In addition to these fixed dues there were other variable or casual burdens which, owing to their very uncertainty, proved disheartening to the peasantry. The tenant on entering into possession of his holding, whether acquired by inheritance or by purchase, was bound to give what was called an *aveu* to the feudal lord.[1] That consisted not only of a formal recognition on the part of the tenant of the lord's right to exact all the dues and privileges attached to the tenure, but also included an exact statement of these burdens and the titles by which the new occupant acquired the land. That process had to be repeated any time, within thirty years, that an error was detected in the original statement, and also whenever the peasant wanted to make an addition to his holding. Obviously that was a costly proceeding, and instances are recorded of where a tenant had to make the *aveu* several times in less than a generation.[2] Avaricious lawyers and middlemen, as anxious to enrich themselves as to swell the *seigneur's* rent-rolls, were constantly reviving old titles by which to squeeze the peasantry.[3]

Another charge levied on the peasant whenever he effected a purchase of land was that known as *lods et ventes*, compelling him to pay a certain proportion of the purchase price to the lord. The proportion varied in different provinces. Sometimes local custom decreed that the seller should shoulder the whole burden, and sometimes again it was jointly shared by the two parties to the sale. A still more iniquitous privilege was that of *retrait (prélation)*, entitling the *seigneur* to acquire the land himself, or to refuse to ratify the sale until an additional charge to that of *lods* and *ventes* had been paid.

It is well known that the *noblesse* were virtually immune from direct taxation in pre-revolutionary France. Rural restlessness and distress, however, probably owed far more to the existence of certain feudal monopolies and private rights of tax and toll than to the taxes levied by the central

1.—See François de Boutaric, *Traité des droits seigneuriaux et des matières féodales*, ed. 1758, p. 3.
2.—H. Sée, *Op. cit.*, p. 80, p. 188.
3.—See *Les Comités des droits féodaux et de législation et l'abolition du régime seigneurial, 1789-1793*, edited by Ph. Sagnac and P. Caron, 1907, p. 271.

government.[1]   The *banalités* formed a particularly vexatious species of feudal privilege.   They gave, in effect, to the lord of the domain control over the commodities necessary for human existence.   The tenant was forced to use only the mills, bake-houses, and wine-presses owned by the lord.   These mills were seldom managed directly by the feudal lords themselves :   they were usually farmed out to middlemen bent on grinding the peasant as well as his corn.   Even after the middleman had taken his pound of flesh, the owners of the mills, bakehouses, and wine-presses still reaped a handsome revenue.[2]   The hunting and fishing rights, and the pigeon trade conducted by the rural nobles, formed another instance of where the industry and welfare of the peasants were sacrificed to the pleasure and profit of the gentry.

Other rights enjoyed by the feudal lords, such as *minage, hallage, étalage*, involved the power of levying taxes on commodities sold in fairs and markets.   *Minage* was a tax levied on corn sold in the market.   The right of *hallage* conferred wider powers ;   it sometimes extended to sales transacted in private houses.[3]   All business transactions in towns, whether conducted by the inhabitants or by outsiders, were subjected to a tax

1.—For a different view, however, see Jean Donat, *Op. cit.*   It is interesting to compare what Hume said of France in this connection :   " The greatest abuses which arise in France .   .   . proceed not from the number or weight of the taxes, beyond what are to be met with in free countries ;   but from the expensive, unequal, arbitrary and intricate method of levying them, by which the industry of the poor, especially of the peasants and farmers, is in a great measure discouraged .   .   ."—*Essays*, The New Universal Library, 1905, p. 67.   When Locke was travelling in France in the second half of the seventeenth century he had some similar observations to make.   " The manner of taxing in the country," he writes in May, 1677, " is this : the tax to be paid being laid on the parish, the collectors for the year assess everyone of the inhabitants, according as they judge him worth, but consider not the land in the parish belonging to any living out of it ;   this is that which so grinds the paisant in France.   The collectors make their rates usually with great inequality ;   there lies an appeal for the over-taxed, but I find not that the remedy is made much use of."—Lord King, *The Life of John Locke, with extracts from his correspondence, journals and commonplace books*, London, 1829, p. 69.   The following year Locke again animadverts on the French tax-system.   He was told by a peasant in the wine district of Grave that the tax collectors sometimes went so far as to seize the peasant's " frying pan and dishes."—*Op. cit.*, p. 76.   The daily fare of this peasant was very meagre and his condition most inhuman.   " In several other parts of France," writes Locke, " the paisants are much more miserable : the peasants who live in Grave they count to be flourishing."—*Ibid.*, p. 77.

2.—H. Sée, *Op. cit.*, pp. 135-6.

3.—See *Dict. des Dicts.*, t. iv., p. 487.

known as *étalage*. The feudal lord not only levied heavy tolls on commodities when they had reached the market but also while they were in transit. The *seigneur's* control over the market also involved the right of selling his wine before any other individual in the parish when the time for marketing had come.[1]

The foregoing privileges might not have proved so irksome were it not for the very substantial powers which the *noblesse* exercised over the law-courts. In all doubtful matters concerning their feudal privileges they had supreme sway. To put it mildly, the judges or legal officers deputed to decide disputes between the tenant and his lord did not usually suffer from the inconvenience of a tender conscience.[2] An obvious example of where the peasant's livelihood might be easily sacrificed to a legal formality occurred in the case of the division of common lands. In the previous century the Crown had frequently to interfere to prevent the nobles from usurping communal rights.[3] The royal edict of 1669, authorising the division of the commons in France, was a real danger to the peasantry, but its effects were not so unfavourable to the rural poor as were those of the enclosures which took place in the eighteenth century. The *cahiers* of the third estate presented to the States General are full of complaints as to the lords' usurpation of communal property rights. As in England in previous centuries, many enclosures took place in France by agreement. The rise in agricultural prices, particularly of corn, necessitated improved methods of production. But the peasants often received few gains for the very real advantages which they were asked or compelled to forego. What was true of England held in France. Enclosures affected the peasant not only in his capacity as grazier or shepherd, but also in his capacity as producer. The profitable working of his arable holding was intimately bound up with the existence of communal rights of fuel and pasture. How could he work his ploughland unless he had some place in which to pasture his oxen ?

1.—*Ibid.*, t. i., p. 729.
2.—Cf. Sée, *Op. cit.*, pp. 123-124.
3.—H. Sée, *La vie économique et les classes sociales en France xviiie siècle*, 1924, pp. 54f.

To complete this brief sketch of agrarian feudalism and to lead up to the legislation of the Revolution with regard to property, some reference may be made to the *droits honorifiques* of the nobility, which included, amongst other things, the right of occupying the first benches in the Church. Although these privileges entailed no great economic disadvantages, they served to intensify the resentment which the peasants felt for burdens which weighed heavily on them during the other six days of the week. Some insight into the psychology of the peasantry may be obtained from a letter addressed to the Committee on Feudal Rights on 19 Nov., 1790, by the Curé of Arrentières.[1] The peasants in this parish, writes Joffroy, think that the abolition of the feudal régime is incomplete as long as certain "*droits honorifiques*" remain. They say that if equality is the "fundamental point in the constitution," it ought, above all, to be observed in the house of God. He is "the creator and father of all men and in His eyes all men are equal."[2] These complaints, however, formed the least important part of the difficult task which confronted the Constituent Assembly and subsequent revolutionary governments. But the peasants erred, as we shall see, in thinking that "equality" was the fundamental point in the constitution framed by the Constituent Assembly.

(3.) PROPERTY AND THE REVOLUTION.

One of the most striking features of French economic history is the manner in which the peasantry, in spite of feudal burdens, not only retained a hold on the land, but actually extended their possessions. A less industrious or a more despondent class might well have disappeared amidst the stormy waters of eighteenth century economic life. The traditional division of French society into nobles, clergy and third estate, confuses rather than clarifies the grand issue of

1.—*Les Comités des droits féodaux . . .* ed. Sagnac and Caron, 1907, p. 192.
2.—*Ibid.*, p. 192. See Aulard, *Op. cit.*, p. 160, who notes that in some places the peasants actually burned the benches reserved for the nobles in the churches.

the Revolution—the abolition of economic privileges. None of these classes was homogeneous. There was a *noblesse de cour* whose privileges were dependent on the tenure of judicial or administrative posts, and there was a *noblesse de campagne* which included individuals of very unequal economic status. In like manner each of the other two classes was composed of persons with divergent interests. While some of the clergy owned large tracts of land and enjoyed every comfort, there were others who had to be content with simple tastes and who, if, on occasion, they lent a little money at interest, frequently gave alms and free loans to their parishioners.[1]

The *cahiers de doléances* drawn up by the third estate for the meeting of the States-General in May 1789 were a mild plea for political and social reform. They contained no radical social theory. Above all, they did not demand " equality," although they asked for many things in its name, such as legislative and administrative reform ; a more equitable distribution of taxation ; a more impartial dispensation of justice ; and, generally speaking, the abolition of those feudal privileges which robbed the people of the fruits of their industry.[2] Quite a number of the *cahiers* would permit the feudal lords to receive compensation for the loss of those privileges to which they could prove a legal title. The keynote of the *cahiers* was that property and liberty are inviolable rights which the State is bound to respect. Property is not only a legitimate right but a sacred one, not to be interfered with except for very sound social reasons. " Feudal rights," however, were privileges rather than legitimate property. They constituted a barrier to individual progress and prevented persons from enjoying the fruits of their labour.

1.—See the very interesting extracts from the diary of Abbé Barrois, (1740-1813), printed in H. Labourasse, *Le Luxe au Presbytère avant 1789*, 1897, p. 5, *et passim*. The diary kept by the Abbé extended over seventeen years, and M. Labourasse infers from the facts which it reveal that the economic condition of the French clergy in 1897 was superior at least to that of the country *curé* in pre-Revolutionary France.

2.—See André Lichtenberger, *Le Socialisme et la Révolution française*, 1899, p. 21, *et passim*, and also the article by the same writer in *L'oeuvre sociale de la Révolution*, ed. Émile Faguet, 1901, pp. 65f. See also the essay by Faguet, *Loc. cit.*, pp. 4-9, and Appendix to Herbert, *Op. cit.*, pp. 202f, for reprint of extract from *cahiers*.

The supreme inactivity of the States-General led the deputies of the third estate, who were joined by a few of the clergy, to form themselves into a Constituent or National Assembly on the 17th June, 1789. Louis XVI., as is well known, endeavoured to suppress what he considered an illegal body, but, finally, in deference to public opinion, commanded the other two orders to join the Assembly. The peasants' up-rising, and particularly the storming of the Bastille in July, speedily convinced the Assembly that the problems which required immediate solution were economic and social rather than constitutional and political. The fall of the Bastille on the 14th July—which typified much that was oppressive and odious in the old régime—had, however, an important effect on the members of the third estate. It strengthened the forces of conservatism. Up to that time the movement for reform was, broadly speaking, a popular one. But now the proprietary classes became alarmed, and two shades of opinion emerged in the third estate. The *bourgeoisie* resolve to become the governing class ; to exploit the revolution for its own profit ; and to silence advanced social views whether expressed in the club or in the press.[1] The debates on the rights of man ; the setting up by the Assembly of a committee of inquiry into feudal rights, with a view to compensating those who were supposed to have renounced their privileges under duress on the famous night of the 4th August ; the Constitution of 1791 ;—all these manifest a tender regard for individual, if not for corporate property,[2] and a desire to confine political power to property-owners.[3] In the preliminary drafts of the new Constitution a property qualification was introduced both for suffrage and the holding of office. A distinction was made between " active " and " passive " citizens. "Active " citizens were property-owners. In order to vote it was necessary that the individual should be paying taxes equal to the price of three

1.—See *Histoire Parlementaire de la Révolution française*, ed. J. B. Buchez and P. C. Roux, 1834, Paris, preface to t. ii., p. 2.
2.—See *Select Documents of the French Revolution*, ed. by L. G. Wickham-Legg, 1905, vol. ii., p. 219. In an explanatory note to the Constitution, 14 Sept., 1791, all church goods are declared national property.
3.—*Ibid.*, vol. i., p. 170.

days' labour on the land. To be elected as a deputy for central or local government, the payment of taxes to the value of a mark of silver (54 livres) was at first required; but that provision gave rise to such opposition that in the revised Constitution of 1791 all active citizens were declared eligible to a place in the Assembly. Thanks to the influence of the Girondins, the distinction between "active" and "passive" citizens was removed by the Convention Parliament.

Some maintained that a declaration of the rights of man was necessary as many people in France believed that they were the property of others.[1] Others thought that such a declaration of rights might prove dangerous and, if necessary, should form an appendix rather than a preface to the new Constitution.[2] M. Malouet contrasted the condition of America in 1776 with France in 1789. A declaration of rights could do no harm in a country like America where all property-owners were "accustomed to equality," and "strangers to luxury as well as to want."[3] Such people were prepared to receive liberty in its plenitude. Their tastes, their customs, and their situation made for democracy. It is different, however, with France. Here we have a large body of propertyless citizens, whose labour affords them but a mere subsistence, and who justly resent the display of wealth by the rich. One, therefore, must proceed with caution. It is more important that men in a dependent condition should "see the just limits of natural liberty than its extension."[4] There are scarcely any natural rights, he goes on to say, that are not modified by positive laws. No useful purpose, therefore, can be served by elaborating a doctrine which, in practice, must be subjected to limitations.[5] In a similar strain, M. de Landine referred to the original equality of men as "a philosophical fiction."[6] Of what avail is it, he asks, to lead men up to a high mountain and show them all their rights when they are obliged to climb down and submit to a

1.—Buchez and Roux, *Hist. Parl.*, 1834, t. ii., p. 196.
2.—*Ibid.*, t. ii., pp. 198-9.
3.—*Ibid.*, t. ii., p. 201.
4.—*Ibid.*, t. ii., p. 202.
5.—*Ibid.*, t. ii., p. 203.
6.—*Ibid.*, t. ii., p. 206.

modification of these rights in actual life.[1]   The right of
property, according to the Declaration of Rights finally
reached by the Assembly in August 1789, was one of the
" natural and imprescriptible rights of man." [2]   This right
being " inviolable and sacred, no one ought to be deprived
of it, except in cases of evident public necessity legally
ascertained, and on condition of a previous just indemnity." [3]

It was the view of property held by Locke, which made it
a natural right derived from human liberty and labour,[4] that
commended itself to the majority of the Assembly, though
they were loath to emphasise the sacredness of all property
as the reformation of feudal abuses was incomplete.   In
England Locke's theory of property was utilised to confirm
the established order.   In France it could only be reasonably
invoked to subvert the existing order, which deprived many
individuals of the free use and disposal of their property.   It
is interesting to compare both the third declaration of the
rights of man in August 1795 and the proclamation of the
Convention on 9th October, 1794, with the first declaration
of rights by the Constituent Assembly in 1789.   The
declaration of 1795 describes the right of property as " le
droit de jouir et de disposer de ses biens, de ses revenus, du
fruit de son travail et de son industrie." [5]   What is important
about it is what it omits.   There is no explicit reference, as
in Art. xvii. of the 1789 declaration of rights, to the State's
right to interfere with property arrangements in the interest
of the public good.   This was probably due to the strange
rumblings of the rights of " sans-culottes," [6] which moved

1.—*Ibid.*, t. ii., p. 209.
2.—Art. ii. English translation printed in Appendix to Dr. R. Price's
Discourse on the love of our Country in Brit. Mus. Tracts, 189(3). See also
Select Documents of the French Revolution, ed. Wickham-Legg, 1905,
vol. ii., p. 218.
3.—Art. xvii., Price, *Loc. cit.*
4.—*Hist. Parl.*, t. ii., pp. 308-9.
5.—*Ibid.*, t. xxxvi., p. 485.
6.—De Boissel's speech to the Jacobins was quoted in parliament to warn
the house of the radical social theories which were being discussed abroad.
See *Hist. Parl.*, t. xxvi., p. 107. François de Boissel published *Le Catéchisme
du genre humain* a few months after the opening of the States-General in
1789. His social views were very extreme and the book was highly irreligious
and immoral. It was condemned in the debates, see *Hist. Parl.*,
t. iii., p. 283.

the Convention Parliament to issue a proclamation to the people in which the following words occur : " Properties are sacred. Far be from us those systems, born of idleness and immorality, which minimise the guilt of robbery and erect it into a system."[1]

Brissot's doctrine that some property is robbery was, as we saw, misrepresented by his political opponents. There were, however, many pamphleteers and editors during the early years of the Revolution who held more radical views. Fauchet, for example, in a paper founded in January 1790, maintained that the amount of land which one may lawfully own is limited by the rights of others.[2] All had a claim to the land, and the State was bound to see to it that nobody was propertyless. In order to understand the attitude of the different Revolutionary governments towards the land question up to the time of Napoleon, it is necessary to describe more fully the various theories of property which were struggling for mastery. The theory that private property was an usurpation, and that communism was the natural and just condition of mankind, was definitely ruled out. The real issue was between those who held that property was a natural right, not to be interfered with except for very grave reasons and with due compensation to the individual whose interests were affected, and those who held that it was primarily a social convention based on human needs and capable of being modified whenever the State deems it necessary. The former point of view found expression in the Rights of Man in 1789, in the speech of Cazalès on inheritance laws in 1791,[3] and in that of Lasource in September 1792. Lasource's language reminds one of Locke. " Everyone entering the social pact," he states " brings with him his

---

1.—*Hist. Parl.*, t. xxxvi., p. 128.—" Les propriétés doivent être sacrées. Loin de nous ces systèmes, dictés par l'immoralité et la paresse, qui attenuent l'horreur du larcin et l'érigent en doctrine."

2.—See *Select Documents of the French Revolution*, ed. L. G. Wickham-Legg, 1905, vol. i., p. 282. See also Ch. R. Gosselin, *Refléxions d'un citoyen adressées aux notables sur la question proposée par un grand roi :* " *En quoi consiste le bonheur des peuples et quels sont les moyens de le procurer ? ou cet autre ' D'où vient la misère et quels sont les moyens d'y remédier,'* " Paris, 1787, p. 65. He advocated confiscation of Church property.

3.—*Hist. Parl.*, t. ix., p. 309.

properties, and the protection of these properties is the object of the social contract. They are, therefore, sacred and the nation cannot dispose of them except for the general good, and then with full compensation." [1]

The other view of property rights is well illustrated by the speeches of Mirabeau and Robespierre in the debate on inheritance laws in April 1791. " The right of property," according to Count Mirabeau, " is a social creation. Not only can the law protect and maintain property, but it may also determine and regulate its scope and content." [2] With regard to inheritance laws, the fundamental question is should the State permit the free disposal of property in the direct line ; that is, can a father or mother bestow their property on whom they wish ? As even the right of private property itself, for him, is not a natural right, it follows that the right to make a will may be abrogated or abolished by positive law.[3] Man's right to property cannot extend beyond this life. Society rather than the individual is the absolute owner of property. Society, therefore, has the right of refusing to its members, in particular cases, the faculty of disposing of their property freely. He would not allow them to dispose of more than one tenth.[4] Roman law allows the individual to decide between different inheritors ; permits parents to discriminate between their children. Mirabeau is not at all sure that a law which served as a beacon light in the past can be fruitfully invoked in this " century of reason." For the authority of Roman Law we must substitute the authority of reason. Equal division of property amongst the children was the most equitable solution. It would abolish favouritism ; promote a better distribution of wealth and lead to an increase of population.[5]

1.—For Lasource's speech from which we quote, see *Hist. Parl.,* t. xix., p. 15.

2.—*Hist. Parl.,* t. ix., p. 287.

3.—*Ibid.,* t. ix., p. 286. Mirabeau admits that there are natural rights, although he does not regard the right of private property or the right of testamentary disposition as belonging to that category of rights. This seems to follow from his statement that " if the right to make a will is a natural right, no positive law can abrogate or destroy that right though it may regulate its usage or exercise.

4.—Cf. Sagnac, *La Législation Civile,* 1898, p. 223.

5.—*Hist. Parl.,* t. ix., pp. 288-9.

On a former occasion, however, Mirabeau gave expression
to views which seem somewhat inconsistent with the doctrine
of property described in the preceding paragraph.   During
the debates on taxation in October 1789, he maintained that
the State, even in a great national emergency, could not,
without acting unjustly, conscript capital.[1]   He would even
exempt creditors of the State from all taxation, for by lending
their money to the government they were in reality paying
the taxes which would have to be paid by others.   At this
point a member challenged his plea for the *rentiers* by making
a distinction which was applauded.   The *rentier*, declared
this speaker, must be considered under a two-fold aspect.[2]
He is a creditor of the State, and, as such, must not suffer
any loss ; but he is also a citizen, and therefore, by virtue
of the income which he enjoys, ought to contribute something
in the way of taxes to the further upkeep of the State.   Again,
Mirabeau's view that the property of the very poor should
not be taxed,[3] though doubtless held on grounds of expediency,
may also be viewed as a tacit admission that there is at least
a certain minimum of property to which the individual has a
natural right and which, therefore, the State may not touch.

Robespierre also, though belonging to the Left Wing or Jacobin Party in politics, was not prepared to accept the full radical
conclusions which might be deduced from the doctrine that
property is a social convention ; that the State rather than the
individual is the real owner.[4]   He admitted that inequality of
wealth was the source of political inequality and destructive of
liberty,[5] but, like other members of the Jacobin Party, he regarded equality of possessions as impracticable in civil society.[6]

1.—*Hist. Parl.*, t. iii., p. 132.
2.—*Ibid.*, t. iii., p. 133.—" The *rentier* has two characters : he is a creditor
of the State and in this capacity he cannot be subjected to any reduction, it
would be bankruptcy ; he is a citizen and by reason of his income he should
contribute to his country."
3.—*Ibid.*, t. iii., p. 131.
4.—*Ibid.*, t. ix., pp. 300f.
5.—*Ibid.*, t. ix., p. 299.
6.—Every member of society, however, had a right to the means of subsistence, and it was the first duty of the State to give that right concrete
expression.   See *Oeuvres de Maximilien Robespierre*, edit. Laponneraye, 1840,
t. iii., p. 353 ; p. 34.—" The first social law is .   .   . that which guarantees
the means of subsistence to all the members of society."—In Lichtenberger,
Le Socialisme et la Révolution française, 1899, p. 105.

In reality what he combated was excessive inequalities or privileges rather than inequalities as such. His party, as Lichtenberger has shown, greeted proposals for "an agrarian law," or the establishment of an agrarian democracy, with derision.[1] In the Convention Parliament Danton, with Robespierre's approbation, demanded a declaration to the effect that property was sacred. And Robespierre approved of the action of the Convention in voting the death penalty against anyone who would propose an agrarian law, (18 March, 1793).[2]

According to Robespierre, however, the State could do much to reduce the existing volume of inequality in property by altering the laws of succession.[3] Society being the owner of all property, the property of the individual after his death should return to the source from which it was derived. The public interest, as well as the nature of the right of property, demand that, as far as possible, there shall be an equal division of property at death. He would not, however, like to see the right of testamentary disposition "entirely destroyed."[4]

M. Cazalès's reply[5] to the foregoing speeches is worth noting as it is typical of another strand of opinion with regard to the nature of property rights. But before doing so, and in order to appreciate the legislation passed by the Constituent Assembly (on the 8 April, 1791), and subsequently by the Convention (7 March, 1793), a word must be said on the laws and customs governing the disposal and transmission of property in pre-Revolutionary France.[6]

Practice with regard to inheritance and disposal of property varied widely, as M. Sagnac has shown.[7] Wherever Roman law or the feudal system of succession had not obtained a

---

1.—*Le Socialisme et la Révolution française*, 1899, ch. iv., pp. 97f. See also his article in *L'Oeuvre sociale de la Révolution*, ed. Émile Faguet, 1901, p. 84.

2.—And on 31 March, 1793, the same penalty was decreed against all who urged people to violate property.

3.—*Hist. Parl.*, t. ix., p. 300.

4.—*Ibid.*, t. ix., p. 301.

5.—*Ibid.*, t. ix., pp. 309f.

6.—See Jean Domat, *The Civil Law in its natural order together with the Publick Law*, tr. Strahan, London, 1722, vol. i., part ii., pp. 542-549.

7.—*La Législation Civile*, 1898, pp. 214f.

footing, the custom was to consider property as belonging to the family rather than to the individual. Fathers were regarded as simply administrators of their property to which all their children had, as a rule, an equal claim. The two other systems of succession in vogue—the feudal and the Roman—favoured concentration of wealth ; and gave rise to a number of voluntary and legal inequalities.[1] According to the Roman system it is the individual's will rather than custom or law which determines who shall inherit his property. He might give it all to one member of the family ; he might divide it between two members, or he might leave it to an outsider. The feudal system of succession prevailed amongst the nobles. They generally adopted the system of primogeniture, chiefly for reasons of prestige. The revolutionaries aimed at reducing these diverse systems to unity. The abolition of the feudal régime decreed, in principle, on the 4th August, 1789, naturally involved the disappearance, in course of time, of the system of inheritance derived from feudal practice.[2] On the 15th March, 1790, the feudal system of succession to property was formally abrogated. All inequalities arising from the accident of noble birth or the holding of noble land were to cease henceforth.[3]

The debates in which Mirabeau, Robespierre and Cazalès participated, led to further legislation as to property. Despite Cazalès's eloquent appeal for legal inequality, the Assembly, on 8th April, 1791, passed a decree establishing the principle of equal division of property in case of intestacy. The inequalities due to human will, from the exercise of the right of testamentary disposition, were left untouched, thanks to the opposition of Cazalès and others. Cazalès sounded a conservative note when he told the Assembly that the decree which it had rushed through in less than an hour would not be passed in England without years of mature deliberation.[4]

1.—*Ibid.*, p. 217.—Cf. Domat, *Op. cit.*, vol. i., p. 648, for contrast between Roman law and French customs.
2.—Sagnac, *Op. cit.*, pp. 217-18.
3.—The decree was prudently enforced so as to cause the minimum amount of inconvenience under the circumstances.—Sagnac, *Op. cit.*, p. 218.
4.—*Hist. Parl.*, t. ix., p. 310.

Fixity of property is essential to the welfare of a nation ; there can be no real patriotism without it. Again, look at the economic and social consequences of equal division. It means that after the death of one member of the family the others will have to sell the whole property in order to effect a new division. This will lead to endless confusion and uncertainty.[1] Division of properties might work all right in the case of lands intensively cultivated, but in the case of pasture, or where great expenditure must be incurred on the land, it would be ruinous. What, for example, would become of the vineyards of Burgundy if they were divided up ?[2] His advice was " to establish the Roman law all over the kingdom with the exceptions which circumstances and local needs may demand."[3] He felt, like De Tocqueville in later years, that the " law of partible inheritance " would not only affect " property itself," but " the minds of the heirs."[4] It would destroy the intimate connection between " family-feeling and the preservation of the paternal estate," and disperse rapidly " both families and fortunes."[5]

Cazalès argued that the right to make a will was a necessary consequence of paternal power.[6] It owed nothing to Roman law or to the custom of feudal lords. It was, moreover, founded on the fact that " property is based on

1.—*Ibid.*, t. ix., p. 314.
2.—*Ibid.*, t. ix., p. 315.
3.—*Ibid.*, t. ix., p. 315.
4.—*Democracy in America*, tr. Reeve, 1838, vol. ii., pp. 41-42.
5.—*Ibid.*, p. 43. It is generally admitted that the " law of descent " as embodied in the Civil Code has been at least one of the principal factors in retarding the normal growth of population in France. See Marcel Thiébault, *Le Principe de propriété individuelle devant l'Assemblée Constituante*, 1899, p. 117. As the Rev. G. de Pascal, in his *La Propriété et le code Napoléon*, 1897, p. 4, points out, Article 826 of the Code, giving every member of the family the right of demanding his or her share of the moveable and immoveable property, puts France in a state of " permanent liquidation." The Spanish code is much better. It avoids the legal expenses so frequently associated with the enforcement of Article 826 of the French code by giving the testator the right of making the division provided he has regard for its legitimacy.
6.—*Hist. Parl.*, t. ix., p. 312. Cazalès interpreted Montesquieu's statement, " the law of nature ordains that fathers shall provide for their children ; but does not oblige them to make them their heirs," (*Hist. Parl.*, t. ix., p. 314), to mean that the father had a right to dispose of his property as he wished. But Montesquieu, as we saw, clearly admitted that the State could interfere with property, and if necessary command " equal division " : the order of succession or inheritance depended upon the " principles of political or civil law."—*Works*, 1777, vol. ii., bk. xxvi., ch. vi., p. 208.

labour." [1] Inequality of property is not a product of the feudal system : it is anterior to it, and due to the industry of individuals. The Convention Parliament of 1793, however, thought otherwise. It proceeded to abolish all feudal rights without compensation, on 17th July, 1793, and on the 7th March, 1793, it abrogated the right of testamentary disposition in the direct line. [2]

The latter decree was in a special sense a product of circumstances. It was directed primarily against those parents who, out of hatred for the Revolution, disinherited their sons because of their attachment to the new régime. In practice, however, this law was sometimes modified. The individual was permitted to dispose of a tenth of his property if he had descendants in the direct line, and one sixth if he had only collateral descendants. [3] Gifts *inter vivos* also could not exceed a certain maximum. These restrictions on gifts and inheritance were made retroactive as far as 14th July, 1789, and thus gave rise to much resentment. The peace of families was frequently disturbed as a result of that provision. But the Convention remained undismayed. [4] Particular interests may have been sacrificed, but the Convention rejoiced in the thought that the general interest was upheld, and that the declaration of the rights of man of July 1789 was no longer an empty formula.

The above legislation was largely inspired by political or patriotic considerations, and was, in a sense, a precautionary measure. But the decree of 10 June, 1793, declaring common lands the property of the communes in which they were located, and that of 17 July, 1793, suppressing all " feudal rights, whether fixed or casual," without indemnity, [5] signify something more than a concession to practical exigencies. They mark, in fact, the triumph of a definite

1.—*Hist. Parl.*, t. ix., p. 313.
2.—See Sagnac, *Op. cit.*, p. 225.
3.—*Ibid.*, pp. 226-27.
4.—See Sagnac, *Op. cit.*, p. 238. M. Sagnac thinks that it was because these laws were regarded as conforming to the general interest and justice that they were not attacked during all the attempted reaction.—*Op. cit.*, p. 239.
5.—See Aulard, *La Révolution française et le régime féodal.* 1919, p. 248, for details of this decree which led to "a revolution within the Revolution."

theory of property. It denotes the supremacy of Rousseau's
doctrine, as expressed in the *Social Contract,* over that held
by the Physiocrats and by the majority of the members of
the Constituent Assembly.

Lord Macaulay's[1] characterisation of the Constituent
Assembly—" they were not constituent "—has a special
relevancy to their method of dealing with the question of
feudal rights. In August 1789 the Assembly declared that
the feudal system was abolished, and at the same time it
proceeded to make distinctions and reservations which, in
effect, largely rehabilitated it. The decrees passed between
the 4th and 12th August included, *inter alia,* the following
clauses.[2] " Of the feudal rights, those which are derived
from real or personal *mainmorte* and personal servitude, and
those corresponding to them, are abolished without indemnity.
All others are redeemable, and the price and method of their
redemption shall be fixed by the National Assembly." All
perpetual rents, whether in money or in kind, whatever their
character and origin, and to whatever persons due, were also
declared redeemable. Also the *champarts* of all kinds, and
under all names, were to be purchased at a rate to be fixed
by the Assembly. Although tithes were also abolished, the
Assembly ordered that they were to be paid until such time
as it could make provision for the different persons affected
by their abolition.

The peasants throughout the country began to take the
first article of the decrees—" The National Assembly entirely
destroys the feudal régime "—quite seriously. They forgot,
or rather they did not understand, the numerous restrictions
which the subsequent clauses of the decrees imposed on the
first article. The Assembly, anxious to carry out reform with
the least possible amount of inconvenience to the feudal
land-owners, set up a committee to deal with the difficult
practical questions which inevitably arose when it came to
applying the decrees. The personnel of the committee com-
prised representatives of the clergy, nobility, and the third

1.—" Essay on Mirabeau " in *Miscellaneous Writings and Essays,*
1889, p. 272.
2.—See *Hist. Parl.,* t. ii., pp. 224f. See Sagnac, *Op. cit.,* p. 91.

estate.[1] The committee, following the lines of the decrees, began by distinguishing between feudal rights which were personal—*droits personnels,* and feudal rights which were real—*droits réels.* The latter were to be bought out, and the former were to be abolished without compensation.[2]

This distinction, as Sagnac has pointed out, was too simple to correspond to the complex character of existing feudal rights. The classification of feudal rights adopted by the committee was clearly out of touch with the economic and political realities of the eighteenth century. For example, the feudal category known as personal rights, that is, rights obliging persons directly, was intelligible in the Middle Ages when the feudal lord provided security and work for his vassals, but it was useless and unjust now that the *seigneurs* no longer performed these functions. The other category, that is, rights " obliging persons only through the intermediary of the land, due from the soil itself and for the concession of which they were established,"[3] included elements which belonged to the former class. An obvious example was that of a *mainmortable* by status or occupation rather than by birth.[4] Here the " personal " dovetails into " real," and, therefore, in strict theory should have been regarded as redeemable. The Assembly, however, was not logical and did not insist on this. But it did insist on other things where to have been illogical would have proved even more meritorious.

Thus the rights of *cens, champart, quint, relief, lods et ventes, etc.,* were declared redeemable unless it could be shown that they were not due to a primitive concession of land.[5] The Assembly put the onus of proof on the peasant. The peasant if unable to produce the title-deeds, or to vindicate his rights in the law courts controlled by feudal interests, was compelled to pay as usual the *cens,* " to carry

1.—For details see Sagnac, *Op. cit.,* pp. 97-120.
2.—See *Les Comités des droits féodaux et de législation et l'abolition du régime seigneurial,* 1789-1793, ed. Ph. Sagnac and P. Caron, 1907, p. 54 ; p. 183.
3.—Cf. Sagnac, *Op. cit.,* p. 98.
4.—Cf. Herbert, *Op. cit.,* p. 131.
5.—See *Les Comités des droits féodaux* . . . ed. Sagnac and Caron, pp. 671-705. Sagnac, *Op. cit.,* p. 104.

a part of his harvest into the *seigneurial* barns that were often miles from his own home, and to quit his farm for several days in the year to work on his master's land." [1]   The decrees passed by the Legislative Assembly in August 1792 were, however, an advance on the work of the National Assembly.   The Legislative Assembly transferred the onus of proof to the feudal lord.   It was he rather than the peasant who was to furnish evidence of his right to the above privileges.   If the right could be justified by original titles or documents, they were still redeemable.   But even then the peasant was faced with the practical difficulty of finding money to compensate the *seigneur* for surrendering rights to which the latter could prove his title.   If the State could declare ecclesiastical goods national property, by what process of logic could it justify the retention of *seigneurial* privileges or demand compensation for their surrender ?   Why confiscate one form of property and buttress another ?   Thus reasoned the Abbé Tardieu and the people of Bas-Vivarais in a petition addressed to the National Assembly on January 16th, 1790.[2]   The Abbé's views did not, however, receive the attention they deserved until the very existence of the nation was imperilled by war abroad, and by civil strife at home.   The Convention, however, made more than an *amende honorable* to the harassed peasants.

The decrees passed on 10th June, and 17th July, 1793, were far more drastic than those sanctioned by the Legislative Assembly between the 20th and 28th of August, 1792.   The latter granted compensation for feudal claims which could be proved to have originated in a concession of land.   The onus of proof, as we saw, was removed from the peasant to the lord.   Again, the legislation of 1792 permitted the feudal

1.—Sagnac, *La Législation civile*, p. 105.
2.—*Mémoire de l'Abbé Tardieu . . .* pour le peuple du Bas-Vivarais, 18 Janvier, 1790, printed in *Les Comités des droits féodaux*, ed. Sagnac and Caron, 1907, pp. 76-78 . . . " You have declared that ecclesiastical goods belong to the nation ; we applaud your wisdom.   But you have left alone the (feudal) rents of the lords. . . .   Yet could it not be said with truth that these goods belong more to the nation than ecclesiastical goods ? . . .   Freedom to buy them out will always be for the small peasants a useless means for peacefully securing their small farms, since the poor can never count on possessing a considerable sum of money."—*Ibid.*, p. 78.

lord to retain any common lands or wastes to which he could prove his title, or at least if he had enjoyed undisputed possession of them for forty years. Even after the so-called self-denying ordinance of the *noblesse* on the famous night of the 4th August, 1789, it appears that many instances of interference with communal rights and usurpations of common lands had been complained of by the peasantry.[1]

The decree passed on 28th August, 1792, however, gave the village communities far-reaching powers to deal with the situation.[2] They could compel the lords to return usurped lands or unpurchased customary rights to their tenants. The law of 10th June, 1793, was even more drastic. It decreed that all commons held by feudal lords, which had not been legitimately purchased, should revert to the village communities without compensation to the *seigneurs*. The decree of 17th July, 1793, declaring all feudal claims abolished without indemnity, explicitly excluded " rentes ou prestations purement foncières et non féodales " [3] from its operation, but in practice it was difficult to distinguish the feudal from the non-feudal element in rents arising from land.[4] The same title frequently included feudal and ordinary rents. In applying the law some judges made a distinction between these two rents, but others declared all rents, into which any feudal element entered, abolished without indemnity.

It had taken four years of strife and suffering before the peasants were completely freed from feudal exactions. The reforming laws passed in August 1789, Karéiew [5] observes,

1.—See *Les Comités des droits féodaux . . .* ed. Sagnac and Caron, pp. 133-4. A petition of a priest named Gauquelin of Avranches to Chapelier, the President of the National Assembly, August 18, 1789, protests against the action of the seigneurs. A similar petition to the Assembly in 1790 complains of interference with the peasants' "long and peaceable possession of the soil," which they had practically created by their labour and, adding, that they were better off in 1785.—*Loc. cit.*, p. 515.

2.—To what extent, or with what consequences, this decree was availed of is not fully known. Mr. Herbert, *Op. cit.*, p. 194, writes, " The history of the application of this decree and its economic results has not yet been written."

3.—Aulard, *Op. cit.*, p. 248.

4.—*Ibid.*, p. 257.

5.—*Op. cit.*, p. 451. Cf. Aulard, *La Révolution française et le régime féodal*, 1919, pp. 282-3.

took four years to elaborate and promulgate, and four more years to apply. Neither the Directory nor the Consulate, however, wanted to re-establish feudal privileges. The question as to how far the small property-owners benefited by the confiscation of Church and other property, such as that of the *émigrés*, is incapable of a precise answer until the historical inquiry now in progress on the subject is completed.[1] The lion's share of the spoil, it is generally admitted, went into the hands of the wealthy land-owners and the *bourgeoisie*.[2] The National Assembly, despite the protestations of the committee of mendicity and the society of agriculture, thought that the State should provide labour rather than land for the poor.[3] In certain parts of the country the peasants acquired some ecclesiastical property, and from November 1793 they were afforded favourable terms on which to purchase the property of *émigrés*, chiefly for political reasons.[4]

The struggle between the adherents of the view that property is a natural right, involving the right of the individual to dispose freely of it by will, and those who held that the right of private property is due to society and gives the individual no strict right to determine who shall possess it after his death, has been described in some detail. It remains to be seen how far these views were embodied in the final legislation at the close of the internal revolutionary period, before noting some of the conclusions suggested by this chapter.

Napoleon had a difficult task to perform in codifying the scattered civil codes which existed in France, and had he done nothing more his name would have an assured place in

1.—See Prof. Aulard's article in *Modern France*, ed. Arthur Tilley, 1922, pp. 121f.

2.—See Sagnac, *La Législation civile*, p. 189. Cf. Georges Lefebvre, *Les Paysans du Nord pendant la Révolution française*, 1924.

3.—Sagnac, *Op. cit.*, p. 172.—The Constitution of 1791 proclaimed that it was the duty of the State to create and organise general institutions for the relief of the poor, to help the helpless, and to provide work for those willing to work. In 1793 the Convention endeavoured to translate these ideas into practice by a system of national relief financed by the treasury, but this ended with the Directory. See Camille Bloch, *L'Assistance et l'Etat en France à la veille de la Révolution*, 1908, p. 111.

4.—Sagnac, *Op. cit.*, pp. 181-82.

history. By a series of financial and other measures he endeavoured to heal the wounds caused to the nation by the Reign of Terror. Reaction does not necessarily mean retrogression. The regulation of inheritance in the Civil Code, though a reaction on the legislation of the Convention, was an improvement. The individual recovers in a large measure the right of testamentary disposition. Napoleon wanted to re-establish, as far as possible under the circumstances, parental authority, and thus the *Code* raised the amount of property of which the father might dispose from one tenth, allowed by the Convention, to one fourth.[1] The testamentary liberty allowed by the *Code* did not, however, prevent each child in the family from claiming his or her share of the property. Article 745 lays down that, in the absence of a will, the property must be divided equally between the children or their descendants. Article 913 allows the father to dispose of half his property when he has only one child; a third of it when he has two children; and a fourth when he has three or more.[2] The power which that article confers has been frequently criticised. It is regarded as too wide by some and too narrow by others.[3] It enables the father to benefit one member of the family at least to the extent of one fourth of the property; that, it is alleged, penalises the other members and is opposed to the democratic spirit of the Revolution.[4] On the other hand, the power which it confers is sometimes considered too narrow; it prevents the father from endowing more liberally members of the family who, owing to physical or mental disabilities, may require far more than the law allows to fit them for the economic struggle of life.

1.—For details see Sagnac, *La Législation civile*, 1898, pp. 348-352, M. A. Franck, *Le Droit de Tester*, 1867, pp. 151f. For further criticism of the Code Civile see P. G. de Pascal, *Op. cit.*, p. 4. Charles G. Doazan, *La Législation française sur la petite propriété*, 1914, p. 33.

2.—Franck, *Op. cit.*, p. 154.

3.—See De Pascal, *Op. cit.*, p. 4 ; Doazan, *Op. cit.*, p. 33.

4.—M. Sagnac seems to regard the legislation governing property and inheritance in the *Code* inferior to that of the Convention, *Op. cit.*, p. 353. For a fuller account of the changes introduced by the *Civil Code* see the article by Prof. A. de Lapradelle in *Modern France*, ed. Tilley, 1922, ch. vi., pp. 323f.

The definition of property adopted in the *Code* and the regulations laid down with regard to the disposal and inheritance of property were of the nature of a compromise. The *Code* represents an attempt to fuse two theories, that of property as a natural right, and that of property as a social creation. It defines property as the right " to enjoy and to dispose of a thing in the most absolute manner, provided one does not use it in a way contrary to the laws or rules of the State." [1] That definition seems to owe more to the inspiration of the Physiocrats and to Locke's *Civil Government*, than to Rousseau's *Social Contract*. In the early years of the Revolutionary period the absolute or individualistic aspect of property rights, stressed by some members of the Constituent Assembly, retarded the growth of a definite or detailed policy towards the abolition of feudal privileges. It was only when the doctrine of property as a social right, held by Mirabeau, Robespierre, and the principal lay writers of the eighteenth century other than the Physiocrats, was accepted by the Convention, that the view expressed by Target in 1789—the property of the poor is as sacred as that of the rich [2]—received practical recognition. But Robespierre and those who held that property rights were due to the State, were anxious to forestall the radical conclusions which might be deduced from that doctrine by insisting that property was not merely a social convention. We know that the Constitution of the Year III. (1795) replaced manhood suffrage by a property qualification, and that the Executive Directory was composed of men of rather conservative social views. The property of the individual, however poor, being now freed from feudal exactions, the time was ripe for a theory which would re-emphasise its sacredness. That, broadly speaking, was the design of the article on property in the *Code Napoléon*.

The definition of property adopted in the *Code* seems to imply that property entails no duties on its owner other than those laid down by positive law. At least the *Code*, unlike the Constitution of 1848, does not explicitly recognise

1.—See Lichtenberger, *Le Socialisme et la Révolution française*, p. **184**.
2.—*Hist. Parl.*, t. i., p. **458**.

the existence of "rights and duties anterior to positive laws." [1]
The doctrine of natural law and natural right should serve
as a criterion as well as a justification of property rights. It
is, perhaps, too frequently employed in the latter rôle. The
Code, however, in so far as it implies that the duties of
property are limited to the observance by the individual of
the regulations laid down with regard to property by the
State, either presupposes that these regulations will be in
conformity with natural right, or else it opens the door to a
violation of natural rights. Some think that because the
rich ordinarily have a predominant influence in making
the laws and regulations governing property, the interests
of those whose property is dependent completely on their
labour are thus endangered. [2]

The Revolution was fundamentally an expression of
individualism. It was a movement to free the individual
from traditional restraints of an economic, social, political,
and religious character. The Church in France, weakened
by dogmatic divisions owing to the Jansenist heresy, and
being itself largely implicated in the feudal system of land
tenure, was unable to adopt a strong Christian attitude
towards feudal abuses ; and, in general, to assert its moral
supremacy in economic and social affairs. Many individual
members of the clergy were ardent advocates of economic
and social reform. And some of them were apostles of
individualism and enthusiasts for economic science when both
individualism and economics needed emphasis. [3] They often
moved in the materialistic atmosphere of the Encyclopedists
without stain to their garments. They made common cause
with them on the question of feudal reform, while they
loathed the materialistic philosophy which was as intent on
depriving the peasants of the heritage of their Faith as it
was on ridding them of the remnants of the feudal system.

1.—See Charles Boucaud, Qu'est ce que le droit naturel ? Paris, 1906, p. 12.

2.—For a rather extreme criticism of the Code from that point of view,
see F. Dugast, La Propriété devant le droit naturel, Paris, 1904, pp. 6-10.
" Labour," he says, " should be the only title to property."—Op. cit., p. 9.

3.—See Abbé Nicolas Baudeau, Principes de la science morale et politique
sur le luxe et les loix sumptuaires, 1767, ed. A. Dubois, Paris, 1912, p. 25. See
Morellet, Mélanges de littérature et de philosophie du xviiie siècle, Paris,
1818, t. iv., p. 309.

Some of the *curés*, as we saw, accepted the confiscation of Church property as a national necessity, though they expressed surprise that less justifiable forms of property were considered sacred. The debates in the National Assembly on Church property, which cannot be considered in detail here, not only illustrate the victory of what one may call the social over the individual view of property rights, but reveal, in part, the reason of the Church's failure to enforce effectively in the eighteenth century its own view on the nature and function of private property.

The partial dependence of the higher ranks of the clergy for their position and revenues on the good-will of the king, which the Concordat of 1516 [1] established, tended to make them unduly submissive towards social evils. During the debates in the National Assembly the Archbishop of Aix maintained that Church property was never given by the nation or to the nation.[2]   The *Curé* de Cuiseaux took a different view, holding that the State was the " owner of all the goods of the clergy," [3] and that only morality and internal discipline belonged to the province of the Church. The Assembly, in deference to the Archbishop's speech, made a distinction between ownership and disposal of property. The Church may own property but the State can dispose of it. As public property, ecclesiastical goods must be at the disposal of the State in time of a national emergency.[4] The army needed reorganisation ;   time was pressing ; and, therefore, said Thouret, we have ordered the sale of some Church property, but " the nation has a right to all." [5]   Abbé d'Eymard's protest, that Thouret had only given the Assembly the " romance of property " while the Archbishop of Aix had given them its " history," [6] went unheeded.

The Revolution, owing to the spoliative policy adopted by its directors towards Church and other property, has

1.—See the article by Henri Hauser in *Modern France*, ed. Tilley, 1922, p. 9.
2.—*Hist. Parl.*, t. v., pp. 330-331.
3.—*Ibid.*, t. v., pp. 364-365.
4.—*Ibid.*, t. v., p. 336.
5.—*Ibid.*, t. v., p. 336.
6.—*Ibid.*, t. v., p. 366-67.

frequently been described as a socialistic movement.[1] Now apart altogether from the consideration that confiscation or spoliation of property is not an essential, though it may be an inevitable, element of socialism as generally understood, it is quite easy to show that the economic and social conditions of a socialistic movement—the existence of a very large class of propertyless workers—were absent from the France of 1789, as indeed they are from the France of to-day. All the directing forces of the Revolution, the proprietary classes, had no intention of sanctioning an economic equalitarianism. The inviolability or sacredness of individual property was stressed even by those who held that all property rights are derived from the State. The Revolution, by abolishing " orders " and " associations " within the State, and by proclaiming freedom of contract and the equality of all before the law, gave an impetus to individualism and capitalism rather than to socialism. The Law Le Chapelier, 1791, decreed that, "As the destruction of every kind of association among citizens of the same state or profession is one of the fundamental bases of the French Constitution, it is forbidden to re-establish these under any pretext or any form whatsoever." [2] It is well known how that law was utilised by the capitalist class to prevent the legalisation of Trade Unions in France until the last quarter of the nineteenth century. The law abolishing associations or favouring competition was passed, it must not be forgotten, by an Assembly which regarded agricultural as far more important than manufacturing industry. There were capitalists and mere wage-earners in France then. What French writers call " mobile " capital was already powerful, but its importance had not yet received full recognition. Even Francois de Boissel, one of the most extreme social theorists of the Revolutionary period, fixed all his attention on the distribution of land, " partage de

1.—The following works, among others, seem to confound the political radicalism of the Revolution with socialistic ideas.—Paul Janet, *Les Origines du Socialisme contemporain*, Paris, 1866. Amédée Lefaure, *Le Socialisme pendant la Révolution française*, Paris, 1867.

2 See *Modern France*, ed. Tilley, p. 346.

terres." [1] He has nothing to say about the distribution of wealth amongst the industrial or manufacturing classes.

The development of capitalistic production in the nineteenth century was intimately connected with the complete victory of economic individualism which the French Revolution secured. On the other hand that individualism, by the logic of facts, led to the growth of associations both amongst employers and employees. The individual was no longer the unit in economic affairs. Economic development had now made freedom to combine essential to freedom to compete. The craving for security is as great as the desire for competition. Reformers and statesmen were led again to envisage private property from the social rather than from the individual standpoint. Those who rely exclusively on State action to check the anti-social aspects of modern capitalism think that the policy of the Revolutionaries towards agrarian feudalism might, with good results, be imitated by an age confronted with the problem of industrial feudalism. Others are of opinion that this remedy might prove worse than the disease. But every right minded person must admit that if property due to personal effort and initiative is a progressive and stabilising influence in society, property divorced from labour and labour which remains merely potential property tend to be subversive of national, as they sometimes are of individual, and family life.

1.—*Le Catéchisme du genre humain*, 1789. See *Hist. Parl.*, t. iii., p. 283, for criticism and condemnation of this book. It is interesting to contrast with De Boissel's book the views set forth in *Le Cadastre Perpétuel*, 1789, by Babeuf and J. P. Audiffered, p. 13, and pp. 80-81. These writers condemn feudal abuses in the name of natural right and suggested a more equitable system of taxation.

CHAPTER VII.

CONCLUSION.

ECONOMISTS have long since recognised the truth of Oscar Wilde's dictum that, " he to whom the present is the only thing that is present, knows nothing of the age in which he lives." [1] The contempt for tradition which, broadly speaking, characterised eighteenth century thought, forms a striking contrast to more modern speculation which is constantly seeking to find its root in former ages. To-day economists and philosophers—and to be a good economist one must, in a sense, be a philosopher—are studying with greater energy and sympathy than ever before the ideas and ideals of the past. The general attitude of eighteenth century writers towards preceding ages now serves merely as a warning that it is nearly as difficult to write history as to make it. The modern student realises that if facts are the body of history, it is by criticism one obtains access to its living spirit. But he also recognises that the criticism which fails to take account of the representative facts can never comprehend the life of a period in all its fullness.

In the eighteenth century Dr. Price [2] was one of the few who knew history sufficiently well to state that the policy of governments towards enclosures, for example, was " more favourable to the higher classes of people," than the policy pursued by Edward VI., or Charles I. Policy with reference to enclosures in the eighteenth century probably owed something to Locke's influence. For not only was he the " prophet of property," [3] but he was also the apostle of individualism. Enclosures and agricultural re-organisation would doubtless

1.—*Intentions*, 1925, p. 172.
2.—*Observations on Reversionary Payments*, 1792, vol. ii., p. 294.
3.—See A. L. Smith's article "English Political Philosophy in the Seventeenth and Eighteenth Centuries," in *Cambridge Modern History*, vol. vi., ch. 23, p. 814.

have taken place in England had Locke never lived.   But there are some grounds for thinking that they would not have involved so much distress to the poor or small property-owner had Locke's theory of property enjoyed less popularity in the eighteenth century than it did.[1]   During our period the State itself assumed, so to speak, an individualistic rôle, and forced men to be free by helping to remove those traditional or customary relationships which placed obstacles to the unrestricted movements of individuals and the unfettered use of their property.

" To conclude this article about customs," wrote a land surveyor [2] in 1727, "I would advise all Noblemen and Gentlemen, whose Tenants hold their Lands by *Copy of Court-Roll* for three Lives, not to let them renew, except they will agree to deliver up their Copy in order to alter the Tenure, by converting it to *Leasehold on Lives*.   This method will put a stop to that *unreasonable* Custom of the Widow's holding a Life by her Free-bench, which is a fourth Life, not covenanted for in the Copy, but only pretended to by *Custom;* which deprives the Lord of an undoubted right of making the best, and *doing what he will with his own*."

Without a detailed investigation it is not easy to say how far Locke's views on education influenced the policy, or lack of policy, of the State with regard to it in the eighteenth century.   It is, however, at least probable that his concentration on the character element in education, and his underration of the differences in the natural endowments of individuals, tended to make education appear a domestic affair rather than a national concern.   The weight of his authority could, therefore, be invoked in favour of non-interference with property by way of special taxes levied for educational purposes.

A full consideration of Locke's ideas on religion and morality, and their influence on the social theory and practice

1.—A book entitled *The Judgement of whole Kingdoms and Nations concerning the Rights and Prerogatives of Kings, and the rights, privileges and properties of the People*, popularising Locke's political philosophy, had reached a tenth edition by 1771.   The author is commonly regarded as Lord Somers.

2.—Edward Lawrence, *The Duty of a Steward to his Lord*, 1727, art. xxiii., p. 60.   (Goldsmiths' Library) Italics in the original.

of the eighteenth century, lay outside the scope of the present work. It may be remarked, however, that he made a stronger plea for the application of religious and ethical criteria and sanctions to economic, social, and political life than is commonly supposed. If, at times, he seems to reduce religion almost entirely to "an attitude of intellectual belief,"[1] he himself was satisfied that the only true rule of life was that contained in the *New Testament*.[2] Although there is an element of inconsistency in his views as to what constitutes the true ethical criterion,[3] it is of interest to note that in one of his miscellaneous papers[4] he regarded a Godless ethic as ineffective. Morality, divorced from a Supreme Lawgiver, with "a right to ordain" and "a power to reward and punish,"[5] appeared to him to strip virtue and vice of their real power and significance, and to reduce them to the level of "reputation" and "disgrace."[6] "The view of Heaven and Hell," he writes in *The Reasonableness of Christianity*, "will cast a Slight upon the short Pleasures and Pains of this present State, and give Attractions and Encouragements to Virtue, which Reason and Interest, and the care of ourselves, cannot but allow and prefer. Upon this Foundation, and upon this only, Morality stands firm, and may defy all Competition."[7] This, he thinks, makes morality "more than a Name, a Substantial Good worth all our Aims and endeavours."[8]

But the tendency of eighteenth century thought to disbelieve in anything that could not be definitely weighed and measured[9] reduced the power of such appeals for virtue, and their influence in economic and social relations. The preoccupation of the century with the material interests of life

1.—W. R. Sorley, *A History of English Philosophy*, 1920, pp. 126-7.
2.—See above ch. iii. and Lord King, *Life of Locke*, 1829, p. 5.
3.—Windelband, *History of Philosophy*, tr. Tufts, pp. 503-513.
4.—"Of Ethics in General," printed in King, *Life of Locke*, 1829, p. 312.
5.—King, *Life of Locke*, 1829, p. 312.
6.—*Ibid.*, p. 307.
7.—Locke, *Works*, 1714, vol. ii., p. 537.
8.—*Ibid.*, vol. ii., p. 537.
9.—"The overthrow of the older authorities had carried along with it nearly all that could serve as an obvious basis for the higher life of mankind."—John S. Mackenzie, *An Introduction to Social Philosophy*, 1890, p. 84.

left little room for the application of the exalted utilitarianism of Locke.   He himself had noted that " Virtue and Prosperity do not often accompany one another ; and, therefore, Virtue seldom had many Followers." [1]   It would be quite unfair to Locke to regard him as an English Machiavelli, or to trace to him the cynical doctrine that private vices are public benefits.   Whatever Mandeville may have thought about the value of riches—and his views have been frequently mis-interpreted—Locke certainly seemed to hold that material prosperity tends to generate an atmosphere which obscures the goal to which our higher interests lead.

Locke's individualistic conception of property, however, tended to make men confuse means with ends.   Had he applied some of that freshness and directness of mind,[2] of which he had an uncommon share, to studying first-hand the views on property held by writers like St. Thomas in the thirteenth, and by others in the sixteenth century, he might have produced a more balanced theory of property.   But the Oxford of his day did not represent what was best in mediaeval thought ; and there were political issues in the seventeenth century which compelled even philosophers to descend to the particular.   It is only in a revisionist age, like the present, that the reasonableness of theories of property held in ages anterior to Locke is beginning to be acknowledged.   Locke cared little for the past.   His mind was mainly directed towards the political, social and philosophical problems of his own time.   Philosopher though he was, he did not con-sider such ordinary things as reform of the coinage and reform of the Poor Law beneath his attention.   With regard to Poor Law reform he wrote thus to his friend Clarke on 25th February, 1697-8.   " It is a matter that requires every

1.—" The Reasonableness of Christianity " in *Works*, 1714, vol. ii., p. 536.
2.—See King, *Life of Locke*, 1829, p. 90.   In his journal of Spring, 1677, Locke noted amongst the causes which retard the growth of knowledge, " the aim and desire to know what hath been other men's opinions."—*Loc. cit.*, p. 92.   " In our inquiry after knowledge," he continues, " it as little concerns us what other men have thought, as it does one who is to go from Oxford to London to know what scholars walk quietly on foot, inquiring the way . . . . who rode post after their guide without minding the way he went . . . . or where one doctor lost or went out of his way, or where another stuck in the mire."

Englishman's best thoughts ; for there is not any one thing that I know upon the right regulation whereof the prosperity of his country more depends.   And whilst I have any breath left I shall always be an Englishman." [1] If our study of Locke does not confirm Voltaire's eulogy of him [2] that there never was a more methodic or logical writer, it at least proves that this patriotic Englishman combined the practical and speculative in a very high degree.

The economic development of the modern world was only in its infancy when Locke wrote.   Trade and commerce had grown to a considerable " height and perfection " [3] even before he was born, but the advent of steam-power and the mechanical inventions of the eighteenth century were destined to make the production of wealth more and more a social process, and to make his explanation of property appear less and less adequate.   While in France (1679) he jotted down several things which might interest an intending visitor to England [4] as, for example, " the iron mills at Wandsworth, four miles from London." [5]   Should the " curious stranger " visit the north he advised him " to see the Peak of Derbyshire." [6]   To-day Wandsworth is part of London ; and the chimney stacks of Lancashire seem to impress the visitor to England more than the mountains of Derbyshire.

Madison, in 1787, had a much better opportunity of visualising the probable trend of economic events in his own country.   We saw that he feared that the " sympathy with the rights of property," which then existed in the United States, would be diminished in the future.   Even in the early nineteenth century a French writer, during his travels in America, was impressed by the respect for private property which existed there.   De Tocqueville noted with joy the steadying influence of property on some people who, when

---

1.— *The Correspondence of John Locke and Edward Clarke*, ed. Benjamin Rand, 1927, p. 533.

2.—Voltaire, *Lettres Philosophiques*, ed. Lanson, 1909, t. i., Lettre xiii., p. 166.

3.—See Lewes Roberts, *The Merchant's Mappe of Commerce*, 1638, ch. x., p. 47.

4.—Lord King, *Life of Locke*, 1829, p. 133.

5.—*Ibid.*, p. 134.

6.—*Ibid.*, p. 135.

in Europe, were "great levellers."[1] One of them, he tells us, was now a " wealthy planter," who discussed " the rights of property as an economist or a landowner might have done."[2] The same writer was also impressed by what he calls " the absence of extreme division of labour "[3] or, as one would now say, the absence of extreme division of occupations. De Tocqueville had known men to have been successively " barristers, farmers, merchants, ministers of the Gospel, and physicians."[4] America, however, was soon to don the cloak of efficiency, and with her, as with England, efficiency implied making the majority of the people dependent upon the " wealth of a few." Madison had foretold it. But he did not foresee that to the Constitution, dear to him, amongst other reasons, because it safeguarded the fruits of men's industry, would be added an Amendment that could be used, at times, to injure them.

The political stability of England contrasts favourably with the political discontent of France in the eighteenth century. To French observers the English government was the most singular one in Europe.[5] Men like D'Argenson, however, could not foresee the national loss to which the imperial policy of that government was leading. By the end of the century the backbone of the English nation, the sturdy rural population, had practically disappeared. During the century France lost most of her colonial possessions, but at its close her people had secured a firmer footing on the land. The small proprietor in France instead of witnessing that which he had being taken from him, as happened to his brother on the other side of the channel, saw that which was not his being added to his estate.

Whatever blunders the ruling aristocracy in England may have committed, they did not think that feudal dues were necessary to make people work.[6] In England the gentry frequently took part in commerce, whereas, in France,

1.—*Democracy in America*, tr. Reeve, 1838, vol. ii., p. 136.
2.—*Ibid.*, vol. ii., p. 136.
3.—*Ibid.*, vol. ii., p. 309.
4.—*Ibid.*, vol. ii., p. 309.
5.—D'Argenson, *Considérations*, Amsterdam, 1765, p. 37.
6.—*Ibid.*, p. 272.

tradition was against it. In France trade was prohibited to gentlemen, " not only that they may not be diverted from the exercise of their proper functions, but also that a liberty of commerce may not be left to persons who by their authority might ingross the whole trade to themselves, and render the condition of the Merchants and Buyers worse." [1] Despite these restrictions on the " liberty of commerce," and the existence of sumptuary laws, France apparently was not free from the evils of luxury when Domat wrote. Locke, who lived in France in 1678, made the following note in his diary : " Sumptuary laws, when the age inclines to luxury, do not restrain, but rather increase the evil ; . . . Perhaps the better way to set bounds to people's expenses, and hinder them from spending their income, would be to enact that no landed men should be obliged to pay any book-debt to tradesmen, whereby the interest of tradesmen would make them very cautious of trusting those who usually are the leaders of fashions, and thereby a great restraint would be brought on the usual excess ; on the other hand, the credit of poor labouring people would be preserved as before for the supply of their necessities." [2]

These observations, which incidentally illustrate Locke's love of the landed interest, will not commend themselves to many. But his view that the right of private property is not dependent on the will of the State is likely always to appeal to the instincts and interests of mankind.

1.—J. Domat, *The Civil Law*, tr. Strahan, 1722, vol. ii., p. 462.
2.—Lord King, *Life of Locke*, 1829, p. 74.

BIBLIOGRAPHY

PRINCIPAL PRIMARY AND SECONDARY SOURCES.

Among these I have included some works dealing with the sixteenth and seventeenth centuries which have been quoted in the text, and also some modern books containing extracts and documents of the eighteenth century. But, to avoid making the bibliography too unwieldy, I have not included well-known collections of papers and tracts. The principal of these are : Domestic State Papers ; The Harleian Miscellany ; Somers' Tracts, the Thomason Tracts, Tracts on Charities, Political and Financial Tracts, in the British Museum ; and the Leaflets issued by the Old South Association, Boston.

(A).—*Works relating to England and America.*

ADAMS, JOHN, *Works.* Ed. C. F. Adams. Boston, 1850-6.

ADAMS, JAMES T., *The Founding of New England.* Boston, 1921.
Revolutionary New England. Boston, 1923.

BACON, FRANCIS, *Essays, including his Moral and Historical Works.* Chandos Classics, 1888.

BASTIDE, CHARLES, *John Locke, ses théories politiques et leur influence en Angleterre.* Paris, 1907.

BEARD, CHARLES A., *An Economic Interpretation of the Constitution of the United States.* N. Y., 1913.
Economic Origins of Jeffersonian Democracy. N. Y., 1915.
Contemporary American History. N. Y., 1920.

BEER, MAX, *The Pioneers of Land Reform.* Bohn's Library, 1920.

BENNET, JOHN, *The National Merchant, or Discussion on Commerce and Colonies.* Lond., 1736.

BERKELEY, BISHOP, *Works*, vol. iii. Ed. Fraser, 1871.

BLACKBURN, F., *A Collection of Important English Statutes showing changes in the Law of Property.* Cambridge, 1885.

BLACKSTONE, WILLIAM, *Commentaries on the Laws of England.* 1783.

BLAND, BROWN, and TAWNEY, *English Economic History ; Select Documents*, 1914.

BRADDON, LAWRENCE, *A Proposal for relieving, reforming and employing all the Poor of Great Britain.* Lond., 1721.

BUCKLE, H. T., *Introduction to the History of Civilization in England.* Ed. Robertson. Lond., 1904.

BURKE, EDMUND, *Select Works.* Ed. Payne, 1904.

CALVIN, *Epistolae et Responsa.* Hanoviae, 1597.

CECIL, EVELYN, *Primogeniture : A short history of its development in various countries and its practical effects.* Lond., 1895.

CHAMBERLAYNE, EDWARD, *Angliae Notitia.* Lond., 1669.
England's Wants. 1689.

CLARKE PAPERS. Ed. Firth.

COLLIER, JEREMY, *Essays upon several Moral Subjects.* Lond., 1698.

CROWLEY, ROBERT, *Select Works.* Ed. Cowper, 1872.

CURTIS, MATTOON M., *An Outline of Locke's Ethical Philosophy.* Leipzig. 1890.

DALRYMPLE, Sir JOHN, *An Essay towards a general history of Feudal Property in Great Britain.* 1758.

DAVENANT, CHARLES, *Political and Commercial Works.* Ed. Whitworth, 1771.

DAVIES, DAVID, *The Case of Labourers in Husbandry.* 1795.

DEFOE, DANIEL, *The Compleat English Tradesman.* Lond., 1732.
The Anatomy of Exchange Alley. Lond., 1719.

De TOCQUEVILLE, C. A. H. M., *Democracy in America.* 2 vols. Eng. trans. Reeve, 1838.

DOWELL, STEPHEN, *A History of Taxation.* 2 vols. Lond., 1888.

FARRAND, MAX, *The Records of the Federal Convention of 1787.* 3 vols. New Haven, 1911.

FERGUSON, ADAM, *Principles of Moral and Political Science.* 2 vols. 1792.

FIRTH, Sir C. H., *The House of Lords during the Civil War.* 1910.

FOLEY, JOHN P., *The Jeffersonian Cyclopedia.* N. Y., 1900.

FORD, PAUL L., *Essays on the Constitution of the United States published during its discussion by the People. 1787-8.* Brooklyn, 1892.
Pamphlets on the Constitution of the United States published during its discussion by the People, 1787-8. Brooklyn, 1888.

FOX-BOURNE, H. R., *Life of John Locke.* 2 vols. 1876.

GARDINER, S. R., *The Constitutional Documents of the Puritan Revolution.* 1906.

GODWIN, WILLIAM, *An Enquiry into Political Justice.* 2 vols. Lond., 1796.

GONNER, E. C. K., *Common Land and Enclosure.* 1912.

HALE, Sir MATHEW, *A Discourse touching Provision for the Poor.* Lond., 1683.

HAMMOND, L. and B., *The Village Labourer.* Lond., 1920.
The Rise of Modern Industry. Lond., 1925.

HAMILTON, ALEXANDER, *Report on the Subject of Manufactures.* Lond., 1793.

HAMILTON, JAY, and MADISON, *The Federalist.* Everyman's Library, 1922.

HARRINGTON, Sir JAMES, *Oceana.* 1656. Ed. Morley, 1887.

HOWELL, T. B. and T. J., *State Trials.* 1817.

HUME, DAVID, *A Treatise of Human Nature.* Ed. Selby-Bigge, 1896.
Essays. The New Universal Library, 1905.

HUTCHESON, FRANCIS, *A Short Introduction to Moral Philosophy.* Glasgow, 1747.
A System of Moral Philosophy. 2 vols. Lond., 1755.

KING, LORD, *The Life of John Locke, with extracts from his Correspondence, Journals and Commonplace Books.* Lond., 1829.

LAMPRECHT, S. P., *The Moral and Political Philosophy of John Locke.* N. Y., 1918.

LE BLANC, JEAN B., L'Abbé, *Letters on the English and French Nations.* 2 vols. Eng. trans. Dublin, 1747.

LEGG, L. G. WICKHAM, *Select Documents illustrative of the French Revolution.* Oxford, 1905.

LOCKE, JOHN, *Civil Government.* Lond., 1694.
 Civil Government and Toleration. Cassell's Library, 1905.
 Civil Government. Ed. Morley. Lond., 1884.
 An Essay concerning Human Understanding. 2 vols. Ed. Fraser. Oxford, 1894.
 The Correspondence of John Locke and Edward Clarke. Ed. B. Rand, 1927.
 Diary, 1679. Brit. Museum, Add. MSS. 15642.
 Works. 3 vols. Lond., 1714.
 Works. 4 vols. Lond., 1777.
 Works. 10 vols. Lond., 1823.

LOWDE. J., *Moral Essays.* York and Lond., 1699.

MACHIAVELLI, N., *Historical, Political and Diplomatic Writings.* 4 vols. Eng. tran., Detmold, Boston. 1882.

MANDEVILLE, BERNARD, *Fable of the Bees : or Private Vices, Public Benefits.* Lond., 1714.
 Fable of the Bees. 2 vols. Ed. Kaye, 1924.

MARION, H., *J. Locke, sa vie, son oeuvre.* Paris, 1878.

MATHER, COTTON, *Magnalia Christi Americana.* Lond., 1702.

MIÈGE, GUY, *The New State of England.* Lond., 1693.

MORISON, S. E., *Sources and Documents illustrating the American Revolution.* Oxford, 1923.

MOSSE, MILES, *The Arraignment and Conviction of Usurie.* 1595.

NEVILE, HENRY, *Plato Redivivus.* Lond., 1681.

O'BRIEN, GEORGE, *An Essay on the Economic Effects of the Reformation.* Lond., 1923.

ORMEROD, OLIVER, *The Picture of a Puritane.* 1605.

PAINE, THOMAS, *Rights of Man.* Part ii. Lond., 1792.

PALEY, WILLIAM, *The Principles of Moral and Political Philosophy.* Lond., 1804.

PORRITT, EDWARD, *The Unreformed House of Commons.* 2 vols. 1903.

PRICE, RICHARD, *Observations on Reversionary Payments.* Lond., 1792.
 Observations on the Nature of Civil Liberty. 1776.

PRIESTLEY, JOSEPH, *An Essay on the First Principles of Government.* Lond., 1771.

PROUD, ROBERT, *History of Pennsylvania.* Phila., 1797.

RITCHIE, DAVID G., *Darwin and Hegel.* 1893.
 Natural Rights. 1924.

ROBERTS, LEWES, *The Merchants' Mappe of Commerce ; wherein the universall manner and matter of Trade is compendiously handled. etc.* Lond., 1638.

ROGERS, ROBERT, *A Concise Account of North America.* Dublin, 1770.

RUTHERFORTH, THOMAS, *Institutes of Natural Law.* American edn., 1832.

SMITH, ADAM, *Wealth of Nations.* Ed. Cannan, 1920.
Theory of Moral Sentiments. Glasgow, 1759.

SMITH, RICHARD, *The Prudentiall Ballance of Religion.* Lond., 1609.

SMITH, SYDNEY, *Works.* Lond., 1850.

SMITH, Sir THOMAS, *De Republica Anglorum,* 1583. Ed. Alston, 1906.

STEPHEN, Sir LESLIE, *History of English Thought in the Eighteenth Century.* 2 vols. Lond., 1902.

STEPHEN, Sir JAMES FITZJAMES, *Horae Sabbaticae.* 2nd series, 1892.

STEUART, Sir JAMES, *An Inquiry into the Principles of Political Economy.* 2 vols. Lond., 1767.

TAGGART, EDWARD, *Locke's Writings and Philosophy.* 1855.

TAWNEY, R. H., *The Agrarian Problem in the Sixteenth Century.* Lond., 1912.
The Acquisitive Society. N. Y., 1920.
Religion and the Rise of Capitalism. Lond., 1926.

TAWNEY, R. H. and POWER, E., *Tudor Economic Documents.* 3 vols. 1924.

TUCKER, JOSIAH, *The Elements of Commerce and Theory of Taxes.* 1755.
A Treatise concerning Civil Government. 1781.
Six Sermons on Important Subjects. Bristol, 1772.

TYRRELL, JAMES, *A Brief Disquisition of the Laws of Nature.* Lond., 1701.

VEITCH, G. S., *The Genesis of Parliamentary Reform.* 1913.

VINCENT, WILLIAM, *Sermons.* Ed. Nares. Lond., 1817.

WALLACE, ROBERT, *Various Prospects of Mankind, Nature and Providence.* Lond., 1761.

WOLLASTON, WILLIAM, *The Religion of Nature delineated.* Lond., 1738.

YOUNG, ARTHUR, *Political Arithmetic.* Lond., 1774.
An Inquiry into the propriety of applying wastes to the better maintenance and support of the Poor. Lond., 1801.

(B).—*Works relating to France.*

ATGER, FRÉDÉRIC, *Essai sur l'histoire des doctrines du contrat social.* Paris, 1906.

AULARD, F. V. A., *La Révolution française et le régime féodal.* Paris, 1919.

BARNI, JULES, *Histoire des idées morales et politiques en France au dix-huitième siècle.* 2 tomes. Paris, 1865.

BAUDEAU, NICOLAS, L'Abbé, *Première introduction à la philosophie économique, 1771.* Ed. Dubois. Paris, 1910.

BREYER, REMI, *Catéchisme des Riches.* Troyes, 1711.

BRISSOT De WARVILLE, J. P., *Bibliothèque philosophique du législateur.* t. vi. Paris, 1782.

BUCHEZ, J. B. and ROUX, P. C., *Histoire parlementaire de la Révolution française*. Paris, 1834.

CARON and SAGNAC, *Collection des documents inédits sur l'histoire économique de la Révolution française*. Paris, 1907.

CONDORCET, M. C., *Œuvres*. Ed. Condorcet O'Connor & Arago. Paris, 1847.

D'ARGENSON, MARQUIS, *Considérations sur le gouvernment ancien et présent de la France*. Amsterdam, 1765.

De BOULAINVILLIERS, Count, *Mémoires présentés à Monseigneur le duc d'Orléans, Régent de France*. 2 tomes. Hague & Amsterdam, 1727.

De P. [PAUL], *Dictionnaire de l'ancien régime et des abus féodaux*. Paris, 1820.

De TOCQUEVILLE, C. A. H. M., *L'Ancien Régime*. Eng. trans. Headlam, 1904.

DOMAT, JEAN, *The Civil Law in its national order together with the Public Law*. 2 vols. Eng. trans. Strahan. Lond., 1722.

ESPINAS, ALFRED, *La Philosophie sociale du xviiie siècle et la Révolution française*. Paris, 1898.

FAGUET, ÉMILE, *Dix-huitième siècle*. Paris, 1890.

FAVRE, JULES, *Le prêt à intérêt dans l'ancienne France*. Paris, 1900.

FRANCK, AD. *Réformateurs et Publicistes de l'Europe : dix-huitième siècle*. Paris, 1893.

HERBERT, SYDNEY, *The Fall of Feudalism in France*. Lond., 1921.

LANSON, GUSTAVE, *Manuel bibliographique de la littérature française moderne*. Paris, 1921.

LEBER, SALGUES and COHEN, *Collection des meilleurs dissertations, notices et traités particuliers relatifs à l'histoire de France composée en grande partie de pièces rares*. Paris, 1826.

LICHTENBERGER, ANDRÉ, *Le Socialisme au xviiie siècle*. Paris, 1895. *Le Socialisme et la Révolution française*. Paris, 1899.

LINGUET, SIMON N. H., *Théorie des Loix Civiles ou principes fondamentaux de la Société*. 2 tomes. Lond., 1767.

LOUIS XIV., King of France, *Œuvres*. Ed. Grouvelle. Paris, 1806.

MÉLON, JEAN F., *A Political Essay upon Commerce*. Eng. trans. Dublin, 1738.

MÉRY, L'Abbé, *L'ami de ceux qui n'en ont point*. Paris, 1767.

MIRABEAU, Marquis de, *Philosophie Rurale*. Amsterdam, 1766.

MONTESQUIEU, C. de S., *Works*. 4 vols. Lond., 1777.

MORELLET, ANDRÉ, *Mélanges de littérature et de philosophie du xviiie siecle*. tomes iii. & iv. Paris, 1818.
Mémoires sur le xviiie siècle. tomes i. ii. iii. Paris, 1821.
Lettres à Lord Shelbourne, 1772-1803. Paris, 1898.

MORELLY, *Code de la Nature*. Ed. Dolléans. Paris, 1910.

QUESNAY, FRANCOIS, *Œuvres économiques et philosophiques*. 2 tomes. Ed. A. Oncken. Paris, 1888.

RATHERY, E. J. B., *Des Relations sociales et intellectuelles entre la France et l'Angleterre depuis la conquête des Normands jusqu' à la Révolution française*. Paris, 1856.

ROUSSEAU, J. J., *Political Writings*. Ed. Vaughan. 1915.
    The Social Contract. Ed. Tozer. Lond., 1905.

ROUSTAN, M., *Pioneers of the French Revolution.* Eng. trans., Whyte. 1926.

SAGNAC, PH., *La Législation civile de la Révolution française.* ¼ Paris, 1898.

SAVATIER, HENRI, *La Théorie moderne du capital et la justice.* Paris, 1898.

SAVATIER, RENÉ, *La Théorie du commerce chez les Physiocrates.* Paris,
    1918.

SÉE, HENRI, *La France économique et sociale au xviiie siécle.* 1925.

SOUCHET, ÉTIENNE, *Traité de l'usure.* Paris, 1776.

TURGOT, A. R. J., *Reflections on the Production and Distribution of Wealth.*
    Economic Classics. Ed. Ashley.
    Œuvres. Ed. Schelle. Paris. 5 tomes 1913-23.

VOLTAIRE, *Lettres Philosophiques.* Ed. Lanson. Paris, 1909.
    A Philosophical Dictionary. 2 vols. Lond., 1843.
    The Philosophy of History. Lond., 1766.
    Candide ou l'optimisme. Ed. Morize. Paris, 1913.

WEULERSSE, GEORGES, *Le Mouvement physiocratique en France, 1756
    à 1770.* 2 tomes. 1910.

INDEX OF NAMES